A Guide to
Crisis Intervention

A Guide to
Crisis Intervention

KRISTI KANEL, PH.D.

Brooks/Cole Publishing Company

I(T)P® *An International Thomson Publishing Company*

Pacific Grove • Albany • Belmont • Bonn • Boston • Cincinnati • Detroit • Johannesburg • London
Madrid • Melbourne • Mexico City • New York • Paris • Singapore • Tokyo • Toronto • Washington

Sponsoring Editor: *Eileen Murphy*
Marketing Team: *Steve Catalano, Aaron Eden*
Editorial Assistant: *Julie Lehmann*
Advertising Communications: *Jean Thompson*
Production Editor: *Karen Ralling*
Manuscript Editor: *Patterson Lamb*

Permissions Editor: *Connie Dowcett*
Interior and Cover Design: *Donna Davis*
Design Coordinator: *Kelly Shoemaker*
Typesetting: *Joan Mueller Cochrane*
Cover Printing: *Webcom*
Printing and Binding: *Webcom*

Copyright 1999 by Brooks/Cole Publishing Company
A division of International Thomson Publishing Inc.
I(T)P The ITP logo is a registered trademark under license.

For more information, contact:

BROOKS/COLE PUBLISHING COMPANY
511 Forest Lodge Road
Pacific Grove, CA 93950
USA

International Thomson Editores
Seneca 53
Col. Polanco
11560 México, D.F., México

International Thomson Publishing Europe
Berkshire House 168–173
High Holborn
London WC1V 7AA
England

International Thomson Publishing GmbH
Königswinterer Strasse 418
53227 Bonn
Germany

Thomas Nelson Australia
102 Dodds Street
South Melbourne, 3205
Victoria, Australia

International Thomson Publishing Asia
60 Albert Street
#15-01 Albert Complex
Singapore 189969

Nelson Canada
1120 Birchmount Road
Scarborough, Ontario
Canada M1K 5G4

International Thomson Publishing Japan
Hirakawacho Kyowa Building, 3F
2-2-1 Hirakawacho
Chiyoda-ku, Tokyo 102
Japan

Printed in Canada

10 9 8 7 6 5 4

Library of Congress Cataloging-in-Publication Data

Kanel, Kristi, 1958–
 A guide to crisis intervention / Kristi Kanel.
  p. cm.
 Includes bibliographical references and index.
 ISBN 0-534-35521-8 (pbk.)
 1. Crisis intervention (Psychiatry) I. Title.
RC480.6.K355 1998
616.89—dc21

97-52343
CIP

About the Author

Kristi Kanel received her doctorate in counseling psychology from the University of Southern California in 1991. Her special areas of research included multicultural sensitivity, existential relationships, and personal therapy for psychotherapists. She earned her master of science in counseling from California State University, Fullerton, in 1982, and has been licensed as a Marriage, Family, Child Counselor since 1983. She has studied family systems approaches extensively as well as Eriksonian approaches to psychotherapy. In 1980, she received her bachelor of science degree in Human Services from California State University, Fullerton. This was her introduction to the concept and experience of the paraprofessional counselor.

In total, Dr. Kanel has 19 years of clinical experience. She brings to her students, clients, and readers knowledge from working at a battered women's shelter, at a free clinic, for a health maintenance organization, in private practice, and for a county mental health agency. In these various work settings, she has seen many types of clients with whom she has used an integrative approach to counseling.

Dr. Kanel also has been an educator since 1983, teaching at a community college, state university, and private university, and has taught doctoral students at professional schools of psychology as well. She has been teaching crisis intervention courses since 1986. This book is a result of all these experiences.

In her spare time, she enjoys sports, tennis, aerobics, and raising her son Gerard with her husband Jerry.

Contents

CHAPTER THREE

Ethical and Professional Issues 32

CHAPTER FOUR

A Multicultural Perspective 39

CHAPTER ELEVEN

Selected Situational Crises of Adolescence, Adulthood, and Old Age 198

Preface

This book was designed to capture the information I would like to continue sharing with graduate and paraprofessional counseling students as well as my colleagues in the counseling profession. In each chapter, I have compiled information on crisis intervention skills and strategies that I find useful every day in my private practice as a licensed Marriage, Family, Child Counselor as I identify and work with the personal issues of each client. I have used these concepts and skills in all the agencies in which I have been a practicing counselor. The particular crisis topics were chosen because of the frequency with which these crises appear in a typical counseling agency environment. The ABC model offered in this book is useful in dealing with almost any crisis, so the student should be able to generalize its techniques to whatever problem may be presented by a typical client for counseling or social work.

Although the book is written for the beginning paraprofessional counselor, some introduction to various psychological and counseling principles will be helpful in understanding the book's material. Please use the book's margins and spaces to jot down ideas, questions, and personal feelings. Students have found this note-taking helpful in creating an active learning process. Your feedback and ideas will stimulate class discussion and further your learning.

Pay close attention to the bold face terms in each chapter. Each is defined or described in the "key terms for study" section at the end of each chapter.

The Instructor's Manual contains short chapter overviews, numerous lecture suggestions and exercises coaching strategies, sample test items and several transparency masters.

I would like to thank the following reviewers for their helpful comments and suggestions: Tammy A. King, Youngstown State University; Mary Moline, Seattle Pacifica University; and Gary Reeves, Hill College.

I would like to express much gratitude to the many human services students who have been enrolled in my classes and who helped refine the strategies for personal crisis intervention by their participation in these courses. Particular thanks go to Dr. Mary Moline, who originally created the crisis intervention course for paraprofessional training, and shared her ideas and structure for presenting these materials. She also conceived the idea of using small group lab sessions to help students learn the practical aspects of implementing these crisis intervention strategies. I also would like to thank Henry Kaiser, Glennda Gilmour, and Peg Tompkins, who have gone beyond the call of duty in serving as lab coaches over the last 11 years.

What Is a Crisis?

Crisis Defined

The term **crisis** has been defined in many ways, but an actual crisis has essentially three parts. The definition reflecting these three is called the **trilogy definition** and is referred to throughout this book. The three aspects of a crisis are these: (1) A **precipitating event** occurs; (2) the *perception* of this event leads to **subjective distress**; and (3) usual **coping methods** fail, leading the person experiencing the event to function psychologically, emotionally, or behaviorally at a lower level than before the precipitating event occurred.

Other authors agree with this general definition. An example is Gilliland and James, who define crisis as "a perception of an event or situation as an intolerable difficulty that exceeds the resources and coping mechanisms of the person" (Gilliland & James, 1988, p. 3). Gerald Caplan, often referred to as the **father of modern crisis intervention**, describes a crisis as "an obstacle that is, for a time, insurmountable by the use of customary methods of problem solving. A period of disorganization ensues, a period of upset, during which many abortive attempts at a solution are made" (1961, p. 18). In its simplest form, according to Caplan, "it is an upset in the steady state of the individual" (1961, p. 18).

Janosik (1986, p. 4) sees the scope of crisis work as including "precipitating events, behavioral response, failed efforts to cope and disrupted equilibrium." She has found the following to occur in a crisis: "a precipitator in the form of a hazardous event intrudes on the life of an individual or group, causing a state of tension that is subjectively uncomfortable and the person experiencing the hazardous event resorts to customary coping behaviors" (p. 7). If these behaviors fail to relieve tension, a crisis occurs.

These three components of a crisis must be recognized and understood as they are the elements the crisis counselor will be identifying and helping the client overcome. The *perception* of the event is by far the most crucial part to identify, for it is the piece that can be most easily and quickly altered by the counselor. It is the focus in this trilogy definition, and the point that differentiates crisis intervention from most other forms of counseling.

By keeping the trilogy definition in mind, the crisis worker can perform the necessary services in a brief time. Whereas other forms of counseling may focus on self-esteem building or personality modification or even extinguishing maladaptive behaviors, *in crisis intervention, the focus is on increasing the client's functioning*. This is addressed in detail in Chapters 2 and 5; for now, look at two useful formulas for the crisis interventionist that utilize the trilogy definition.

Formula for Understanding the Process of Crisis Formation

Precipitating Event ⟶ Perception ⟶ Subjective Distress ⟶ Lowered Functioning

If the goal of crisis work is to increase functioning, the following formula aids the crisis worker in understanding the process for leading a client out of a crisis.

Formula to increase functioning

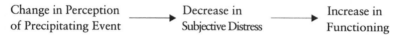

Change in Perception ⟶ Decrease in ⟶ Increase in
of Precipitating Event   Subjective Distress   Functioning

Again, notice that the method of change has to do with how the precipitating event is perceived rather than with making a change in the precipitating event itself. Usually, changing the facts and actual events that have occurred is not possible. The best we can do is work at changing or altering the client's cognitions and perceptions of these events. These ideas are explored further in subsequent chapters.

One additional thought about crises in general: often the word *crisis* conjures up images of panic, emergency, and feeling out of control. This is not necessarily the case. Crises are a part of life and should not be considered abnormal. Crises occur in the lives of *normal, average* individuals who are just having difficulty coping with stress; therefore, they represent a state to which most of us can relate.

Because of the universal nature of crises, it is understandable that a specific approach for intervening in these situations was developed out of the experience of helpers; they discovered that the more traditional, long-term counseling approaches weren't appropriate in dealing with crises and found that short-term crisis intervention was much more effective. Short-term and brief therapy models are discussed in Chapter 2.

Crises as Danger and Opportunity

Crisis states are seen by many as somewhat normal developments that can occur episodically during "the normal life span of individuals" (Janosik, 1984, p. 3). Whether the individual comes out of the crisis state productively or unproductively depends on how he or she deals with it. In Chinese, crisis means both **danger and opportunity**. This dichotomous meaning helps to highlight the potentially beneficial as well as potentially hazardous aspects of a crisis state. A person might face the challenge of the precipitating event adaptively, or he or she might respond with a neurotic disturbance, psychotic illness, or even death.

According to Caplan (1961, p. 19), growth is preceded by a state of imbalance or crisis that serves as the basis for future development. Without crisis,

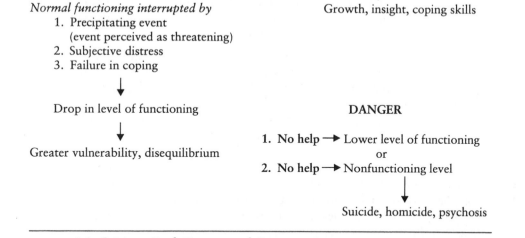

FIGURE 1.1 *Crisis as Both Danger and Opportunity*

development is not possible. As a person strives to achieve stability during a crisis, the coping process itself can help him or her achieve a qualitatively different stability, at either a higher or lower **functioning level** than in the pre-crisis state (see Figure 1.1).

Process of Crises

Even if the person receives no outside intervention or help, the crisis state will eventually cease, usually within 4 to 6 weeks. A crisis is by nature a time-limited event in that a person cannot tolerate the extreme tension and psychological disequilibrium characteristic of this state for more than a few weeks (Caplan, 1964; Janosik, 1986, p. 9; Roberts, 1990; Slaikeu, 1990, p. 21). Whether a person emerges stronger or weaker from a crisis is not based so much on previous character makeup—although this factor is relevant—as on the kind of help he or she receives during the actual crisis. A person is more receptive to suggestions and help in a crisis state than in a steady state. A crisis worker can gain significant leverage at this time because of greater client vulnerability. Instead of stabilizing at a lowered level of functioning, an individual who receives help during a crisis state is more likely to create a new state of functioning at higher, more adaptive levels, relieving erratic behaviors and emotions.

Example After having been raped, a woman might not seek help or even tell anyone about the trauma. About a month after the violation, she may slip into a state of denial with reduced contact in the world, lowered trust levels, increased substance abuse, poor interpersonal relations, and a state of dissociation. However, she may continue to be able to work, go to school, put on a front with family and friends, and appear to be functioning normally. In reality, however, she is functioning at a lower level than prior to the rape and will be somewhat impaired until she gets intervention. The longer she waits to get help, the more resistant she will be to it because of the amount of energy she will have invested in the denial process.

This scenario is especially common in cases of incest. It seems fairly obvious that a 3-year-old girl brought in for counseling after being molested one time will respond better than a 30-year-old woman who was molested at age 3 and had repressed acknowledgment of the molestation for 27 years.

A very important aspect in regard to greater client vulnerability during crises is the ethics and integrity of the crisis worker. It would be easy for an unscrupulous worker to take advantage of a client in crisis. Chapter 3 is devoted to ethical issues.

Once the client has returned to the previous or a higher level of functioning, he or she may opt to continue with therapy. Brief therapy is a reasonably cost-effective approach for dealing with aspects of life that have plagued a person regularly but have not necessarily caused a crisis state. A counselor may work with an individual for 6 to 20 sessions and obtain excellent results in behavioral and emotional changes. Once people have benefited from crisis intervention, they are often more open to continuing to work on more in-depth personal issues because of increased trust in the therapeutic process and the therapist. The choice to continue in post-crisis counseling will of course depend on financial ability and time availability.

The Crisis-Prone Person

Not everyone who experiences a stressor in life will succumb to a crisis state. No one is sure why certain people seem to cope with stress easily whereas others deteriorate into disequilibrium when faced with stress or trauma. Figure 1.2 extends Figure 1.1 to include the **crisis-prone** person. If a person does not receive adequate crisis intervention during a crisis state, but instead comes out of the crisis by use of ego defense mechanisms such as repression, denial, or dissociation, he or she is likely to function at a lower level than before the stressing event. The ego then must use its strength to maintain the denial of the anxiety or pain associated with the precipitating event. This effort takes away the individual's strength to deal with future stressors, thereby leading to another crisis state the next time a stressor hits. This crisis state may then be resolved by the use of more ego defense mechanisms after several weeks, leading to an even lower level of functioning if the person does not receive adequate crisis intervention.

This pattern can go on for many years until the person's ego is completely drained of its capacity to deal with reality; often such people commit suicide, kill someone, or have a psychotic breakdown. Until then, this type of individual is often

Higher functioning level:
growth, coping skills learned for use with future stressors

↑

Receives help

State of disequilibrium

Receives no help

↓

Lower functioning:
defense mechanisms

New stressor hits; lack of ego strength
to cope with it leads to new crisis state

↓

NO HELP
Lower functioning than before, fewer coping skills
for future stressors

New stressor hits

↓

Another state of disequilibrium

↓

Lower level of functioning, death or psychosis, severe
personality disorder

FIGURE **1.2** *Crisis as Danger: The Development of a Crisis-Prone Person*

viewed as having a personality disorder. People with personality disorders are usually seen as suffering from emotional instability, inability to master reality, poor interpersonal and occupational functioning, and chronic depression. Defense mechanisms and substance abuse are common ways in which people overcome crisis states when they don't seek professional help. Quite possibly, if the person had received help prior to the use of defense mechanisms to overcome the crisis state, the personality disorder would not have evolved.

Traditional psychotherapy has been the usual course of counseling for this type of person. In today's economy and with health maintenance organizations (HMOs) dictating mental health treatment, clinicians are often not in a position to take the traditional road with the crisis-prone person. Short-term treatment is required in most settings. Therefore, it is essential to begin working with people as soon as possible after the crisis state sets in to prevent this chronic cycle from developing.

Other Determining Factors

Other factors may also determine whether a crisis presents a danger or an opportunity. These factors are generally found in the client's own environment. In addition to receiving outside help, having access to (1) material resources, (2) personal resources, and (3) social resources seems to determine the level an individual reaches after a crisis.

> **Example** A battered woman with minimal **material resources** (money, food, housing, and transportation) will suffer more in a crisis than a woman with her own income and transportation. According to Maslow's (1970) hierarchy of needs, material needs must be met before the other needs of personal integration and social contact can receive attention. Not until she is housed, fed, and safe can the battered woman process the crisis psychologically.
>
> How the woman then begins to work through the crisis will also affect the outcome. Her **personal resources** such as ego strength, previous history of coping with stressful situations, the existence of any personality problems, and physical well-being will help determine how well she accepts intervention.

Ego strength refers to the ability to understand the world realistically and act on it to get one's needs and wishes met. Many times a crisis worker will be called on to be the client's ego strength temporarily (as when a person is psychotic or vegetatively depressed) until the client can take over for himself or herself. These clients cannot see reality clearly nor put into action realistic, coping behaviors. They need someone to structure their behavior until the crisis is managed successfully, often with medication, family intervention, and individual counseling. When someone has coped successfully in the past with various stressors, then usually his or her ego strength is high. However, as was shown in Figure 1.2, when someone does not cope successfully with stressors, the person's ego strength is lowered. A crisis worker can be tuned into the client's level of mastering reality to help set up realistic goals and problem-solving strategies.

Personality problems may also interfere with crisis intervention. Some people have problems accepting help or being strong. Others are paranoid or avoid conflict. These people will require a different style of intervention from that offered to an open, trusting person.

Clients' physical well-being will also affect how well they deal with crises. Healthy people have more energy and greater ability to use personal and social resources. The ability to move about and exercise is essential in coping with stress.

Level of intelligence and education will also affect the outcome of a person's crisis state. A well-educated person will be able to utilize cognitive reframes and logical arguments to help him or her in integrating traumas psychologically. People with lower IQ levels will have more difficulty understanding events and their own reactions in general and they will tend to be less flexible in problem solving.

A person's **social resources** also affect the outcome of a crisis. A person with strong support from family, friends, church, work, and school will have natural help available if these support systems are healthy. A lone individual will struggle more in crisis and will tend to depend on outside support systems instead. Part of the crisis worker's responsibility is to link clients with their natural support systems so their dependency on mental health workers is reduced.

Precipitating Events

Personal crises have identifiable beginnings or precipitating events. These can be new adjustments as the family evolves, loss of a loved one or of one's health, cultural contradictions and stresses involved in acculturation, normal psycho-social stages of development, or unexpected situational stressors. Perhaps the most important aspect of any crisis is how the person perceives the situation. The meaning given to the event/adjustment will determine whether the person can cope with the added stress in his or her life. This meaning has been termed the **cognitive key** (Slaikeu, 1990, p. 18). It is the key with which the counselor unlocks the door to understanding the nature of the client's crisis. Once the helper identifies the cognitive meanings the client ascribes to the precipitating events, he or she can work actively to reframe these cognitions. This new way of perceiving the event aids the client in reducing subjective distress and increasing coping abilities.

The way the precipitating event interacts with the person's *life view* is what makes a situation critical. If people cannot cope with new situations with their usual mechanisms, a state of disequilibrium will occur. However, if their cognitive perspective of a potential hazard/precipitating event allows people to relieve the stress effectively and resolve the problem, the crisis will end—or not occur in the first place.

Stress is different from crisis, though they are often confused. If people cope with precipitating events without suffering subjective distress, they will likely experience stress but not a crisis. Stress is part of modern life; in fact, it is part of daily life. That does not mean that crises are part of daily life, however, because people typically cope with stress without falling apart emotionally.

Developmental Crises

The idea of **developmental crises** was first proposed by Erik Erikson (1963) and is well documented and accepted by social scientists. Erikson spoke of developmental crises induced by special tasks, and role changes required by each new stage in the sequence of psychosocial maturation. People are more vulnerable to crises at these stages in their lives. This normal process of growth and development is gradual as a person moves from one stage of psychological, biological, and social development to another. It is the short periods of psychological upset that occur during a critical transition point in the normal development of a person from birth to old age that will be a major focus for the crisis worker.

In working with developmental crises, the crisis interventionist must acknowledge that role development does not exist in a vacuum. When one person changes in her or his role, other people in the family system change as well. Because of the involvement of the family in the completion of a role change, these crises can take as long as 5 years to complete.

Having a baby is an example of a psychosocial stage that creates the need for accomplishing various tasks. The first year of a child's life creates many stresses in the home, and these often lead parents to seek out the services of a mental health provider. The baby needs unconditional love, attention, and nurture. These do not come naturally to all parents. The addition of a baby definitely upsets the steady state that existed when the family was only a husband and wife. In other cases, perhaps the mother is not married or is a teenager. Providing for an infant to grow up trusting that all his or her needs will be met is quite a task. Parenting education is very helpful during this first year. Parents also need support and encouragement to take care of themselves. A crisis worker may suggest that they go out on a date or ask in-laws to baby-sit so they can get a rest. Empathy goes a long way during this most difficult psychosocial stage.

The next stage of parenting brings many families in for counseling. Helping toddlers work through their power needs to reach a point of balanced independence/dependence is quite a challenge. Parents often need very structured behavior modification strategies to get through this transitional process. The crisis worker should teach parents how to set boundaries and limits without shaming the child. It can be quite scary for a 2-year-old to be in charge of a home. Parents need to take control without being tyrants.

Once children enter school, social acceptance, assertion, self-esteem, and identity become the tasks they must master. Children of school age often experience crises related to social rejection. The crisis worker can help by exploring suitable alternatives by which the child can get his or her needs met. Parents should be involved in these sessions and can be of great support to their children.

As individuals enter adulthood, new tasks arise. These start with the person's sense of being responsible for himself or herself economically and socially. Young adults will eventually seek partners to fulfill their emotional needs as they move away from their parents. Making the transition from parental affection to partner intimacy is no easy task. Generally, a decade is needed for young people to work through this stage. Relationship breakups are at an all-time high during the ages of 18 to 28, and a crisis worker will be dealing with lonely young adults who are trying to find intimacy as they separate from their parents.

Another typical developmental crisis is often referred to as the midlife crisis. It can occur over a period of several years as the individual's life becomes routine. Usually, people at this point have stabilized in a career, their children are grown and independent for the most part, and their marriage has lost its fire. To bring themselves out of this rut and reduce their feelings of boredom, many will attempt to create circumstances that renew their youth, such as getting a sports car, having an affair, searching for a new job, or enrolling in college. The counselor can aid individuals at this time by showing them that their feelings are normal and helping them focus on productive ways to eliminate their depression. Marital counseling can be very useful at this point so that both spouses can grow together and create a relationship without the children that incorporates new activities into their lifestyle.

The last psychosocial stage is often referred to as integrity versus despair as the older adult begins accepting the knowledge that his or her life is approaching its climax. Retirement, illness, and death are some of the stressors normally found during this time. The crisis worker needs to help this age group adjust to a new way of life. Retirees can be encouraged to play golf, volunteer at charity organizations, or take classes at a senior center. Also, couples may need marital therapy to help them find a new love for one another. They can then be at peace during their twilight years.

In Table 1.1, the author has used **Erickson's (1963) eight stages of development** as a beginning point, showing particular changes they involve and interventions that can be helpful to clients experiencing crises in these stages.

Evolutional Crises

Another way to understand crisis states is to look at the normal passages, or **evolutional crises**, that typical families go through as the years pass. This model is helpful for crisis workers who can explain it to clients when their particular crisis is clearly due to problems in adjusting to the growing family unit.

FIRST STAGE OF A FAMILY: CREATING A MARITAL SUBSYSTEM

(For purposes of explanation, a typical nuclear family is explored.) The first adjustment must be made when a man and a woman decide to get married. Both the couple and their respective parents must change. Each member of the couple comes from a family in which certain values and behaviors are accepted and practiced. The new husband and wife need to create their own behavior patterns for their new home—their own **marital subsystem**. They will adjust to each other, try to change one another, and adapt. Sometimes conflicts occur because of inability to adjust. Sometimes this conflict results from the interference of in-laws who discourage this adjustment, albeit in subtle ways. Power struggles are common during this time. The parents still want to control their adult child, and the adult child wants to assert independence without total alienation from the parents—a definite setup for a crisis.

Education and reframing are helpful here. The couple needs to be encouraged to set up their own home without completely negating their parents' wishes. Compromise is helpful when possible. Also, cultural considerations need to be explored.

TABLE 1.1 Crisis Intervention as Related to Erikson's Psychosocial Stages of Development

Stage	Crisis	Possible Problematic Social Role Changes	Interventions
Infancy	Trust versus Mistrust	Mother fails to bond/nurture infant	Teach mother proper parenting skills; discuss fears about intimacy with baby
		Father fails to join in as a nurturer; father unable to maintain sense of belonging to family unit	Encourage communication and expression of sense of being left out with no function; educate mother on the need for father's involvement with infant
Toddlerhood	Autonomy versus Self-Doubt	Parents fail to allow independence and are overcontrolling	Educate parents about the needs of toddler to feel powerful over self
		Parents fail to set appropriate boundaries and limits	Educate parents about ways to set limits without creating uncontrollable power struggles
Preschool Years	Initiative versus Guilt	Child is unable to interact with children and initiate play	Support parents in their efforts to role-model proper assertive behavior for their child within the family and with extrafamilial relationships
		Child is overly competitive and aggressive and unable to share or cooperate	Teach parents how to help child submit without feeling completely worthless
Childhood Years	Industry versus Inferiority	Child fails to master skills at school, either academic, physical, or social	Encourage child to develop competence at some task or game

		Child fails to demonstrate competence in areas parents perceive as appropriate	Teach parents about the need for child to develop an identity and skills appropriate for the child rather than expecting behaviors that meet the parents' emotional needs and desires
Adolescence	Identity versus Role Confusion	Parents fail to allow child freedoms and responsibilities	Introduce family therapy that focuses on negotiation and compromise
		Parents fail to listen and understand the needs of the child	Teach parents active listening and empathetic understanding skills
		Child fails to transfer emotional need fulfillment to peers	Support child to interact with peers and encourage social involvement
		Child fails to manage increased responsibilities and stress of growing up	Support child to accept reality of growing up, pointing out the advantages that go along with stress and responsibility
Young Adult Years	Intimacy versus Isolation	Young adult fails to form intimate relationships; experiences loneliness	Teach healthy social interaction skills; help work through grief and depression
		Young adult fails to experience independence from parents emotionally, financially, or physically	Educate young adult about normalcy of fears regarding independence, life cycle; give practical suggestions on how to manage daily stresses and let go of parents
		Parents fail to let go of young adult, attempt to control his or her life	Help parents grieve loss and focus on new involvements

Continued

TABLE 1.1 *Continued*

Stage	Crisis	Possible Problematic Social Role Changes	Interventions
Middle Adult Years	Generativity versus Stagnation	Spouses fail to rekindle marital bond after children move out	Suggest marital counseling to address feelings of loss, increase marital interactions and activities
		Adult fails to involve self in new and fulfilling activities	Encourage career change, enrolling in college, starting a hobby, doing volunteer work
		Adult fails to adapt to grandparent role appropriately	Teach appropriate role behaviors and boundaries for grandparents
		Parents fail to let go of adult children, experience profound depression because of their loss	Help parents grieve loss and work through depression
Mature Adult Years	Ego-Integrity versus Despair	Older adult fails to continue participation in life	Encourage involvement in senior centers and support groups
		Older person experiences depression about his or her life	Provide supportive counseling focusing on positives in life
		Older person experiences anger and shame about dependence on family	Use family therapy to address feelings and communicate needs

Source: Adapted from Erikson, 1963; expanded by author.

The couple needs to decide how each set of parents is going to influence their marriage. Also, they need to set boundaries that say "We are united for each other" versus "We are united against you." We will look more at boundaries in Chapter 2 under "Structural Therapy."

CREATING A PARENTAL SUBSYSTEM

The next potential for crisis in the evolving family occurs when a child is born. Now, the parents have to adjust to a third individual who will have quite a profound effect on the family unit they have been creating. **Parental** nurturance of the baby needs to be learned; this will be quite different from the affection and intimacy of the marital unit. Each parent will need to develop skills and behaviors to help raise the child. Also, in-law involvement must be determined. Grandparents have rights, and children benefit greatly from healthy grandparent involvement. If the parents have not come to terms with their own parents, however, the birth of a child can create tension and conflict.

It is vital to have a strong marital subsystem before creating a parental subsystem. The crisis worker needs to help the couple strengthen their marriage before any real change in parenting function can be made.

CREATING SIBLING SUBSYSTEMS

As the children grow and as new children are added to the family, new tasks of evolution are faced. Parents need to acknowledge that **siblings** share certain ideas and behaviors that belong to them and not to the parents. Good, strong, even conflictual sibling relationships should be encouraged (though abuse should not be tolerated). These experiences are important to healthy interpersonal functioning later in life. If the parents interfere too much, the siblings do not learn how to cope interpersonally outside the family.

Also, parents need to understand that children of different ages need different expectations, responsibilities and privileges. A 5-year-old must be treated differently from a 15-year-old in regard to bedtime, curfew, eating habits, and social activities as well as household chores.

CREATING GRANDPARENT SUBSYSTEMS

As children grow up and marry, the parents must relinquish control and move into a more collaborative relationship with the adult children. This means that the parents must strengthen their marital unit and accept the boundaries that the adult children will set. Also, when they become **grandparents**, the parents need to set boundaries so as not to be taken advantage of by their children, either financially or for baby-sitting services.

Often a grandparent must sit by quietly as he or she watches a child or child-in-law make mistakes with the grandchildren. Interference is usually not appreciated and can cause problems in the family. The crisis worker needs to explain to these well-meaning grandparents that their child and his or her spouse need to make their own mistakes, which they themselves were allowed to make. The counselor can also point out ways the older parents can be supportive of their children without being intrusive.

Situational Crises

The crises discussed above were *developmental crises*, events that occur in the normal flow of human growth and evolvement. They involve a dramatic change or shift that produces abnormal responses. A **situational crisis,** on the other hand, is one that emerges with the occurrence of uncommon and extraordinary events that an individual has no way of forecasting or controlling (Gilliland, 1988, p. 15). Some examples of situational crises are crime, rape, death, divorce, illness, and community disaster. The chief characteristics that differentiate these from developmental crises are their (1) sudden onset, (2) unexpectedness, (3) emergency quality, and (4) potential impact on the community (Slaikeu, 1990, pp. 64–65). Situational crises are discussed in detail in the second half of the book.

Subjective Distress

A rise in anxiety is a typical reaction to the initial impact of a hazardous event. A person may experience shock, disbelief, distress, and panic. The increased anxiety is often a defense mechanism as it may allow the person a brief respite if the precipitating event is too overwhelming (e.g., Stage I of rape trauma syndrome). If this initial anxiety is not resolved, the person may experience a period of disorganization (e.g., Stage II of rape trauma syndrome). During this phase of the crisis, the person often experiences feelings of guilt, anger, helplessness, hopelessness, dissociation, confusion, and fatigue, leaving her in a vulnerable state. She is now unable to function at her previous level at work, school, or home. Ironically, in certain circumstances, anxiety has the power to generate energy and increase coping, as when a child is in danger and the parent experiences a surge of adrenaline, allowing him to rescue her, or when a natural disaster hits and everyone has increased physical strength and endurance to carry bodies and sandbags.

Anxiety, however, seems to fit the **curvilinear model** in that too much or too little leaves a person in a state of inertia or with undirected and disintegrative energy (Janosik, 1986, p. 30). When the anxiety level is moderate and manageable, the crisis worker can utilize it to help motivate the client to make changes. In summary, anxiety is not always a bad thing; it is considered necessary, at moderate levels, to spur people to make changes in their lives.

Curvilinear Model of Anxiety as Motivator for Change

Moderate Anxiety (highest level of performance)

Low Anxiety (low level of performance inertia)　　　　High Anxiety (low level of performance, undirected energy)

Anxiety is an internal experience; therefore, interventions might first be aimed at alleviating the internal component of stress. This action makes sense because the external component of a crisis often cannot be undone. The only remedy for distress is to change the internal experience.

This can be done in several ways. One would be to medicate the person to relieve the anxiety or grief. The benefit of this intervention is removal of subjective distress. Sometimes clients cannot benefit from cognitive crisis intervention because their anxiety or grief is too great; in these cases medication can provide temporary relief until their cognitions can be altered. Crisis workers need to learn to work jointly with psychiatrists when medication is necessary.

The crisis worker, however, would not want to rid the client of all subjective distress too soon without helping the person change his or her perception of the precipitating event. Without any discomfort, the client will not be as motivated to change. The crisis counselor depends on the client to be in a state of disequilibrium and vulnerability if cognitive change is to occur. Clients with good ego strength and no history of mental illness often can work through a crisis without any medication. Some people, though, absolutely need medication, and the crisis worker must be skilled at knowing when the situation calls for more than just "talk" therapy.

Medication should be used discriminately for crisis states. The decision is up to the psychiatrist. The crisis worker should discuss his or her treatment plan with the psychiatrist and how medication fits into it. Often, the psychiatrist will have suggestions for the counselor and can be a valuable resource for the client. Keeping an open mind to medication can benefit your client.

For clients who do not seem to need medication to relieve subjective distress, the internal experience is best changed through cognitive restructuring, discussed in subsequent chapters. This can be done in a number of ways.

The essential idea to remember is that the crisis interventionist should not focus on changing precipitating events but rather the way in which clients experience them. Changing perceptions will lower clients' subjective distress and increase their functioning levels.

Coping Methods Fail

When people in crisis are experiencing feelings of bewilderment, confusion, and conflict, they will be in a vulnerable position. Ethical behavior on the part of crisis workers is vital as they offer support, education, and reframing statements. Beginning counselors must learn their limitations in using the various intervention skills. They must not naively expect clients in crisis to utilize easily the reframes and education that counselors offer. These interventions can be effective in helping clients return to pre-crisis or higher levels of functioning if they are offered in a sensitive and thoughtful manner. According to Caplan (1964, p. 18), there are seven characteristics of effective coping behavior (see Table 1.2). Crisis workers might want to assess clients' coping in these areas and work toward increasing the areas not being demonstrated. These characteristics should be remembered as the

TABLE 1.2 **Effective Coping Behavior**

1. Actively exploring reality issues and searching for information

2. Freely expressing both positive and negative feelings and tolerating frustration

3. Actively invoking help from others

4. Breaking problems into manageable bits and working through them one at a time

5. Being aware of fatigue and pacing coping efforts while maintaining control in as many areas of functioning as possible

6. Mastering feelings where possible, being flexible and willing to change

7. Trusting in oneself and others and having a basic optimism about the outcome

Source: Caplan, 1964.

crisis worker begins to provide services to the client, keeping in mind these strengths and weaknesses. The behaviors can serve as a guide for working with the client.

When a person is not able to use these coping behaviors and is faced with stress, a crisis state will generally evolve. Often the subjective distress, such as anxiety or grief, overwhelms the individual and the coping behaviors just aren't functioning. It is no wonder that the person's functioning level in a variety of areas will be affected. When such individuals realize they can no longer function at work, at home, socially, or emotionally, they may then seek mental health treatment. During treatment, they will slowly begin to function again by reducing their subjective distress and increasing their coping behaviors.

Key Terms for Study

Caplan's seven characteristics of effective coping behavior: Behaviors proposed by Gerald Caplan (1964) as essential for getting through a crisis state. They can be learned through formal crisis intervention, through experience, or while growing up. In any case, the crisis worker needs to acknowledge these characteristics and to transmit them to clients when possible.

cognitive key: The perception the person has about the precipitating events that led to subjective distress. The crisis worker must identify the perception if he or she is to help the client change it and thereby increase functioning.

coping methods: The behaviors, thinking, and emotional processes that a person uses to handle stress and continue to function.

crisis: A state of disequilibrium that occurs after a stressor (precipitating event). The person then is unable to function in one or more areas of his or her life because customary coping mechanisms have failed.

crisis prone: The condition that persists when people fail to grow from a crisis experience and instead come out of the crisis state by using ego defense mechanisms. They will be crisis prone because their ego strength will be weakened, leaving them unable to cope with future stresses.

curvilinear model of anxiety: Model showing that anxiety has the potential to be either a positive or a negative influence for someone in crisis. Too much anxiety may overwhelm the person and lead to lowered functioning. However, moderate anxiety may offer an opportunity for growth and transition from one stage of life to another or as a motivator for a person to grow from experiencing a trauma. Without any anxiety, people tend not to be motivated to make any changes at all.

danger and opportunity: Dichotomy associated with a crisis: A crisis can be an opportunity when the person grows from the crisis by developing new coping skills and altering perceptions. It can be a danger when the person does not seek help and instead comes out of the crisis state by use of defense mechanisms, resulting in a lowered functioning level and possibly psychosis or even death.

developmental crises: Normal transitional stages that all people pass through while growing through the life span. They often trigger crisis states.

ego strength: The degree to which a person can see reality clearly and meet his or her needs realistically. People with strong egos usually cope with stress better than people with weaker egos.

Erikson's (1963) eight stages of development: Often called the psychosocial stages of development, the tasks of growing up that everyone experiences and that often lead to crisis states. They include the following:

1. Infancy: Trust versus mistrust

2. Toddlerhood: Autonomy versus self-doubt

3. Preschool: Initiative versus guilt

4. Middle school: Industry versus inferiority

5. Adolescence: Identity versus role confusion

6. Young adulthood: Intimacy versus isolation

7. Middle adulthood: Generativity versus stagnation

8. Maturity: Ego-integrity versus despair

evolutional crises: The normal stages a family experiences while it evolves through the life span of its members. The crises result from having to adjust to the formation of the following subsystems:

marital: The system that refers to the new couple. The couple needs to learn how to set boundaries with each family of origin and set rules for the new family.

parental: The system concerned with parenting. The couple now must establish behaviors that deal with raising children and the ways the marital system will change in response to children.

sibling: The system concerned with relations between siblings in the new family. Another boundary as well as new rules are established with brothers and sisters.

grandparent: The system establishing the relationship of the couple with their parents after the parents become grandparents. The role of a grandparent must be defined, with boundaries and support.

father of modern crisis intervention: Title given to Gerald Caplan.

functioning level: The way a person behaves socially, occupationally, academically, behaviorally, and emotionally. Functioning level is impaired when a person is in a crisis. The goal of crisis intervention is to increase this level to pre-crisis levels or higher.

material resources: Tangible things such as money, transportation, clothes, and food. It is one determinant of how well a person will be able to deal with a crisis.

precipitating event: An actual event in a person's life that triggers a crisis state. It can be situational or developmental.

personal resources: Determinants of how well a person will deal with a crisis; they include intelligence, ego strength, and physical health.

situational crisis: Unexpected trauma having a sudden onset that impairs one's functioning level.

social resources: A person's friends, family, and co-workers. The more resources one has, the better the person will weather a crisis.

subjective distress: Painful and uncomfortable feelings a person experiences when in a crisis.

stress: A natural, though trying, part of life. Difficult events happen and we feel anxiety, but when we can cope with them and our functioning is not impaired, they do not become crises.

trilogy definition: The three-part approach to understanding what a crisis is. It includes the precipitating event, subjective distress (caused by cognitions), and usually failure to cope, which leads to lowered functioning.

CHAPTER TWO

Crisis Intervention

The History of Crisis Intervention

The first major work focused on crisis intervention was done by **Eric Lindemann** (1944). He studied the grief reactions experienced by relatives of the victims in the **Coconut Grove fire** in Boston on November 28, 1942. On that night, 493 people perished in the Coconut Grove nightclub, destroyed in the largest single building fire in the country's history. Lindemann and others from Massachusetts General Hospital played an active role in helping survivors who had lost loved ones that day. He came to believe that clergy and other community caretakers could help people with their **grief work**. Prior to this, only psychiatrists had provided services for those with emotional symptoms of anxiety and depression, and these symptoms were thought to stem from personality disorders or biochemical illnesses.

After his study, Lindemann and Gerald Caplan established a communitywide program of mental health in Cambridge, Massachusetts, that became known as the **Wellesley project**. Their work began with references to the personal reactions of individuals to such traumatic events as sudden bereavement or the birth of a premature child. Caplan's focus on preventive psychiatry, which attempted early intervention to promote positive growth and minimize the chance of psychological impairment, led to an emphasis on mental health consultation (Slaikeu, 1990, p. 7). Much of current-day crisis intervention theory has come from this Wellesley project.

Continuing the trend of crisis intervention, in the early 1960s, the suicide prevention movement grew rapidly, and many community centers offered 24-hour hot lines. Developing from the social activist mentality of the 1960s and Caplan's theory, these centers relied on nonprofessional volunteers in their telephone counseling programs. Caplan's focus on critical life crises attracted the nontraditionalists who were dissatisfied with medical model psychoanalytic treatments. Many nonprofit organizations specializing in the treatment of certain personal crises evolved from **grassroots** efforts—free clinics for abortion of unwanted pregnancies, battered women's shelters, rape centers, and now AIDS centers.

Parallel to the suicide prevention movement was the emergence of the community mental health movement in the United States. In 1957, the

Short-Doyle Act provided funding for each county throughout the United States to provide mental health clinics. This act was the impetus for the monumental deinstitutionalization of mental patients from federally funded state mental hospitals. Prior to this time, patients would stay in these hospitals for an indefinite period of time—sometimes to fade away, forgotten. Six years later, the U.S. Congress Joint Commission on Mental Illness and Health, with the support of the Kennedy administration, passed the **Community Mental Health Centers Act of 1963.**

When mental health services were placed in the community, these services became an area of specialty for psychiatry. The Community Mental Health Centers Act was originally intended to serve chronically mentally ill patients, but soon mental health workers began seeing healthier, more affluent patients suffering from emotional disorders that were typically dealt with in private psychologists' offices. As a result, the chronically mentally ill were receiving less care than intended. This development led to passage of the Lanterman Petris Short Bill in 1968, which established more specific requirements for the provision of mental health services in the community. The focus was to be on short-term crisis intervention when the clients were non-chronically mentally ill patients. The legislation was also designed to prevent the public from being harmed by mentally ill people and to prevent the mentally ill from committing crimes by providing long-term case management and conservatorship for them. Last, the bill created the 5150 involuntary hospitalization code and provided protection for the civil rights of mentally ill individuals, assuring them a fair hearing in cases of involuntary confinement.

A major part of this community effort was 24-hour emergency service, which later became Psychiatric Emergency Treatment or PET services. In 1998, community mental health is still based on this act. Procedures for dealing with psychotic, suicidal, and homicidal crises and how they relate to community mental health are discussed in Chapter 6.

In the late 1960s and early 1970s, journals appeared, such as *Crisis Intervention* and *Journal of Life Threatening Behavior*, dealing specifically with crisis topics. Program evaluations began to be conducted in crisis centers, and researchers concluded that short-term crisis intervention models were more effective than long-term psychotherapy. Crisis intervention became more valued in the 1970s as economic conditions led to greater use of community resources (Slaikeu, 1990, p. 8).

The short-term crisis intervention model is by far the most cost effective and thus the approach sought after by most **health maintenance organizations (HMOs)**, preferred provider organizations (PPOs), and other insurance carriers. Community mental health and nonprofit organizations also use the brief therapy model. Utilization review committees often limit treatment to four to six professional sessions and encourage the completion of therapy in community resources such as 12-step programs and other support groups. This method of treatment fits well with a crisis intervention approach for both the professional therapist and the paraprofessional counselor working in community agencies.

One controversy in the field of crisis intervention centers around **paraprofessionals**. Some licensed professionals feel that these workers, who have traditionally provided crisis intervention, should not be doing so. Instead, the professionals have proposed that only those with at least master's degrees be allowed to give services to those in crisis. Such a move could have a negative impact on poorer communities that cannot afford the costs of such expertise, however. The volunteer worker seems vital, especially during times of economic downturn. Understandably, politics and perhaps professional jealousy and fear play a part in the opposition to paraprofessional counseling. No doubt, many clients in need would go untreated if these workers were prohibited from practicing crisis intervention.

Contributions from Other Theoretical Modalities

No one discipline or school of thought can claim crisis theory as its own, for this theory has been derived from a variety of sources. The result, therefore, is an eclectic framework drawn from psychoanalytic, existential, humanistic, cognitive-behavioral, and general systems theories.

PSYCHOANALYTIC THEORY

Psychoanalytic theory has contributed to the treatment of people in crisis. Freud postulated an idea that is extremely applicable to crisis intervention and crisis theory. His assumption about *psychic energy* was that it is finite and only a limited amount exists for each of us. This assumption helps explain the disequilibrium that develops when a person's customary coping skills fail and his or her psychological energy is depleted. It also helps to explain why people with personality disorders, neurosis, and psychosis react more poorly in a crisis, as much of their psychic energy is used in maintaining their disorder, leaving no unused energy to combat unforeseen emergencies (Brenner, 1974, pp. 31–80).

In crisis theory probably more than in any other psychological theory, the counselor is advised to assess the client's ego strength and at times take over the function of the ego. The concept of ego strength is directly related to psychic energy in that people with personality disorders or psychotic disorders are usually unable to cope effectively with most precipitating events because their psychic energy is being used to deal with previous stressors, losses, and traumas.

EXISTENTIAL THEORY

Another contributor to crisis treatment is **existential theory**. Although true existential psychotherapy is considered a long-term therapy whose goal is basic revision of life perspective (Bugental, 1978, p. 13), some ideas from this approach are useful in a short-term adjustment model. Certainly, the existential thought that anxiety is a normal part of existence and can help self-development is useful to the crisis worker. This idea coincides with the Chinese idea of *danger and* *opportunity*. Without anxieties caused by new life situations, we would never grow. Therefore, anxiety as a motivator to risk and grow is a key concept from existential theory. The notion that we will all suffer in life at one time or another and that it will strengthen us can be seen as a reframe for the person in crisis.

Another concept from existential theory that is useful to crisis theory has to do with the individual's accepting personal responsibility and realizing that many problems are self-caused. Choice then becomes a major focus for the person in crisis. Empowering clients with choices and encouraging them to accept responsibility are useful strategies in many crisis situations. Consider a person recently confronted with her cocaine abuse. A crisis worker can assist this person in accepting responsibility for her addiction; the worker can offer alternative choices and be supportive while the client struggles with the anxiety of withdrawing from the cocaine habit.

HUMANISTIC APPROACH

The **humanistic approach** and person-centered therapies have much to offer to crisis intervention. This style of helping stresses the importance of trusting clients to realize their potential in the context of a therapeutic relationship. This optimism and hope that clients will recognize and overcome blocks to growth is the foundation for a counselor trying to help someone work through a difficult situation (Bugental, 1978, pp. 35–36). If I, as a crisis interventionist, do not truly believe my clients can work through their problems, why would I waste my effort on them? True, they may not resolve their difficulties *my* way, or at *my* time exactly, but I need to respect clients at their level and work from there. As long as they grow and develop, I can feel that I have contributed to the resolution of the crisis.

Carl Rogers, the founder of person-centered counseling (considered a humanistic therapy), has also contributed to the field of crisis intervention by his focus on reflective and empathetic techniques. These techniques, shown to be effective in treatment outcome, help clients acknowledge and freely express their emotions (Corsini & Wedding, 1989, pp. 175–179). In addition to these outcomes, humanistic techniques create an environment that is special.

Practitioners of person-centered counseling believe that people can grow in a beneficial direction if they can experience a relationship of true acceptance, genuineness, and empathetic understanding. Crises are seen as blocks to growth and *potential* for growth. By being present with the clients, counselors help clients begin to accept themselves, to trust in themselves, and to make new choices based on this self-acceptance and trust.

COGNITIVE-BEHAVIORAL THEORIES

Basically, every crisis model is based on the **behavioral problem-solving model,** which has three parts:

1. Define the problem.

2. Review what you have already tried to correct the problem.

3. Decide what you want when the problem is solved.

4. Brainstorm alternatives.

5. Select alternatives and commit to following through with them.

6. Follow up.

The **cognitive approaches** that blossomed in the 1970s and 1980s are also important in crisis work. As mentioned in Chapter 1, a person's cognitions, meanings, and perspectives about the precipitating event are important in the counselor's determining whether a crisis state develops. The cognitive approaches are largely based on Albert Ellis's rational-emotive therapy, Beck's cognitive therapy, Meichenbaum's self-instructional training and stress inoculation, and Lazarus's multimodal therapy. All these approaches are concerned with understanding the person's cognitive view of the problem, then restructuring and reframing the maladaptive cognitions (Peake, Borduin, & Archer, 1988, pp. 69–71). The cognitive approaches also stress homework assignments and follow-up.

FAMILY SYSTEMS THEORY

Systems theory is particularly useful in developmental crises and with clients of various cultural backgrounds, so the focus in this section is on these. Keep in mind that a situational crisis will also impact a person's interpersonal and occupational systems.

General systems theory is based on Newton's law of physics, which says that for every action, there is an equal and opposite reaction. Terms like *self-regulating mechanism, feedback, counteraction,* and *calibration* can be used to describe an interpersonal system as well as mechanical systems.

The idea is that if a member in a family unit makes any major changes in behavior, others in the family will behave in ways to prevent the change from happening. This is most likely due to fear of change at subconscious levels. Change often makes people feel anxious. Counteractive behaviors are used to lessen anxiety, often without the family members realizing what they are doing. Therapists will point out these processes and make clients conscious of them. Helpers must be sure that clients' anxiety is contained, that clients are supported, and that their perceptions are reframed. Typical counteractive behaviors used by family members include shaming the target member, threatening the person, and excluding or punishing the person. The one who is behaving outside the calibrated range of behaviors is often put in a position of preferring the acceptable behavior, even if it is pathological, rather than endure the counteraction from the family unit. Family systems theory helps explain why pathology exists in families so regularly and why change takes a long time to occur in a family. Stability (homeostasis) is a preferred state for us all—even if the consequence is to retain the symptoms.

Runaways *Runaway* is the term used in the family systems model to describe a true family crisis. This term has a very particular meaning in family systems theory. A runaway exists when the counteractive/negative feedback mechanisms fail to bring the situation back into calibration—that is, family members cannot create homeostasis by normal coping mechanisms. This runaway state often triggers a family to seek family counseling.

Of course, the family therapy models have usually focused on providing brief interventions, very much in keeping with the crisis model. Reframing and assigning positive connotations are two major intervention strategies in the family systems approaches, particularly the strategic models. Both these techniques aim at changing the internal cognitive experience of family members.

Just as a maintenance worker must come in and reset a thermostat if its mechanisms do not work to maintain temperature stability, a family worker comes in and resets the calibration of family rules after a runaway to help the family return to homeostasis, albeit a new stability. Figure 2.1 illustrates general systems theory for both a thermostat and a family. Crisis intervention often makes use of systems theory by employing techniques from structural and strategic problem-solving therapies (Peake et al., 1988, pp. 90–95).

Structural Family Therapy Some families may inadvertently maintain a crisis state in a family member because of their resistance to allowing passage through a critical developmental stage. **Structural family therapy** attempts to help everyone in the family move through new developmental stages at the same time by learning new roles in the family that are more adaptive. The range for allowable behaviors will be recalibrated with the effect of reducing counteractions (resistance). New boundaries are established that allow for age-appropriate independence and nurturance. Minuchin (1974) points out that these are the two main functions of a family: to provide support and nurturance and to create individuals who can function in society independent of their family of origin. Crisis workers must keep this in mind when assessing the nature of a client's crisis. It could be due to problems of closeness/support or distance/independence.

Certain terms may be helpful at this point to identify healthy versus unhealthy structures in families. They also shed light on why certain problems exist in families. These are words that describe specific types of roles and structures that become part of homeostasis in a family and that may need to be altered to move the family out of a runaway.

> *Enmeshed:* In an enmeshed situation, everyone in the family interferes and is overly involved in everyone else's decisions, feelings, wishes, and behaviors. Children may know too much about their parents and vice versa. An enmeshed family is observed when one sees *a lack of independence* of thought and feeling among family members. These families

THERMOSTAT AS SELF-REGULATING MECHANISM

	Range	
Counteraction/Negative Feedback Mechanisms (Below 68 degrees)	68 ·············· 72 Homeostasis	Counteraction/Negative Feedback Mechanisms (Above 72 degrees)

This thermostat allows the temperature to be between 68 degrees and 72 degrees. If the room becomes any colder or warmer, the mechanism will turn the heating unit on or off to cool or heat the room.

FAMILY AS SELF-REGULATING MECHANISM

Out-of-Range Behavior	Range			Out-of-Range Behavior
13-year-old talks about suicide	Moody	Cheerful	Excited	13-year-old is busy with friends and school; is too excited to eat or spend time with parents; is overly verbose
Counteraction/Negative Feedback Mechanism				Counteraction/Negative Feedback Mechanism
Parents take her to psychiatrist and listen more to her				Parents listen to her and encourage her to slow down and take deep breaths, and try to show interest in her life

Out-of-Range Behavior	Range			Out-of-Range Behavior
More than 15 minutes late	15 mins. late	On time	Early	No desire to go out with friends
Counteraction/Negative Feedback Mechanisms				Counteraction/Negative Feedback Mechanism
Parents impose restrictions/punishment; teenager can't go out next weekend				Parents talk to teen to find out what the problems are with her friends

In the first example, the acceptable range of behavior in this family allows the 13-year-old to display behavior from moody to excited, but when it dips as low as being suicidal or rises so high as to appear out of control at the other end of the spectrum, the family mechanisms break down and cannot restore the homeostasis. Similarly, the family can't control the behavior of a teenager who will not observe a family's curfew or, at the other extreme, has no desire to spend time with friends. *Continued*

FIGURE 2.1 *General Systems Theory*

FAMILY IN A RUNAWAY SITUATION

Out-of-Range Behavior	Range			Out-of-Range Behavior
	B	A–	A	
8-year-old refuses to do homework and fails the grade				8-year-old develops performance anxiety and severe compulsions trying to ensure perfection

Counteraction/Negative Feedback Mechanism	Counteraction/Negative Feedback Mechanism
Parents attempt punishment, scolding, but nothing helps	Parents try to tell child not to worry so much, but it does not help

CHANGE TO FAMILY SYSTEM TO OVERCOME RUNAWAY SITUATION

Out-of-Range Behavior	Range			Out-of-Range Behavior
D	C	B	B+	A

Successful Counteraction	Successful Counteraction
Parents engage tutor, help with homework, talk to teachers, use a behavior modification reward system	Parents display surprise, nonchalance, low-keyed celebration, and reinforcement

In the runaway situation, although the allowable behaviors in this family are for children to earn grades no lower than B on their report cards, the family is not able to stabilize itself with children who either will make no effort to do their schoolwork, even when it means failing the grade, or who experience extreme grade anxiety, trying to ensure perfection. The parents cannot fix these problems by helping, scolding, or coercing; they must seek outside help if the family is to return to a manageable level of homeostasis. The crisis worker might help the family set a range of acceptable academic achievement that would allow the children's behavior to change. Perhaps the parents could accept a C on some subjects or provide tutoring for very difficult subjects. On the other end, allowing the gifted child to make mistakes and even encouraging her to relax about her grades may be setting homeostasis at C through B. If the child gets an A, it's a surprise. These changes should relieve the child of anxiety and oppositional behaviors.

FIGURE 2.1 *Continued*

typically see themselves as very close or *too close*. Children from enmeshed families often grow up to find themselves in unhealthy relationships where battering, alcoholism, and other forms of abuse exist. A child grows up feeling no sense of separateness and has problems making decisions and functioning in other adult situations. Depression and anxiety are common in regard to relationships. A crisis state may occur when someone in the family attempts to break out of the enmeshment. Others may react by subtly punishing the individual—perhaps by the silent treatment or by noninclusion in family affairs. A healthy balance between closeness and separateness is the goal of counseling in these circumstances.

Diffuse: A family is diffuse when family members are not clear about who is to do what. Roles are not well defined or may be inconsistent (as when a 16-year-old girl raises a baby in the same home with her own parents. The baby will be confused about the role of his mother as he watches her be parented while she parents him). A pathological variation of this is called *cross-generational coalition*; here a parent and child team up against the other parent, thereby crossing the parent/child boundary. Incest, for example, is one of the worst cases of cross-generational coalition and results in moderate to severe disturbances to the child throughout her or his life. Clear age-appropriate boundaries are essential to healthy emotional functioning.

Disengaged: In a disengaged family, *distance* is the pattern. The rule in these families is not to get too close emotionally or socially. The relationship between parents and children and between spouses tends to be more functional than in some other troubled families. Independence is encouraged. However, children may feel unsupported and unloved in families where disengagement is strong. This feeling could lead to gang involvement, substance abuse, or teen pregnancy as a way for children to seek love and support or not to feel anything (substance abuse). Crisis workers can intervene by helping family members learn how to show support to one another to increase a sense of belonging.

Rigid: In families with rigid boundaries, spouses and children are treated only one way. There is no crossing over between generations: Children are to be seen and not heard. Wives clean, husbands work. Children obey. Father disciplines. Mother takes care of children. These rules are typical and can lead to rigid personality structures in the children who are brought up this way. Counselors need much skill to be able to reframe and educate parents with rigid boundaries. They must carefully respect cultural factors and be creative in their approaches. The following vignette is of a family with a problem. The approach used here combines structural family therapy with the family systems model.

Example   A family comes for help to straighten out the 13-year-old girl's behavior. She likes to be in her room alone, talks back to her parents, prefers her friends over her family, and is interested in boys. Her parents have been restricting her out-of-house activities, but that hasn't helped. As a crisis interventionist, I might restructure and reframe the whole system. Now, instead of two adults and a child, the home consists of two adults and a maturing adolescent who is behaving normally. The rules for behavior need to be changed to accommodate the structure change, thereby lessening negative feedback. This less restricted atmosphere will encourage the 13-year-old to communicate more with her parents. The parents must be made aware of the family's enmeshment. They must see that their teenager needs a sense of independence. This will be good training for her. She will soon be an adult.

In the **strategic family therapy** model, the goal is to shift the rules in the family to bring about a new homeostasis that doesn't include pathological behaviors. Insight into why the family behaves the way it does is not necessary. Short-term homeostatic systems therapy can be done in less than ten sessions and includes the following stages:

1. Introduction to treatment

2. Definition of the problem

3. Estimation of the behaviors maintaining the problem

4. Setting goals for treatment

5. Selecting and making interventions

6. Termination

Reframing a developmental crisis as a family or marital problem or a simple matter of adjustment is a common intervention. Additionally, prescribing the symptom is also a technique (albeit sophisticated) in alleviating crisis states (Haley, 1976). When using this technique, the counselor suggests that the client or family members engage in the problematic behavior, but with a slight modification. For example, clients who are very depressed might be told that they are not letting themselves really feel depressed and that they should close all the windows and curtains and sit in the dark. They are to focus on their sad feelings and cry for one hour. This episode will allow the clients to experience their symptoms in a new way. Usually, it results in an alleviation of the symptoms. A counselor must take great care with this technique and be well trained or receive expert supervision in using it. It is not recommended for suicidal clients.

Brief Therapy

Brief therapy can also be useful with an individual client. In this type of approach, clients explore their past patterns of behavior and how these have prevented the clients from succeeding at life the way they have wanted to succeed. They may explore interpersonal relationships, self-concept, and family patterns. The focus is on creative change and incorporating new styles of relating to the world. Sometimes the precipitating event is the best thing that could happen to a particular person because it leads him or her to a counselor's office where some of these chronic debilitating patterns can be identified. If past ineffective patterns can be recognized, they can be eliminated; the client can learn more effective behaviors with which to deal with the current as well as future stressors.

Brief therapy seems to be as effective as long-term therapy. According to Garfield (1980, p. 282), "the evidence to date suggests that time-limited marital-family therapy is not inferior to open-ended treatment." The average length reported in his research was seven sessions, a duration that certainly fits with the crisis intervention philosophy.

The ABC Model of Crisis Intervention

The **ABC model** of crisis intervention will be useful in most nonprofit agencies, county agencies, hospitals, HMOs, and with most insurance plans. It is a convenient way to organize a crisis interviewing session, either in person or on the phone. It can be completed in a 10-minute phone conversation, in one session, or over six sessions.

The ABC model was developed by the author. It is loosely based on Jones's (1968) A-B-C method of crisis management as well as lecture notes from and discussions with Mary Moline at California State University, Fullerton, in the 1980s. A brief outline of the model is presented here, and later chapters explore in detail the different aspects of the model. In general, the crisis intervention model is an action-oriented effort between a helper and a person immobilized by an emergency situation; the purpose is to provide temporary but immediate relief. This treatment differs from psychotherapy, which is usually a more intensive, introspective analysis between a professional therapist and a client; its goal is to provide self-understanding and reconstruction of long-standing personality traits and behavior (Cormier, Cormier, & Weisser, 1986, p. 19).

The focus of the ABC model is to identify the precipitating event, the client's cognitions about the precipitating event, subjective distress, failed coping mechanisms, and impaired functioning. Remember that these are the aspects of a crisis. The goal is to help the client integrate the precipitating event into his or her daily functioning and return to pre-crisis levels emotionally, occupationally, and interpersonally.

Developing and Maintaining Contact (A) is the first phase of a crisis intervention interview. Rapport building via basic attending skills is the foundation of the therapeutic encounter. Without establishing contact with the counselor that the client perceives as empathic, present, nonjudgmental, and genuine, the client will not move into parts B and C of the model. Beginning crisis intervention students are often told that before they give advice, they should make sure clients trust them and themselves to follow through with it.

Identifying the Problem and Therapeutic Interaction (B), the second phase, focuses on delineating the problem. Because crisis intervention is brief and time limited, the interventionist needs to zoom in quickly on why the client is seeking help at this particular time. A sharp focus on the problem will prevent distracting issues from confusing the crisis and depleting the client's needed coping energy.

The B section is most important. Identifying perspective, subjective distress, and current and previous functioning takes up most of the middle part of the model. With the basic attending skills of part A, the crisis worker collects the necessary information to understand the nature of the crisis and then provide new ways for the client to think about, perceive, and cognitively process the situation.

Coping (C) is the last phase of the model. Once the crisis interventionist achieves contact with the client and identifies the crisis, together they explore new coping methods. The worker encourages the client to examine alternative ways to cope, and then presents his or her own suggestions. Last, the counselor does a follow-up of some type.

Key Terms for Study

ABC model: One way to structure crisis intervention. It includes (A) developing and maintaining contact, (B) identifying the problem, and (C) coping.

behavioral problem-solving model: Approach focusing on goal setting, problem solving, and brainstorming alternatives.

brief therapy: May be confused with crisis intervention; however, its focus is on changing long-standing behavior patterns rather than on focusing only on the current precipitating event.

Coconut Grove fire: Occurred in 1942; over 400 people died, leaving many survivors in crisis. It is considered one of the major events leading to the development of crisis intervention as a form of mental health treatment.

cognitive approaches: Approaches focusing on a person's perceptions and thinking processes and how these lead to crisis states.

Community Mental Health Centers Act of 1963: Legislation enacted during the Kennedy administration directing all states to provide mental health treatment for people in crisis.

existential theory: Theory from which crisis intervention took the ideas of choice and anxiety. The crisis worker believes that anxiety can be a motivator for change and encourages the client to master anxiety realistically by making choices and accepting responsibility for the choices.

grassroots: Upward movement from local groups that led to the creation in the 1960s and 1970s of many agencies to meet the needs of various populations not being helped by traditional governmental agencies.

grief work: Crisis intervention largely based on working with survivors and family members of victims of the Coconut Grove fire. It was with this population that Caplan and Lindemann learned how to conduct short-term interventions.

health maintenance organization (HMO): The current trend in health insurance. These organizations focus on maintaining health rather than curing illness. The orientation of mental health care under this style of management is definitely crisis intervention.

humanistic approach: Model using a person-centered approach in developing rapport with clients. Its focus is the use of basic attending skills and attention to the inherent growth potential in the client.

Eric Lindemann: Worked with Caplan on the Wellesley project and helped create crisis intervention as we know it. He is recognized for his contributions to grief work.

paraprofessionals: Originally community volunteers. Because of the tremendous number of clients needing help at the same time after the Coconut Grove fire, it was necessary to employ community volunteers who were not professionally trained to conduct crisis intervention sessions. These "paraprofessionals" became part of many agencies in later decades.

psychoanalytic theory: An approach considered the opposite of crisis intervention but with certain ideas useful for the crisis worker. The notion that we have only a certain amount of psychic energy to deal with life stressors leads us to keep our clients proceeding at a slow pace so they don't deplete this energy. Also, ego strength is a useful concept, as shown in Chapter 1.

strategic family therapy: An approach for treating the entire family when a crisis affects any or all members. It is brief, problem solving, and goal oriented and largely based on systems theory.

structural family therapy: An approach focusing on the boundaries and roles of family members and the crises that arise when families must adjust to changing roles because of normal evolution.

systems theory: An approach useful in understanding families in crisis. The idea is that a family is a self-regulating system and that when any member behaves outside the norms, other members will attempt to cope with this behavior by counteraction. When this counteraction fails (coping fails), a runaway develops in the family dynamics. This runaway is a crisis and often requires the intervention of a family counselor.

Wellesley project: The first organized attempt at introducing crisis intervention into a community, developed by Caplan and Lindemann.

Ethical and Professional Issues

The Need for Ethics

Strong ethical practice is especially important in the field of crisis intervention because clients in crisis come to a counselor in a vulnerable state, one of disequilibrium and instability. To take advantage of someone in such an unsteady state would be fairly easy. At the outset of counseling, clients often feel hopeless and scared. They might view a counselor who reaches out with empathy and seems to have all the answers as a hero or savior of some type. Crisis interventionists must adhere to strong ethical behaviors to help clients see them and their abilities in a realistic light.

Use of Paraprofessionals

Some mental health professionals may feel that crisis intervention should be provided only by professionals, those with at least a master's degree or license. However, as discussed in Chapter 2, crisis intervention began with the use of community workers or so-called paraprofessionals. These workers often functioned in multidisciplinary team settings such as county agencies and grassroots nonprofit organizations. Effective crisis intervention can be conducted by undergraduate student trainees or community volunteers as well as graduate level and professional counselors, if their training is appropriate and they are properly supervised.

The use of the paraprofessional crisis worker will be especially important in the next few years for several reasons. The economic recession of the early 1990s plus a decided shift in governmental policies have led to cutbacks in government spending on human services programs. This has meant less money or *no* money available to pay mental health workers. In these circumstances, the use of volunteers and paraprofessionals makes excellent economic sense as most professional therapists will not provide crisis intervention consistently for the $6.00 to $9.00 an hour that is paid to many paraprofessionals.

Also, many situations—including the AIDS epidemic and family deterioration—will ensure that crises will be plentiful and intervention will be desired. When immediate, low-cost help is needed, using paraprofessionals makes the community stronger by ensuring that its population is functioning and coping with stress.

Self-Awareness and Countertransference

Self-awareness is a tool available to crisis workers if they are willing to bring themselves into the interview therapeutically. Therapeutic awareness means being conscious of your own emotions, values, opinions, and behavior. Understanding your own psychological processes and dynamics can help you guide another through her or his processes (Corey, Corey, & Callanan, 1993, pp. 30–32). Students can learn therapeutic awareness in training sessions of crisis intervention classes; such training can help students take an honest, in-depth look at themselves in relation to the crisis of interest. It can be a valuable learning experience, enhancing the crisis worker's skills in helping clients. If a worker learns to deal with all the issues surrounding AIDS, for example, he or she has a better chance of helping a client deal with them.

Countertransference is an issue that often must be addressed in the helping professions. Countertransference can be defined as an "unconsciously determined attitudinal set held by the therapist which interferes with his work" (Singer, 1970, p. 290). It can be worked through effectively with personal therapy, lab sessions, and active self-exploration. A very common occurrence for beginning crisis intervention students is for them to have experienced one or more of the situational crises practiced in coaching sessions. If they have not worked through the crisis completely, their own feelings may interfere with their ability to remain calm, objective, and client focused. However, once the students' unresolved issues are discovered and processed, both in their own counseling and in lab group, they often are able to work quite effectively with clients going through that same type of crisis. Countertransference is not restricted to students in training. In actuality, this concept was first developed by Freud in his training of psychoanalysts. Even the highly trained professional is liable to experience countertransference from time to time—and this is the primary reason that personal analysis has been encouraged for psychoanalysts from the very beginning of the discipline.

Dual Relationships

Another ethical issue involves **dual relationships**—a counselor's having more than one kind of relationship with a client. When counselors are providing crisis intervention to a client, they should not be involved with that client on a personal level of any kind. This includes prohibition of any sexual relationship, social relationship, employee relationship, or financial relationship that is not directly related to the provision of crisis intervention. This separation is necessary because a person in crisis is often in a vulnerable state and could be taken advantage of quite easily by a counselor (who is viewed as an expert). Another reason to avoid dual relationships is because of the possible emotional damage clients might sustain if they were to experience the counselor in a different role and then be disillusioned or disappointed. Also, the power differential between counselor and client is enormous. The counselor knows quite a bit about the client, and this knowledge can be a source of awkwardness for the client when he or she is out of the therapeutic situation.

The most potent word on the subject is this: Don't make friends or lovers of your clients. It is unethical and in some cases, illegal.

Confidentiality

Confidentiality is one of the hallmarks of any trusting relationship. It is also an important part of the ethical code for mental health providers. A broad concept that refers to safeguarding clients from unauthorized disclosures of information made in the therapeutic relationship, confidentiality is an explicit promise by the counselor to reveal nothing unless agreed on by the client. *Privileged* communication, which is sometimes confused with confidentiality, is the legal right in statute that protects clients from having their confidences revealed publicly (Corey et al., 1993, pp. 102–103).

As they relate to crisis intervention, however, some **exceptions to privilege and confidentiality** do exist. **Privilege** is waived if the client signs a document giving the helper permission to disclose the communications between the client and the counselor. Clients may be asked to waive privilege to assure continuity of care among mental health professionals, to provide for appropriate supervision, when access to records is needed for court testimony, and if the information is needed for submitting health insurance claims. *Confidentiality* can be broken in cases of child abuse or elder abuse, when the client is gravely disabled, and when the client is a danger to self or others.

Sometimes, a client's mental condition will be the focus of a lawsuit and in some cases confidentiality can be ethically and legally broken. For example, a client who sues a therapist for malpractice and claims to have suffered emotional damage because of the therapist's incompetence gives up privilege to communications from the therapy sessions. The therapist may use any case notes to defend against the malpractice charge. A similar example in which a client would forfeit the protection of privilege would be in a case in which the client is attempting to prove emotional injury in a worker's compensation lawsuit.

The other exceptions to confidentiality fit under the adage, "Privileged communication ends where public peril begins." This includes peril to clients if they endanger *themselves* because of a mental disorder. If clients are considered suicidal or gravely disabled and unable to care for themselves, helpers may breach confidentiality to protect them. The spirit of this allowance is that sharing of information is meant to be among professionals, family, and friends, not for frivolous purposes.

Gravely disabled clients are those who, because of a mental disorder, cannot take care of their daily needs for food, shelter, medical care, clothing, and so on. Clearly, it is more important to break confidentiality to save someone with Alzheimer's disease who is delusional about the food in the house than to maintain confidentiality and let the person starve.

The other situations in which privileged communications should be broken involve trying to prevent the client from harming others. These conditions include elder abuse, child abuse, and the possibility that the client might cause different kinds of **danger to others**.

Elder Abuse Reporting Act

The department of social services in some states has an adult protective services program that responds to reports of abuse of the elderly (adults over 65 years old). **Elder abuse** refers to any of the following acts inflicted by other than accidental means on an elder by another person: physical abuse, fiduciary abuse (involves trust and money), and neglect or abandonment. In many states, knowledge of such abuse must be reported to social services, the police, or a nursing home ombudsman (governmental investigator).

Some agencies have also begun taking reports of abuse of the disabled adult population. This could cover any adult who suffers from mental or physical disability such as mental retardation or blindness.

Child Abuse Reporting Act

Since passage by Congress of the National Child Abuse Prevention and Treatment Act in 1974, many states have enacted laws requiring professionals to report child abuse. States differ on the indicators for reporting and whether sanctions will be imposed on individuals for not reporting. According to most professional associations, protecting children from harm is an ethical obligation, and there is a growing trend to ensure that reporting professionals are given immunity from being sued if the suspicion proves to be false (Carey, 1996, p. 179). **Child abuse reporting** includes suspicions of physical abuse, sexual abuse, general neglect, and emotional abuse.

In many states, child abuse must be reported within 36 hours of its discovery to the department of social services or the police. The child protective services program will then investigate the suspicion. Remember that as a mental health provider, you are not required to have evidence of abuse before you report; you need only the suspicion that it exists. If you suspect abuse that is later proved and you failed to report it, you may be fined by the state. On the other hand, more and more states are ensuring immunity from suit for false reports.

The Tarasoff Case

The consequences of failing to warn an individual of possible danger to her or him by another are dramatically illustrated in the Tarasoff case. In 1969, Prosenjit Poddar was seeing a therapist at the campus counseling center of the University of California, Berkeley. Poddar confided to the therapist that he intended to kill

Tatiana Tarasoff when she returned from Brazil. The therapist considered Poddar dangerous and called campus police, requesting that Poddar be confined. This confinement was not done; worse, the therapist's supervisor ordered that all case notes be destroyed. Tarasoff was later killed by Poddar, and her parents filed suit against the California Board of Regents. The decision from this case requires any therapist to notify the police and intended victim when possible if he or she has reasonable belief that the client is dangerous toward others. This is known as the "duty to warn" (Corey et al., 1993, pp. 117–119).

Informed Consent

Informed consent is a way of "providing clients with information they need to become active participants in the therapeutic relationship" (Corey et al., 1993, p. 87). Although there are no specific rules on how much information a therapist is to provide, there are three legal elements to informed consent. First, the clinician must make sure the client has the ability to make rational decisions and if not, must ensure that a parent or guardian takes responsibility for giving consent. Second, therapists must give clients information in a clear way and check their understanding of the risks and benefits of treatment and alternate procedures available. Third, the client must consent freely to treatment. The exceptions to these elements occur when clients are dangerous to themselves and others or they are gravely disabled. Electroconvulsive shock treatments and psychosurgery (lobotomies) cannot be done without consent; however, there are times when medication is given without client consent.

Supervision and Training

The ethical code requiring counselors to receive appropriate supervision and training must be followed for both the benefit of the client and the clinician's growth and confidence. Unless paraprofessionals are supervised by a licensed professional, most agencies—county, state, and nonprofit—do not let them provide crisis intervention and counseling. Even seasoned therapists should consult with colleagues on cases for which they have minimal training or experience. Referring a client to another helper is often done by crisis workers because the crisis worker's duties are largely assessing and brokering out. These tasks require a sound knowledge of community resources for a variety of problems.

Being able to assess for organic illnesses and severe mental illness is especially important when a helper is conducting a crisis interview. Some cases require a multidisciplinary team approach with medical doctor involvement and they must be identified if the patient is to receive the total help needed. Even though making technical diagnoses is not usually considered appropriate for paraprofessionals, knowledge of the **Mental Status Exam** and the *Diagnostic and Statistical Manual of Mental Disorders* (American Psychiatric Association, 1994) will be helpful in assuring that clients receive services from the type of professional appropriate to their needs.

> **Example**   Suppose that a 45-year-old woman comes to a community center because her 70-year-old mother has been behaving strangely, doesn't recognize her family members, and leaves the gas stove burners on all day. Knowing that these symptoms are indicative of Alzheimer's disease or other organic brain disorder will help the crisis worker develop treatment strategies. Most important is having the woman examined neurologically to rule out any medical cause for her unusual behavior.

A brief outline of a formal Mental Status Exam and its use is presented in Chapter 5.

Key Terms for Study

child abuse reporting: Required of anyone working with children as a counselor, doctor, teacher, or in any other capacity since passage of the 1974 Child Abuse Prevention and Treatment Act by Congress. These people must report any suspicions of child abuse to the child protective services agency in their state. This requirement is mandatory and in many states overrides the client's right to confidentiality.

confidentiality: An ethical standard providing the client with the right for all disclosures in counseling to be kept private.

countertransference: A situation in a counseling relationship that arises from unresolved feelings experienced by a counselor in a session with a client. These feelings come out of the counselor's personal life and cause him or her to act out these feelings with a client, behavior that may cause emotional harm to the client.

danger to others: Condition in which a client is deemed to be a threat to others. At this time, the counselor must breach confidentiality and report his or her concerns to the police and/or the intended victim. This is called the "duty to warn."

Diagnostic and Statistical Manual of Mental Disorders: The guide developed by the American Psychiatric Association that describes mental disorders, now in its fourth edition.

dual relationship: A relationship that a counselor engages in with the client outside the professional one—for example, a social, sexual, or business relationship.

elder abuse: Physical abuse, fiduciary abuse, neglect, or abandonment of someone 65 years old or older. In many states, anyone working with clients over 65 years of age must report suspected cases of elder abuse to the state's adult protective services agency. This reporting is often mandatory and grounds for breaching confidentiality.

exceptions to privilege and confidentiality: Situations in which communications between therapist and client can be legally and ethically shared with others. In the case of confidentiality, these include elder abuse and child abuse; when the client is gravely disabled; and when the client is a danger to self or others. In the case of privilege, these include voluntary waivers given by the client for information to be shared in a limited forum as well as some involuntary disclosure, as in certain court cases.

informed consent: Permission for treatment given by a client to a therapist after the client has been thoroughly informed about all aspects of the treatment. Anyone entering a counseling relationship has the right to understand the nature of therapy, give his or her consent for it, understand that it is voluntary, and be told the limits of confidentiality.

Mental Status Exam: An examination used to rule out severe forms of mental illness and organic disorders. As part of their ethical responsibility, crisis interventionists must know when to refer a client to a physician. Use of this exam can help in making those determinations.

privilege: The legal counterpart of confidentiality. Clients may waive the right to privilege if they wish the counselor to share certain information in court or other limited venues.

CHAPTER FOUR

A Multicultural Perspective

Interest in the sensitivity of counselors and therapists to culturally diverse clients has been growing in the past few decades. It began in the 1960s when civil rights and affirmative action emerged and became a part of formal education in the late 1980s and 1990s. Arredondo and colleagues (1996) describe specific behaviors and attitudes of the multiculturally aware counselor. According to Arredondo et al. (1996), "Multicultural counseling refers to preparation and practices that integrate multicultural and culture-specific awareness, knowledge, and skills into counseling interactions" (p. 43). They suggest that *multicultural* refers to five major cultural groups in the United States: **African-American**, **Asian-American**, Caucasian, Hispanic, and Native American. The reader is encouraged to obtain a copy of their article and keep it for reference.

In this chapter, we look briefly at the **help-seeking attitudes** of females versus males as well as help-seeking behaviors of Hispanics, African-Americans, and Asian-Americans. Next, the process of becoming a culturally sensitive therapist is reviewed. Last, we examine various issues important for the crisis worker regarding certain ethnic groups.

The Role of Ethnicity and Gender on Help-Seeking Attitudes

Gender seems to be related to help-seeking attitudes. Johnson (1988) found women to be more tolerant of the stigma related to receiving personal counseling and that they therefore sought help more often than did men. And Pomales and Williams (1989) found that level of ethnicity interacted with gender in the willingness of Hispanic undergraduate subjects to see a white counselor; that is, female Hispanics were more open to seeking help than were male Hispanics. The root of these findings might be lack of knowledge of what is expected, because of cultural differences, as well as differences in socialization patterns between male and female Hispanics.

Other studies (e.g., Levine & Franco, 1983; Marshall & Kratz, 1988) also found that gender and ethnicity were related to subjects' willingness to seek therapy. Levine and Franco (1988) found that Anglo males and females and Mexican-American females signed up for a follow-up interview with the directive-style therapist more often than did Mexican-American males. Marshall and Kratz (1988), however, found that familiarity with therapy increased the ratings of the counselor's expertness and trustworthiness among all respondents—males and females.

Other researchers have explored the impact of the trust factor on African-Americans' help-seeking attitudes. In their examination of African-American clients' expectations about counseling, Watkins and Terrell (1988) found that mistrust of mainstream Caucasian counselors was a factor in negative attitudes about counseling.

These study results suggest that there will be differences in attitudes toward the crisis worker and the process of receiving help among various ethnic groups and between men and women. To be effective, crisis workers must be sensitive to these differences.

Development of Culturally Sensitive Psychotherapists

As part of a course in a doctoral program at the University of Southern California, several students co-authored an article that describes the **development of cultural sensitivity** among therapists. The seven students and the professor found similar patterns happening as they all struggled with gender and ethnic issues involved in diagnosing and treating various groups. Based on case vignettes and class discussion, a model of developmental stages was created and is shown in Table 4.1. Counselors don't have to be perfect in their interventions with all cultures, but they need, at minimum, to be aware of possible cultural, ethnic, religious, and gender issues that may bear on the crisis intervention process.

It can be helpful for counselors to have knowledge about various cultures ahead of time, but more important is following the client's lead to arrive at a place that she or he can feel understood and validated. The consequences when a counselor fails to respect cultural differences may very well be the end of any crisis intervention. Following is a case example in which the therapist did not display cultural sensitivity; the consequences were that the client dropped out of therapy prematurely.

A 41-year-old man requested an emergency session in regard to his marriage. At his request, I saw him Saturday morning. He spoke with an Asian accent and identified himself as half-Chinese and half-Spanish. He was born in China.

As we discussed his presenting problem, he resisted any of my suggestions that part of his problem might derive from his wife's being Caucasian and the disapproval that her parents and siblings expressed toward him. He had come to my office to appease his wife who said she would leave him unless he sought counseling. They have a poor sex life and he was resistant to discuss this openly with me. He kept insisting that he had the problem; he described himself as cold and not liking to be around people.

I noticed myself becoming very frustrated. He refused to accept the idea that he and his wife had a relationship problem. I guess he sensed my frustration because he asked me if I could refer him to another therapist. He had many demands regarding the times

TABLE 4.1 Proposed Stages and Stage-Specific Consequences in Therapists' Development of Cultural Sensitivity

Stage	Description	Consequence
Unawareness of cultural issues	Therapist does not consider a cultural hypothesis in diagnosis.	Therapist does not understand the significance of the clients' cultural background to their functioning.
Heightened awareness of culture	Therapist is aware that cultural factors are important in fully understanding clients.	Therapist feels unprepared to work with culturally different clients; frequently applies own perception of the client's cultural background and therefore fails to understand the cultural significance for the specific client; can at times accurately recognize the influence of clients' cultural background on their functioning.
Burden of considering culture	Therapist is hypervigilant in identifying cultural factors and is, at times, confused in determining the cultural significance of the client's actions.	Therapist believes that consideration of culture is perceived as detracting from his or her clinical effectiveness.
Movement toward cultural sensitivity	Therapist entertains cultural hypotheses and carefully tests these hypotheses from multiple sources before accepting cultural explanations.	Therapist has increased likelihood of accurately understanding the role of culture on clients' functioning.

Source: Lopez et al. (1989). Copyright 1989 by the American Psychological Association. Adapted with permission.

he was available for appointments, and he refused marital therapy, which I had recommended. I can only guess that part of his issues are cultural in nature, but unfortunately, I will not have the opportunity to explore this with him (Lopez et al., 1989, p. 370).

"This vignette indicated that the therapist did not consider cultural factors in her work with this ethnic minority client. She appears to be defining the problem for the client without considering the client's definition of the problem and working from there. This is not to say that the therapist is wrong in her assessment; the client is likely having marital problems. However, her failure to validate his explanatory model or interpretation of the problem may have led to his request for another therapist"(Lopez et al., 1989, p. 371).

The intent with this chapter is for readers to learn how, looking at certain groups, to get a beginning working model. This model should help them understand various norms and family structures of the group, various crises that often arise, and interventions to alleviate them.

Mexican-American Families

Over 6.5 million **Mexican-Americans** are estimated to live in the United States. They often suffer discrimination in housing, employment, and education. Their school dropout rate is high and they are often exploited by employers who keep them in low-paying and low-prestige jobs. They often do not receive welfare benefits despite their high unemployment rates.

Most Mexicans are *mestizos*, a mix of American Indian and Spanish. During the 17th to 19th centuries, Spain extended its rule over the region that is now Mexico into California and other southwestern states. The Spaniards and Indians shared much with each other, but the Spaniards took Mexico's riches and kept the natives poor. Spanish priests taught Catholicism to the natives, who combined it with their own religions. From these interchanges, a new culture was created—the Mexican culture.

After the 1848 gold rush in California, settlers from the eastern part of the United States came west, and conflicts began to erupt between them and the Mexicans. The two groups lived separately, and Mexicans lost much of their property and rights. The United States citizens were happy to settle in the areas where there was gold and other natural resources, such as agricultural land and water. The Mexicans were pushed far into Mexico where the land is arid and not suitable for agriculture. Industrial development has been slow, and Mexico has become a poor country (McGoldrick, Pearce, & Giordana, 1982).

Many Mexicans stayed in the United States and created pockets of subculture, which are sometimes called barrios. They speak English and have adopted some mainstream values. However, they still maintain certain distinguishing behaviors. Because the United States and Mexico are so close to each other geographically, Mexicans continue to immigrate, but many enter the United States illegally. Their resulting undocumented status is an important factor in understanding their behavior. Sensitivity to this history can help the crisis counselor approach the Mexican- American client in a more empathic frame of reference.

CULTURAL PATTERNS

Mexican-American cultural patterns include certain beliefs, developmental norms, and family roles and rules. One particular Mexican ideal that may differ from Anglo norms has to do with certain child-rearing practices. In Anglo-American culture, autonomy is stressed; in Mexican culture, however, nurturance and obedience to authority are stressed. Mexican-American children will often appear to be delayed developmentally (e.g., a 5-year-old sitting on his mother's lap, a 3-year-old drinking out of a bottle, a 14-year-old still spending all her time with her mother), but these are well within their cultural norms.

Physical distance among Mexican-Americans is another cultural variation that is different. Interpreted by Anglo standards, Mexican-Americans might seem overinvolved with, enmeshed with, or overprotective of one another. This interpretation could simply mean that the family members sit close together or that various family members assume they are to be included in any individual family member's crisis (McGoldrick et al., 1982, p. 151). Keeping in mind **the role of systems theory** is imperative in working with Mexican-American families because of this strong norm of family involvement by each member.

> **Example** If an 18-year-old daughter were to be raped or a 22-year-old daughter were being battered, it is likely that each young woman's family would become involved in helping her through the crisis. This is not to say they would tell her to leave her husband or go to trial for the rape, but she would most likely tell them of her distress. In many Anglo cultures, victims might well deal with these crises with the help of professionals and community support groups, without even telling the family.

Sometimes Mexican-American families may seek help because they do not have knowledge of community resources (McGoldrick et al., 1982, p. 154). With language barriers, racism, or lack of exposure, they might not know even the most basic services available. Rather than try to conduct extensive introspective, psychodynamic psychotherapy (which, by the way, is counter to most Mexican-American norms), serving as a broker for services is often an extremely helpful role for a counselor who is working with a Mexican-American family in crisis.

> **Example** In some families, the children are bilingual although a parent may speak only Spanish. Sometimes the children do not get the services they need because the parents feel embarrassed or frustrated when trying to communicate their needs to professionals and agencies. Often, the job of a crisis worker is to make contact with a school official or a legal advocacy program and connect the family with the service. Such action is very useful in alleviating this type of crisis.

DYSFUNCTIONAL PATTERNS OF CULTURAL TRANSITION

Other crises that may emerge in Mexican-American families could reflect patterns that developed and were functional when the family first immigrated but have now become rigid and restricting for certain family members. For example, many parents have depended on their children to be intermediaries with the larger culture, and allowing the children to separate from them in later years can be very difficult (McGoldrick et al., 1982, p. 155).

Another example has to do with the adolescent who incorporates certain Anglo values that are contrary to traditional Mexican cultural patterns. Rejection of old Mexican values may be the precipitating event for a crisis in a Mexican mother or father.

> **Example**   A 15-year-old girl may act out rebelliously by dating boys, staying out late, or dressing less than modestly. A crisis interventionist may suggest that the parents take a more active role in their daughter's growing up by structuring traditional activities for her such as a *quincinera*—a party to announce entrance to womanhood. The girl's acting-out behavior can then be reframed as her confusion about whether she's growing up or not. With a structured ritual, everyone will more easily accept role changes; this structure should help reduce the family's distress (McGoldrick et al., 1982, p. 156).

Using negotiation skills and finding compromises are essential for the interventionist working with dual-culture families. Remember that the parents have chosen to live in the United States; this decision says something about their desire to be connected with some parts of American culture. A counselor can weave this idea with positive reframes, pointing out the opportunity afforded the family by adopting certain Anglo behavioral norms.

African–American Families

In an ideal world, we would pay no attention to skin color. However, if we as mental health providers don't realize that African-Americans differ in various ways from mainstream American culture, we may do disservice to this group in our efforts to be nonracists or liberals. You personally may not be a bigot or discriminate against African-Americans, but you might want to be aware of your own naivete when you try to understand how being African-American may impact a person's crisis state.

When one considers the history of African-Americans, much of their family structure and value systems make sense. Raised in slavery, the African-American family learned to exist in settings where roles were flexible and families were usually extended to several generations. These aspects can be readily seen in modern-day African-American families. Elderly people as well as young adults "tend to be supported by the collective efforts of family members both within and outside the nuclear family" (McGoldrick et al., 1982, p. 90).

This history certainly has implications for the crisis interventionist in terms of utilizing naturally existing support systems for any particular individual. Also, exploring the role norms of the family system is important for the therapist so as not to see a problem when none exists.

Example A child may be brought in by his parents for misbehaving in school. You may discover that the parents do not understand this behavior and seem to be ineffective in eliminating it. Perhaps the child's grandmother is perceived by all to be the primary disciplinarian and nurturer. Instead of trying to lay those responsibilities onto the parents and disengage the grandmother from the problem, you may instead bring in the grandmother and work with her alongside the parents. You would be exhibiting culturally biased behavior to insist that only the parents be involved in their child's therapy in this case.

THE ROLE OF RELIGION

Slaves found solace in the view that God would provide a better world for them after life in this world of suffering. This tradition of strong religious beliefs and practices has been passed down through the generations and must be kept in mind by the crisis worker.

The church has been a forum in which many African-American women and men have expressed their talents and leadership skills (McGoldrick et al., 1982, p. 96), a kind of haven from a racist society. For the crisis interventionist, incorporating the church—whether seeking support from a minister or encouraging client involvement in church activities—is a valuable tool in working with African-Americans. Even though trust in mainstream, middle-class mental health counselors may not be high among many in this community, usually it will be strong with an African-American minister. Sometimes, however, paranoia and suspicion of the mainstream system and its agents are warranted; in some cases, appeals for help to the church do not produce the desired results. If the crisis worker encounters extremely distrusting African-Americans, instead of trying to convince them that he or she can be trusted, the counselor might more productively empathize with the distrust and help these clients into various long-standing, trustworthy support systems.

PROBLEM-SOLVING MODEL

Not all African-American families in crisis need to be referred to traditional support systems. A growing number have moved quite easily into the mainstream, middle-American value systems and will use the appropriate interventions. Focusing on the presenting problems and setting up goal-specific plans will often work well. Even insight-oriented therapy will be accepted and sought by some African-Americans. The most important idea is to try to get a feel for the needs of any particular client/family and, with cultural sensitivity, attempt to meet them. Always, the reality that racism exists in society must be acknowledged by any counselor so he or she can understand the world of the client.

Wright (1993) emphasizes the importance of cultural sensitivity when dealing with African-American males about issues of sexual behavior and the risk of HIV infection. His research shows that mainstream thinking about various sexual categories and other cultural values related to sexual behavior may be insensitive to the African-American male's enduring cultural values. Because AIDS is widespread among the African-American population and is primarily spread by men, intervention strategies must be developed to take these differing values into consideration.

Specifically, Wright suggests that current educational materials, health facilities, and community-based AIDS education and prevention programs are inadequate in their cultural and racial sensitivity. He states that "the AIDS epidemic is not merely a medical dilemma but is a socio-cultural medical dilemma. For African-American men, AIDS has become an overwhelming and devastating blow that has torn away at their already threatened health and social status" (Wright, 1993, p. 430). Wright recommends that future policy address cultural issues when programs are created to help prevent and reduce the risk of AIDS transmission among African-Americans.

Although this research suggests that social policy be culturally sensitive, individual crisis workers can also benefit from these studies into the nature of the sexual behaviors of African-American males. Particularly, the crisis worker must realize that for this group, their sexual behavior does not necessarily fit with their identity as a homosexual, heterosexual, or bisexual. Asking questions such as, "Are you gay?" to assess for level of risk for AIDS would be inappropriate for this population because even though the man may be engaging in homosexual behavior, he may not regard himself as a homosexual. More suitable questions might be simply to identify specific behaviors known to be high risk and to provide information about high-risk behaviors and ways to prevent transmission of the HIV virus. (See Chapter 8 for more details.)

Once you understand the client's perspective, you have managed the most important part of your task. Using it to help the person cope is the next challenge.

Asian–American Families

Members of Asian-American families have their roots in East Asia—China, Japan, and Korea. This area is distinguished by having the oldest continually recorded civilization in the world. Its history gives it a background very different from that of the West in a variety of ways. For example, there are differences in philosophical approaches to life that are dictated in the East by Confucianism and Buddhism rather than Judeo-Christianity. These systems do not stress independence and autonomy but rather emphasize the importance of the family and the specific hierarchical roles established for all members. Rules for behavior are extremely strong and more formalized than in other cultures. Because these people lived for years under oppressive dynastic rule and needed to maintain a large labor force capable of heavy manual and agricultural labor, male offspring became more valued than females (McGoldrick et al., 1982, pp. 208–210).

There are also historical differences among the various Asian cultures. Language represents one difference; another is the specific immigration problems and circumstances for each of the groups. For example, many Vietnamese immigrated in boats to escape Communist rule whereas many Japanese are able to come to America because of financial investments and employment opportunities.

CRISIS INTERVENTION ISSUES

Although not all persons of Asian descent will be identical, certain characteristics can be observed regarding the expression of a crisis state and coping skills. The typical middle-class Judeo-Christian attitude of many mainstream training programs and work settings in the mental health field often does not address the special needs of Asian-Americans.

The idea that family should be placed ahead of individualism is one cultural difference that can definitely affect the counselor's work. Asian-Americans are traditionally reinforced to respect the family more highly than their own personal needs. Kashiwagi (1993) states that "back in the old country the people had to band together, work together cooperatively, just to survive. I think because this value system worked then it was handed down" (p. 46). He further proposes that Asians who came to America felt the need to prove themselves and this set up the "model minority" stereotype. This tradition of being overachieving, hardworking, and industrious may lead to stress and pressures to maintain the status quo inside and outside the Asian-American community; it is something the crisis worker should keep in mind when working with this population.

SOUTHEAST ASIANS AND POSTTRAUMATIC STRESS DISORDER

Kinzie and his colleagues (1984) have noted certain values held by Southeast Asian patients that affect the course of psychotherapy when they are treated for posttraumatic stress disorder (PTSD):

1. An orientation to the past, including great respect for ancestors;

2. a primary reliance on the family as the basis of personal identity and self-esteem;

3. the tolerance of multiple belief systems in regard to religion and cosmology; an acceptance of life as it is, rather than what it could be. (pp. 645–646)

The mainstream-oriented crisis worker must consider these aspects when dealing with this population so as not to force values onto them that do not fit with their cultural norms. However, Boehnlein (1987) believes that the mainstream cognitive psychotherapeutic approaches do have relevance for working with Cambodian patients with posttraumatic stress disorder. "This approach facilitates an ongoing dialogue allowing the therapist to directly address issues in treatment that may relate to conflicting beliefs and values, along with doubts about one's personal and social identities that may affect interpersonal functioning. This is especially helpful in PTSD patients who have such profound doubts about their self-worth and their abilities to make effective changes in their lives based on personal traumatic histories and religious belief systems which often lead to a pessimistic view of fate" (p. 525).

Boehnlein (1987) offers some very specific questions a crisis worker might ask of the PTSD Southeast Asian client:

"Do you have to attain perfection in order to not consider yourself a failure?"

"Given the progress you have steadily been making, is your life still fated to be continuously and forever difficult?"

"You have been viewing yourself as a weak and ineffective person, yet you had the strength as an adolescent to survive years of starvation and brutality. There must be strengths that you and your family possess that you have not been aware of in recent years." (p. 526) [Note that these statements are an example of reframing.]

Boehnlein further notes that these patients tend to minimize outward emotional expression, which, in the case of posttraumatic stress disorder, can consume a lot of psychic energy because of the patient's perceived need to defend against emotional display. Therefore, when working with Asian patients with PTSD, the crisis worker needs to be aware of his or her own affective responses and of the subtle cues of internal distress communicated by the patient. These cues may be communicated through reports of dreams or perhaps behavioral signs of depression such as somatic distress or sleep disturbance.

Finally, he suggests that the "therapist can communicate a sense of warmth, genuineness, and competence by being direct, yet compassionate; by being assertive in the recommendation of treatment approaches, yet responsive to possibly conflicting cultural concepts of illness and healing, and by allowing the patient to report difficult historical information or express intense emotion without a sense of shame. Explaining to patients in a matter-of-fact way that a number of their experiences and feelings are shared by many other Cambodians does not trivialize their personal situation but instead serves to minimize their fear of going crazy" (p. 527). This is a good example of how educational comments and reframing can be utilized.

In his work with Asian-Americans, Hong (1988) has found that mental health workers would do well to adopt a general family practice model whereby they maintain an ongoing interaction with the family and serve as a resource for the family to consult in difficulty. A counselor should use knowledge of the client, as well as knowledge of the client's family, community, and social environment. This approach seems particularly suitable for Asian-Americans whose culture emphasizes the role of the family. It helps to minimize the client's inhibition against seeking mental health services (Haney, 1988, p. 60) and provides the crisis worker with the advantage of having family support and less resistance from the system.

Whenever possible, the crisis worker must take into consideration the effect any intervention will have on the client's family, bringing in the family whenever possible. To suggest that a client focus exclusively on her or his own problems will undoubtedly wreak havoc on the family system.

Example   A 26-year-old Vietnamese female came for crisis intervention because of depression and increasing tension in her house. She was a medical student and working full-time. Her father expected her to serve him, support the family financially, and stay at home when she was not at school or work. Her older brother was permitted to lie around the house, contributing nothing; the client was very angered by this inequality. She realized that she had become quite Anglicized in her value system and felt taken advantage of by her family. She was miserable and pondered suicide.

In analyzing this case, the helper realized that cultural sensitivity was vital. If the counselor thought only in terms of middle-class, Caucasian values, then he would be supporting separation/individuation processes and would be encouraging to client to assert her own needs and rights. However, if this client were to go against the wishes of her father, she would be ostracized from her family. A few concepts can help explain this dilemma.

THE FAMILY STRUCTURE

In most Asian families, males are respected more than females. The oldest son has more privileges than his own mother, though he must respect her at certain levels. The mother plays the stereotypical role of nurturer, providing domestic structure, whereas the father dictates all family decisions. The daughter contributes to the household until she marries, then she belongs to her husband's household and family. The concept of individualism is not part of this culture.

SHAME AND OBLIGATION

If the norms are not followed, an individual and the family will experience a sense of shame—not only for their own actions but for the entire family line. This factor makes it necessary at times to reject a family member completely so as not to bring shame on the family itself. The differentiation between the family and its members often does not exist as it does in European cultures. Obligation arises in any situation in which the rules of family structure arise. The child is obligated to respect these structures or bring shame. These choices often bring on feelings of depression and anxiety. The crisis worker needs to be sensitive to these struggles and search for ways to negotiate compromises when possible.

In the case of the young medical student, instead of suggesting that she move out and tell her father she is an adult and does not have to support him, the counselor encouraged her to use the counseling sessions as a venting system for her frustrations. The crisis worker let her know that she understood her dilemma, and that by choosing to maintain status quo she was able to be a part of her family. The consequences for violating the system would be complete alienation from her mother and sisters as well as the men in her family. If she could learn to keep her focus on the value of family, perhaps she could learn to let go of her feelings of unfairness. In reframing the situation, the worker pointed out that although the client felt a lot of pressure to keep the family out of shame, her father felt this obligation even more. In actuality, it is the father who carries the burden of keeping his family in line. He would experience incredible shame if his daughter were to move out unmarried and refused to support his family financially.

Kashiwagi (1993) provides another example of how "certain traditional Asian cultural influences, such as bringing shame to the family and losing face in the community" (p. 46), will have an effect on mental health problems and intervention. He asserts that when an Asian-American teenager has a drug or alcohol addiction, the family will often deny the condition and perpetuate the problem. This denial results in large part from the lack of connection, communication, and understanding in the parent/child relationship. If the counselor recommends a "tough love" approach—that is, refusing to continue being enablers for the teenager's behavior and setting standards that he must meet—the parents probably will not follow through adequately because of the cultural tendency to care for family members at a surface level.

Another example of the importance of avoiding family shame was presented by Carol Cole (1993). In her role as an emergency response worker with a county mental health unit, she received a call from some neighbors who complained of an awful stench coming from a house next door. When she arrived, she found a 40-year-old Asian-American who was completely psychotic. She was delusional, disheveled, disoriented, with no food in the house and no signs of reality orientation. This Asian family had immigrated to the United States five years earlier and the parents had kept this 40-year-old daughter in the home with no treatment because acknowledging that a child was mentally ill would put shame on the family. Two weeks earlier, the parents had been in a car wreck and no one was home to take care of the daughter. In this case, although the client was hospitalized involuntarily, the action was reframed as an opportunity to help stabilize the daughter and to teach the family about available resources—in this χασε, ιν τηε ςιετναμεσε χομμυνιτψ.

Strict approaches that require setting firm limits, such as making a child sleep outside or go to school in dirty clothes, bring shame to the whole family; therefore, parents tend to enable irresponsible behaviors to avoid this shame. To confront a child about how her or his behavior makes the family feel would be shameful, so parents' true feelings are often hidden inside. The child usually knows this, can take advantage, and can abuse the parents' acts of kindness. This situation is especially damaging in dealing with drug addicts. These teenagers know that their parents will bail them out of jail if they are arrested, or will always allow them to stay at home. Not to do so would bring shame to the family. Unfortunately, many parents of drug-addicted Asian-American teenagers believe they are helping their children by taking care of their basic needs and buying them material things. This, however, reinforces the addicts' behaviors and enables further drug use. The crisis counselor must be sensitive to these cultural norms and slowly encourage open communication between generations rather than force programs such as "tough love."

THE COMMUNICATION PROCESS

Another area in which sensitivity is needed is communication style. Asian-Americans have been conditioned to avoid eye contact and direct confrontations, especially with doctors and authority figures. This trait may create complications during an interview if the counselor is not aware of this cultural style. Whereas mainstream Americans may consider avoiding eye contact to be rude, the Asian may feel that looking someone in the eyes is rude behavior. Also, Asian clients may feel that they cannot disagree with the counselor because of respect for the authority position. The counselor may have to encourage disagreement and define it as part of the interview process at times.

Also, if a crisis worker is doing family therapy, the tendency to ask family members to confront each other directly may be culturally insensitive. They will probably do best with more educational, problem-solving approaches that focus on a presenting problem. Reframing the solution as strengthening the family unit will probably be well received by Asian-American clients. The crisis worker needs to be aware of the hierarchy in the family and include the most powerful family members in any decision making.

> **Example**   A 19-year-old Asian-American youth was very depressed about having received a C in a chemistry course. He felt very ashamed and was sure his father would be angry with him for bringing disgrace on the family. He believed that his only solution was to kill himself by jumping off a tall building.

Instead of working only with this client, the counselor would be well advised to bring in the young man's parents. The client needs to be told that his suicide might bring more shame to the family than making a C in chemistry. After all, the lower grade in that course could be balanced by a high grade in another class—a reframing of the problem. By asking his parents for their opinions and possible solutions, the client will feel more secure in the fact that he won't bring shame to them. Instead, the family may be brought closer together. The counselor should emphasize to the parents that their son cares so much about the family name that he was willing to sacrifice his own life for the family honor—another reframing of the situation.

Having information about various cultural groups as a guide when providing mental health services is helpful, but it is not always readily accessible. Current theoretical approaches to diagnosing and treating various psychiatric symptoms do not consider these symptoms from a multicultural perspective. Vega and Rumbaut (1991) recommend that further research and studies be conducted to help formulate new theories, diagnostic procedures, and interventions that encompass cultural characteristics of minorities. They note that "theories coined at the turn of the century to describe the assimilation process of European immigrants are poorly suited to grapple with the current diversity. In addition, studies of the mental health of nonimmigrant racial-ethnic groups need to distinguish between different U.S. generations and to identify the effects of new interracial-interethnic formation" (p. 379).

Vega and Rumbaut (1991) suggest that research explore the ways psychological and emotional functioning may be affected by long-term adaptation to specific conditions of life change. They have concluded that if mental health practitioners are to be adequately prepared to assist various ethnic groups through acculturation crises, more studies are needed to help workers understand why the acculturation process is distressing. It seems obvious that acquiring a new language and new cultural information and behavior would be taxing for an immigrant, but knowing why this is so can help the crisis worker perform.

Vega and Rumbaut (1991) also point out the need to consider the mental health consequences of racism and racial discrimination as well as the personal and social costs to an individual. Last, they encourage mental health workers to "explore the meaning of psychiatric signs, symptoms and dysfunctions within diverse ethnic minority communities" (pp. 379–380). Again, this is very much in keeping with the spirit of capturing the cognitive element in the understanding and resolution of crises and other dysfunctions.

As a final thought, even though having knowledge of different cultural needs and behaviors is helpful, the crisis interventionist must always focus more on the *individual* client than on any preconceived idea of how that client should behave. Although counselors may be well intentioned, they may come across as patronizing if they treat clients according to what they expect rather than what they actually see. An example would be for a counselor to structure his or her behavior toward an Asian-American according to what the counselor knew of that culture only to find that the client and his or her family had thoroughly assimilated mainstream American culture. The client could be insulted and the counselor could feel foolish. Counselors must listen to their clients!

Other ethnic groups traditionally thought of as Caucasian may also have rules in their family systems that need to be understood. By remembering systems theory, the counselor can identify any rules established by ethnic identification and ward off resistance to interventions. Counselors should try to work within the rules of the system unless the system is extremely pathological. When expanding or tightening rules, do it slowly and with regard for the feelings of all in the family. When possible, find a positive way to reframe new rules that you may offer; after all, there must be a good reason for you to want to change the system.

Key Terms for Study

African-Americans: As seen by the crisis worker, a minority group that does not utilize the mental health system often. The historical roots of this group help explain why its members tend to resolve crises through extended family and the clergy rather than with governmental or other mainstream agencies. Racism and discrimination are still prominent with this group and must be kept in mind by crisis workers. Religion has historically been important in getting this group through the many daily stressors that are part of being black in America.

Asian-Americans: As seen by the crisis worker, a minority group whose members may seek the services of mental health workers in crises, but who prefer a problem-solving approach similar to that used by a family doctor to treat physical illnesses. The crisis worker must be aware of issues of shame and obligation as they may very well come into play when a family member is in crisis.

Crisis workers must also respect family structure to prevent resistance to proposed coping alternatives.

development of cultural sensitivity: A four-stage process proposed to explain how counselors learn to consider cultural factors when they conduct counseling sessions. The stages are as follows:

1. Lack of awareness of cultural issues

2. Heightened awareness of culture

3. Realization of the burden of considering culture

4. Beginnings of cultural sensitivity

help-seeking attitudes: Behavior that encourages certain groups to seek out counseling more than others—females more than males, Caucasians more than minorities, for example.

Mexican-Americans: As seen by the crisis worker, a cultural group whose members seek mental health services more often than the other two minority groups studied here. Mexican-Americans suffer crises related to language barriers, religious differences, and cultural differences in child rearing. Families tend to be enmeshed, and children are encouraged to be dependent.

the role of systems theory: An important element in working with clients from minority groups. The crisis worker must identify family roles and allowable behavior for a particular cultural group; these may be very different from mainstream roles and behaviors. Imposing mainstream theories of pathology on other cultures is often counterproductive.

The ABC Model of Crisis Intervention

The ABC model of crisis intervention is a method for conducting very brief mental health interviews with clients whose functioning level has decreased following a psychosocial stressor. This model follows the formula presented in Chapter 1 regarding the process of crisis formation. It is a problem-focused approach and is most effectively applied within four to six weeks of the stressor. Identifying the cognitions of the client as they relate to the precipitating event and then altering them to help decrease unmanageable feelings is the central focus of the method. Additionally, providing community referrals and other resources such as reading material is also essential in applying this model.

Caplan and Lindemann first conceptualized the crisis intervention approach in the 1940s (Caplan, 1964; Lindemann, 1944); others have since developed models that utilize the principles and techniques of these founders. The ABC model of crisis intervention presented in this text has its origins in a variety of sources. It is loosely based on Jones's (1968) A-B-C method of crisis management; in this model, he proposed a three-stage process: A, achieving contact; B, boiling the problem down to basics; and C, coping. Moline (1986), a former professor at California State University, Fullerton, developed a course called Crisis Intervention in which she used a modified version of Jones's model. Through her lecture notes and from discussions with her about how she organized the course, the author developed the ABC model of crisis intervention discussed in this book. Over 10 years, using information from experts in the community who provide crisis intervention to a variety of populations, she has added to the ABC model. Finally, her own experience with clients, as a mental health provider for the past 18 years, and extensive study of typical intake forms from public, private, and non-profit agencies have contributed to her expansion of the model to its current form.

Other models have also influenced the ABC model of crisis intervention in terms of the particular structure and use of stages. Structuring the counseling process around certain phases or stages is not a new phenomenon but has been practiced by mental health practitioners since the days of founding theorists such as Sullivan (1954) and Adler (Corey, 1996, p. 143). The phases are not linear, but like those of the ABC model, are best "understood as a weaving that leads to a tapestry" (Corey, 1996, p. 143). Adler developed a four-phase model for the therapeutic process that includes Phase I, establishing the relationship; Phase II, exploring the individual's dynamics; Phase III, encouraging insight; and Phase IV, helping with reorientation (Corey, 1996, pp. 143–150). These four phases are similar to those of the ABC model:

A, Developing and Maintaining Contact, corresponds with Adler's Phase I.

B, Identifying the Problem and Therapeutic Interaction, corresponds with Adler's Phase II and Phase III.

C, Coping, corresponds with Adler's Phase IV.

Sullivan (1954) also structured psychiatric interviews using a phase model. His stages, which can be seen to correspond with the stages of the ABC model, are I, the formal inception (analogous to A of the ABC model); II, the reconnaissance, and III, the detailed inquiry (analogous to B); and IV, termination (analogous to C).

Although the ABC model of crisis intervention is presented as a three-stage approach, in practice, the components of any one of the stages might be used throughout an interview. Keeping that in mind, we begin with a discussion of each stage. The crisis worker will learn how to integrate the stages through practice and experience.

A: Developing and Maintaining Rapport

The foundation of crisis intervention is the development of **rapport** between the client and the counselor. Rapport is a state of understanding and comfort. As the client begins to feel this rapport, trust and openness follow, allowing the interview to proceed. Before delving into the client's personal world, the counselor must achieve this personal contact. The counseling relationship is unique in this regard. Before any work can be done, the client must feel understood and accepted by the counselor.

By learning several basic attending skills, the beginning crisis counselor can develop the self-confidence needed to make contact with someone in crisis. Use of these basic rapport-building communication skills invites the client to talk, brings calm control to the situation, allows the facts of the situation as well as the client's feelings to be heard and empathized with, and communicates the counselor's concern and respect. Remember that the interview process does not proceed in a linear fashion; the various attending skills can be interwoven as appropriate. For example, the counselor may ask a question before reflecting or may reflect before asking a question.

Unlike other approaches to counseling, crisis intervention does not typically include the use of techniques such as interpretation or direct advice giving. These techniques generally require a therapeutic relationship of long duration before they are effective; in crisis intervention, developing such a relationship is not practical. Although it may be tempting to jump in and tell clients what is wrong with them and what to do about it, the crisis interventionist is encouraged not to do this. The basic attending skills are a useful alternative to the sometimes rote practice of asking routine questions and giving routine advice and interpretations. Sometimes, clients are just not routine!

The primary purpose of using the basic attending skills is to help the counselor gain a very clear understanding of the internal experience of the crisis as the client sees it. Only by true understanding can the counselor help to bring change in the client's subjective distress and assist the client to improve his or her functioning.

Table 5.1 can be used as a guide for the beginning counselor. It is not meant to be followed as a linear script but rather to be a reminder of the skills the counselor

TABLE 5.1 Basic Attending Skills

	Skill Proficiency		
	Good	*Fair*	*Poor*
Attending Behavior			
Eye contact			
Warmth			
Body posture			
Vocal style			
Verbal following			
Overall empathy (focus on client)			
Questioning			
Open-ended			
Closed			
Clarifying			
Paraphrasing			
Verifying			
Reflecting			
Positive feelings			
Painful feelings			
Ambivalent feelings			
Nonverbal feelings			
Summarizing			
Tying together feelings and facts			
Tying together precipitating events, subjective distress, and meanings			

is to utilize throughout the interview. Skill proficiency columns are built into the table to allow for evaluation of student performance by the course instructor.

ATTENDING BEHAVIOR

The most basic skill of helping is listening. Appropriate verbal and nonverbal behavior—or **attending behavior**—is the hallmark of a helping interview. Good eye contact, attentive body language, expressive vocal style, and verbal following are valuable listening tools, but they are not always present. The next time you carry on a conversation with a friend, observe whether these behaviors are in evidence. Using a soft, soothing voice, showing an interested face, having relaxed posture, leaning toward the client, making direct eye contact, and maintaining close physical proximity (Cormier et al., 1986, p. 30) are all ways to convey warmth and are part of active listening. These attending behaviors "demonstrate to the client that you are with him or her and indeed are listening," enabling the client to talk more freely (Ivey, Gluckstern, & Ivey, 1997, p. 19).

Active listening requires being able to observe the client and at the same time pay attention to one's own reactions—such as questions asked, supportive statements made, or other feedback. This is often quite difficult. Try the following exercise.*

::::::::::::::::::::::::::::::::

Exercise

Break into groups of three or four; using the Basic Attending Skills outline evaluation sheet in Table 5.1, rate each other on the attending behaviors. One person can play the client and another can be a crisis worker. A third can be the rater. If there is a fourth, that person can be an observer. The rater also enhances her or his skills of observation while giving feedback to the counselor. After this exercise, have some fun exaggerating an interview in which the crisis worker does not employ these behaviors (i.e., has poor eye contact, is cold, keeps arms folded, does not pay attention verbally). This behavior will really leave an impression of what *not* to do!

::::::::::::::::::::::::::::::::

Crisis workers must remember that the attending behavior of different cultural and ethnic groups may vary in style, and these helpers may need to adapt when working with the groups discussed earlier. Ivey et al. (1997, pp. 20–21) have summarized typical variations:

Eye Contact	African-Americans, Hispanic-Americans, and Native Americans may avoid eye contact as a sign of respect. With Hispanics, direct sustained eye contact can represent a challenge to authority. A bowed head may be a sign of respect from Native Americans.

*Reprinted with permission from *Basic Attending Skills,* 3rd Ed., by Ivey, A. E., Gluckstern, N. B., & Ivey, M. B., pp. 19, 20–21, 35, 56, and 92. Copyright © 1997 Microtraining Associates.

Body Language	The public behavior of African-Americans may seem emotionally intense and demonstrative to European-Americans. A slap on the back may be insulting to an Asian-American or a Hispanic-American.
Vocal Style	Hispanic-Americans often begin meetings with lengthy greetings and pleasant talk before addressing key issues. European-Americans tend to value a quiet, controlled vocal style; other groups may see this as manipulative or cold.
Verbal Following	Asian-Americans may prefer a more indirect and subtle communication and consider the African-American or European-American styles too direct and confrontational. Personal questions may be especially offensive to Native Americans.

QUESTIONING

Asking pertinent questions of the client is an invitation to the client to talk. Open-ended questions provide room for the clients to express their real selves without the imposed categories of the interviewer. They allow clients an opportunity to explore themselves with the support of the interviewer. **Closed questions** can help the interviewer gather factual information such as age or marital status. However, clients frequently feel attacked or defensive with certain closed questions, such as *why* questions; these should be used sparingly if at all (Ivey et al., 1997, p. 35). Beginning counseling students tend to ask "do you, have you, could you, and would you" questions. These types of closed questions can be answered yes or no by the client, with the result of bogging down the interview. Counselors should avoid these types of closed questions, asking more specific open-ended questions instead. Try to tie your open-ended questions to what the client has just said.

Examples of poorly and appropriately worded questions are shown here:

Poorly Worded Counselor Question	*Appropriately Worded Counselor Question*
Do you feel sad about losing your husband?	How do you feel about losing your husband?
Have you tried to talk to your father?	What have you done?
Could you tell me more about your sadness?	What is your sadness like for you?

Providing information in response to open-ended questions is generally more comfortable for clients than giving answers to 20 closed intake questions. Interweaving closed questions in with open-ended questions, reflection, and paraphrasing should allow a counselor to complete the intake forms in most agencies. This takes practice, but clients will benefit from this style.

Following are some examples of effective open-ended and closed questions. Included are suggestions for changing *why* questions into open-ended questions.

Effective Open-Ended Questions	*Appropriate Closed Questions*
How did that make you feel?	How long have you been married?
What happened that caused you to come?	Have you been checked out by a doctor today?
Could you tell me more about your family?	Are you taking any medications?
What is the worst part about being raped?	Are you afraid for your kids?

Why Questions	*Open-Ended Questions*
Why did you ask him into your apartment?	How did things get out of control in your apartment?
Why did you smoke the crack?	What was it like to decide to smoke crack?
Why did you try to kill yourself?	What was going through your mind when you took the pills?

How do these questions make you feel? Role-play these questions with friends.

CLARIFYING

A particular type of questioning called **clarifying** is used to clear up confusion or ambiguity so as to avoid misunderstanding and to confirm the accuracy of what the counselor heard. The client is asked to rephrase or restate a previous message. This type of question is used for **verifying** that what the crisis worker heard is what the client intended to say.

Paraphrasing is also a clarifying technique that feeds back to the client the essence of what was said (Ivey et al., 1997, p. 56). Its focus is on the cognitive and factual part of the client's message; its intent is to encourage elaboration of the statements to let the client know you have understood or heard the message; to help the client focus on a specific situation, idea, or action; and to highlight content when attention on affect would be premature or inappropriate (Slaikeu, 1990, p. 38).

::::::::::::::::::::::::::::::

Exercise

Form into dyads or include a third observer while one person plays the crisis interviewer and one plays a client in crisis. After the client tells the counselor about the crisis, the counselor is to restate in her or his own words what was heard. Do not parrot and repeat exactly what was said. Sometimes it is helpful to break character and tell the observer what was heard in the third person and then practice paraphrasing directly back to the client what you heard her or him say, as shown here:

Client: I've been depressed since I had to have my dog put to sleep last week. I can't sleep or concentrate at work and everyone thinks I'm a big baby.

(Verifying)

Crisis Worker: Are you saying that you have felt very bad since your dog died and aren't receiving any support from your co-workers?

(Paraphrase)

Crisis Worker: I hear you saying that since putting your dog to sleep last week you've been unable to sleep and feel depressed, and no one at work seems to understand your feelings.

REFLECTION OF FEELINGS

Empathy is integral to achieving and maintaining contact with clients. This means being able to let clients know you understand their feelings. The technique of **reflection,** which is a statement rephrasing the affective part or emotional tone of the client's message, is a powerful tool in creating an empathic environment. Not only does it help clarify the client's feelings in a particular situation, but it also helps the client feel understood. Clients can then express their own feelings about a situation; learn to manage their feelings, especially negative ones; and express their feelings toward the mental health care provider and agency.

From Freud to Rogers, catharsis and experiential awareness of feelings have been the curative factor in therapy. The crisis interview might be the only time the client has ever felt validated in her or his feelings, and that is a good experience!

Exercise

In dyads or in a group, have someone role-play a client in crisis. Tell the others of your problem and feelings. Each student/counselor then restates just the feelings to the client. Listen to the emotional tone and look for nonverbal cues such as eyes watering or fist pounding. Try using these openings: "You seem to feel . . . ," "Sounds like you feel . . . ," "I sense you are . . . ." Look for ambivalent feelings and contradictory feelings as well as positive feelings.

Here are some examples:

Painful feelings: "Sounds like you are furious with your wife."

Positive feelings: "You seem to be happiest when you don't drink."

Positive feelings: "You seem to be happiest when you don't drink."

Ambivalent feelings: "Although you say you hate your husband, you also seem to pity him."

Nonverbal feelings: "I can see by the tears in your eyes how painful this loss is."

SUMMARIZATION

The key purpose of **summarization** is to help another individual pull his or her thoughts together. A secondary purpose is to check on whether you as a helper have distorted the client's frame of reference. Summarization may be helpful in beginning an interview if you've already seen the client previously; it may help to bring together threads of data over several interviews, or simply to clarify what has gone on in the present interview (Ivey et al., 1997, p. 92). Here is an example of a summarization:

"So, your husband beat you last night and this time hit your daughter. You are scared and lonely and don't know where to turn."

The next chapter shows that summarization can help make a smooth transition from identifying the problem to finding coping strategies. Usually the cognitive and affective content are restated as well as the precipitating events and coping efforts. These aspects are easy to remember if you keep in mind the three aspects of any crisis: (1) the precipitating event; (2) the perception of the event by the client, which leads to subjective distress; and (3) failure of the client to cope successfully with the distress.

Now that you've learned the basic attending skills, practice them in seven- to 10-minute role-plays using the evaluation sheet in Table 6.1. Once you have mastered these skills, you are ready to move on to more advanced communication skills. The basic attending skills will be used throughout every session. They help counselors maintain rapport and allow them access to delicate information about the client.

Key Terms for Study

attending behavior: Behavior that has to do with following the client's lead, actively listening, and demonstrating presence.

clarifying: A basic attending skill with several uses. It can let clients know they are understood and let the counselor know that she or he understands the clients. It usually focuses on facts and cognitions.

closed question: A type of question that can be answered with yes or no or some other one-word answer. Its best use is for obtaining facts such as age, number of children, or number of years married. Forced-choice questions or "do you, have you" questions are generally not effective. These types of questions can lead the interview to a dead end or sound like an interrogation.

paraphrasing: A form of clarifying in which counselors say to the client in their own words what they think the client said. Sometimes they simply repeat the client's words.

rapport: A special type of bonding that a counselor seeks with a client. The more rapport there is between client and counselor, the greater will be the client's sense of trust and security.

reflection: The best way to show emotional empathy for a client. The counselor points out the client's emotions by stating them as either seen or heard.

summarization: A skill useful in tying ideas together, wrapping up a session, or moving from B to C. It is also useful when the counselor does not know where to go next. It is a statement that pulls together the various facts and feelings discussed in the session.

verifying: A form of clarifying in which the counselor questions what was just said to make sure he or she understands it accurately.

B: Identifying the Problem

After demographic information has been gathered and as rapport is developing, the crisis worker starts to focus on the client's presenting crisis. This is the second step in the ABC method and the most crucial one. Refer to the ABC Model of Crisis Intervention outline in Table 5.2 for a look at the interview process. Each aspect is examined individually as well as in context with the others in the process. Beginning counselors should become fluent with the various aspects of this model so as not to appear mechanical to the client. Keeping in mind the definition of crisis will help counselors remember what to identify: precipitating events, perceptions, subjective distress, and functioning.

Although the model is presented in a linear outline form, interviews do not have to be conducted in a linear fashion. Unfortunately for beginning counselors, having a script for each crisis situation is just not practical. However, the examples presented can be used in conjunction with the counselors' creative processes and intuition.

This outline will be useful for you as you practice each situational crisis in Chapters 6–11. In each of those chapters, examples are given for practice in role-playing. Do not be restricted to using only the ideas given. Create your own ideas whenever possible. The outline can be used for a 10-minute phone call, a 50-minute session, or over 6 weeks of weekly crisis intervention sessions. Each week, new issues can be addressed and new coping strategies sought; also, changes in functioning can be assessed from week to week.

Notice that the model has several areas to assess. This does not mean that on every visit the counselor must assess for each area. Rather, each area should be addressed at least on the first or second visit and then reassessed thereafter as necessary to evaluate the client's progress.

Of particular importance in crisis intervention and in brief therapy is the ability to explore the client's perceptions. Most sessions will be spent in this process. It is through these explorations that the client will gain knowledge of the source of her or his pain. Once the client's perceptions and frame of reference

TABLE 5.2 The ABC Model of Crisis Intervention

	SKILL PROFICIENCY		
	Good	*Fair*	*Poor*
A: BASIC ATTENDING SKILLS	___	___	___
B: IDENTIFYING THE PROBLEM AND THERAPEUTIC INTERACTION	*Assessed*	*Not Assessed*	*Not Applicable*
Identify the precipitating event	___	___	___
Explore meanings, cognitions, and perceptions	___	___	___
Identify subjective distress (emotional distress)	___	___	___
Identify impairments in functioning in the following areas:			
1. behavioral	___	___	___
2. social	___	___	___
3. academic	___	___	___
4. occupational	___	___	___
Identify pre-crisis level of functioning in 1–4 above	___	___	___
Identify any ethical concerns:			
1. suicide assessment	___	___	___
2. child abuse, elder abuse, homicide	___	___	___
3. organic or other medical concerns	___	___	___
Identify substance abuse issues	___	___	___
Use therapeutic interactions:	*Done*	*Not Done*	
1. educational comments	___	___	
2. empowerment statements	___	___	
3. support statements	___	___	
4. reframes	___	___	
C: COPING			
Identify client's current coping attempts	___	___	
Encourage client to think of other coping strategies	___	___	
Present alternative coping ideas:			
1. Refer to support groups, 12-step groups	___	___	
2. Refer to long-term therapy, family therapy	___	___	
3. Refer to medical doctor or psychiatrist	___	___	
4. Refer to lawyer	___	___	
5. Refer to shelter, other agency	___	___	
6. Recommend books	___	___	
Get commitment; do follow-up	___	___	

regarding various situations are understood, the crisis worker is in a position to guide the client into new ways of thinking and experiencing himself or herself and the world. Also, once the person's cognitions are changed, subjective distress will be reduced, coping skills can be implemented, and functioning will be increased. This, as you will recall, is the goal of crisis intervention.

Probably the most important reason for exploring the client's internal frame of reference is that changing internal perceptions is easier than changing external situations. If the crisis worker spends too much time focusing on the significant others and the details of the situation—elements that generally cannot be changed—the client might experience increased frustration.

At the end of this chapter, a "script" is presented utilizing the ABC model of crisis intervention. It offers specific questions and statements a crisis worker might use. It is presented after the reader has had a chance to learn about each section of the model individually. Then he or she should be able to understand how to integrate all the sections together in a typical interview.

IDENTIFYING THE PRECIPITATING EVENT

Shortly into the interview, the counselor should begin to ask about the precipitating event. To ask, "What happened that made you call for an appointment?" is appropriate. It is an opening for the client to tell what is going on with her or him. If the client cannot think of any particular event that brought her or him to counseling, the crisis worker must probe further, explaining that understanding the trigger of the client's crisis will aid in relieving the crisis state.

The precipitating event may have happened yesterday or three months ago. A helpful strategy is learning when the client started to feel bad. This will help pinpoint the triggering event. "The straw that broke the camel's back" is a common expression that can help the client focus on the beginning of the crisis.

Another reason for specifying the precipitating event is to be able, later on, to explore how the client has been trying to cope since it happened. When the client's denial is strong, the crisis worker must confront the person about why exactly she or he decided to come for counseling. The reason is usually because of trouble coping with a precipitating event. If the event is not clearly defined, the counselor will have problems presenting alternative coping strategies. Last, identification of the precipitating event is vital because the crisis worker must identify the client's perceptions about this episode. If these cognitions are not identified properly, there can be no therapeutic interactive comments about or altering of them, and change in the way the event is perceived is essential for increased functioning. In Chapter 1, two formulas were presented; they are repeated here. Refer to them as you practice using the ABC model.

Formula for understanding the process of crisis formation

Precipitating Event $\longrightarrow$ Perception $\longrightarrow$ Subjective Distress $\longrightarrow$ Lowered Functioning

If the goal of crisis work is to increase the client's functioning, the following formula aids the crisis worker in understanding how to move the client out of a crisis.

Formula to increase functioning

Change in Perception $\longrightarrow$ Decrease in Subjective $\longrightarrow$ Increase in Functioning
of Precipitating Event   Distress

No matter how much clients profess that "nothing has happened, really," something drove them to seek help. Squeeze it out of them! They need to see that their current state of subjective distress is tied to an actual event or fact.

RECOGNIZING THE MEANING/PERCEPTION OF THE PRECIPITATING EVENT

In addition to identifying precipitating events, the crisis worker will actively explore the meaning the client ascribes to these events. It is the person's perception of stressful situations that causes him or her to be in a crisis state. Usually, stress originates from one of three areas: loss of control, loss of nurturance, or forced adjustment to a change in life or role.

All aspects of the situation should be examined. For example, suppose a woman is raped. Not only does the actual rape cause stress, but her perception of how her husband will react also contributes to her stress as she struggles with her perceived new role with him.

Some questions the crisis worker may ask to elicit the client's frame of reference regarding the crisis situation include these: "How do you put it together in your head?" "What do you think about this?" "What does it mean to you that . . . ?" "What are you telling yourself about . . . ?" "What assumptions are you making about . . . ?"

Cognitive restructuring/reframing is a valuable tool for the counselor but can be done only if the client's current cognitions are known. It is impossible to develop a coping plan for the client without examining the cognitive and perceptual experience. Think of yourself as a mechanic who needs to analyze and experience the trouble firsthand before tinkering with the engine.

Assessing the client's perception of the precipitating event is the most important part of the interview and must be done thoroughly on every visit to check for changing views as well as long-standing views on a variety of issues.

IDENTIFYING SUBJECTIVE DISTRESS AND FUNCTIONING LEVEL

In addition to exploring stressors and client perceptions of them, counselors must inquire about the client's functioning and how the precipitating events are affecting it. Clients seem to benefit from expressing painful feelings and sharing other symptoms. These are symptoms that may impair the client's occupational, academic, behavioral, social, interpersonal, or family functioning. Counselors should ask how the clients' perceptions about the precipitating event are affecting their functioning in each area. Often each area in which the person is suffering distress is dealt with separately because a specific perception might be associated with that area and not another.

The crisis worker is advised to explore each area affected during the crisis state in as much detail as possible. This probing gives the counselor a feel for the degree of impairment the client is experiencing and can be used later to help select coping strategies. When clients discuss their symptoms and impairments in functioning, they can receive feedback, education, and support from the counselor. Often, understanding one's feelings and behaviors is the first step in coping with them.

> **Example** A battered woman might be experiencing much anxiety at work because she believes that her husband will come there and cause a scene, which would probably result in her being fired. This perception might be dealt with by letting her know that bosses can often be sympathetic and helpful, and that her boss might even provide her with support and initiate legal action for her.

In addition to identifying the client's current level of functioning, the crisis worker needs to assess the client's pre-crisis level of functioning so as to compare the two. This will help the counselor to determine the level of coping the client can realistically achieve; it also gives the counselor an idea of the severity of the crisis for the person. The comparison will serve as a basis for evaluating the outcome of crisis intervention. Remember that the goal of crisis intervention is to bring the client back to the pre-crisis level of functioning.

> **Example** If a woman was getting straight A's in college prior to being raped, and afterward her grades went down to C's and D's, her crisis was worse for her than for a woman who was raped but showed only minimal disturbance at work or school. In these cases, it is probable that the first woman's perception of the rape was more drastic than the second woman's. Maybe she told herself that she was at fault, that she is dirty and that no one will ever love her again. The second woman might have a more realistic view of the rape and be able to tell herself that it was the rapist's fault and that no one is going to hold her responsible or think differently about her.

Most intake forms ask for a comparison between current and previous functioning on a regular basis. It is important to include this information as part of any crisis assessment procedure.

MAKING ETHICAL CHECKS

Several other areas need identification in this stage of the interview. These have ethical implications and must be assessed either directly or indirectly with every client. However, in order not to behave like a prosecuting attorney, the crisis worker is encouraged to extract this information in a fluid, relevant manner. Rather than going down a list and asking one question after another, the counselor should weave the questions in as the issues arise in the normal flow of the conversation.

Suicide Check Because people in crisis are vulnerable and often confused and overwhelmed, suicide sometimes becomes an alternative for them. Every crisis worker must assess for suicidality, particularly when the client is depressed or impulsive. A separate chapter discusses suicide prevention and assessment.

Homicidal/Abuse Issues   As discussed in the ethics chapter, mental health workers in many states are required to report child and elder abuse and any suspicion that a client may harm someone. Assessment of these issues must be done during the course of an interview. Often, the counselor's intuition will provide the basis for detailed inquiry.

> **Example**   A 43-year-old male may say that he hates his father for having beaten his mother and can see himself smashing the father's face. This statement alone does not warrant an attempt to take the client into custody. However, I would inquire about how he deals with this anger, especially toward his wife and children.

Child abuse is discussed later, but it is important for counselors to know that suspected abuse of children must be assessed in all cases. Sometimes, turning away and collaborating in denial with an abusive family is easier than facing the issue, but doing so is never in the best interest of the child. Such action is unethical and might be illegal, depending on the laws of the state where the action occurs.

MENTAL STATUS EXAM AND THE *DIAGNOSTIC AND STATISTICAL MANUAL OF MENTAL DISORDERS*

When a helper first sees a client, the counselor is obligated to ensure that obvious client symptoms—physical or mental—are not overlooked. Granted, paraprofessional counselors or community workers are not expected to be proficient at psychiatric diagnosis; but any crisis worker must, for ethical reasons, be familiar with the symptoms of severe mental illness and **organic brain disorders**. If the counselor observes abnormal behaviors in a client, he or she can use the **Mental Status Exam** to determine whether adjunct medical treatment is called for. This exam is a useful tool for detecting a client's strengths, personality weaknesses, and overall functioning. The results can help indicate organic disorders found in the *Diagnostic and Statistical Manual of Mental Disorders* (4th ed.), commonly referred to as the *DSM-IV* (American Psychiatric Association, 1994). When such disorders are found, the involvement of a physician would be indicated. The parts of the Mental Status Exam are explained next.

> *Appearance:* A person's overall **appearance** indicates her or his relationship to self and to society. Good grooming and hygiene indicate good self-esteem and consideration for others. As the appearance deteriorates, the likelihood of an emotional disturbance increases.
>
> *Attitude:* **Attitude** reflects the client's overall manner in relation to the counselor and the counseling situation. Interpersonal functioning is often a clue to severe mental disturbances or drug intoxication.
>
> *Psychomotor behavior:* How a person carries herself or himself physically—the **psychomotor behavior**—can help the crisis worker determine the severity of

depression or detect other problems such as tics, stuttering, muscular disorders, or level of agitation.

Speech: The rate at which a person talks often indicates his or her level of anxiety, depression, mania, or intoxication. Also, speech impediments can be observed and noted.

Mood: **Mood** is the client's overall emotional tone during the interview. It is an indicator of the severity of impairment and the kind of impairment. Most people who seek help are in an anxious or depressed mood. If the emotional tone seems extreme, the crisis worker should note it and consider referral to a physician.

Affect: Counselors commonly look for the client's feelings during the interview and assess the appropriateness of them to the content. *Appropriate in direction* means that the feeling matches the content (e.g., the client cries when talking about his or her father's death). *Appropriate in intensity* means that the level or demonstration of the feeling matches the content (e.g., the client sheds a tear rather than sobbing uncontrollably when talking about a child getting his first shots). *Flat* and *blunted* **affect** are seen in cases of severe depression and psychotic disorders. These terms refer to a lack of emotion, indicating that the counselor can't quite connect emotionally with the client.

Thought processes: **Thought processes** refer to the rate, form, and content of the client's thoughts. Individuals who suffer from psychoses often present with disturbed thought processes. They suffer from **delusions** (false beliefs)—a definite indication that they need medical attention. Following is a list of common delusions observed in individuals with **schizophrenia:**

> **Thought insertion**—the clients believe someone is putting thoughts into their heads against their will.
>
> **Thought broadcasting**—clients believe that their thoughts are being put out into the air and that others know what they are thinking.
>
> **Delusions of reference**—clients think that things and people are focused on them and people are talking about them.
>
> **Delusions of persecution**—clients believe someone is out to get them, that there are plots against them.
>
> **Delusions of jealousy**—clients believe their spouses are cheating on them, despite lack of evidence.
>
> **Religious delusions**—clients believe they have a special relationship with God or the Devil.
>
> **Delusions of grandiosity**—clients believe they have special powers and abilities—can read minds, can talk to God.
>
> **Somatic delusions**—clients believe their bodies are rotting or sick or possessed.

Delusions of sin—clients believe they have committed some horrible sin and should be punished.

In addition to assessing for delusions, the crisis worker can observe the way the client talks. Individuals who are incoherent may be intoxicated. *Loose associations* is a term used to describe the fleeting conversations of a schizophrenic patient who doesn't make sense in logical terms. *Tangential thinking* describes a person's going off on a topic unrelated to the original subject. These all indicate serious pathology. How much a person says also indicates pathology. A client who does not say anything or very little may be very depressed. On the other hand, long-winded clients may be in a **manic state**.

Sensory perception: **Hallucinations** are false sensory experiences. They can involve any of the senses, with the person hearing voices or noises, seeing things or people, smelling odors, tasting things, or feeling something on the body. In each case, there is no actual stimulus to cause the perception. Any hallucination is indicative of serious pathology.

Sensorium: **Sensorium** refers to the client's mental faculties such as memory, concentration, intelligence, and orientation to the surroundings and to herself or himself. Certain questions and tests, such as the following, can be used to assess for these:

Proverbs—these can help the counselor ascertain whether the client has abstract reasoning abilities and is connected to reality (e.g., what does it mean when one says "People who live in glass houses shouldn't throw stones"?).

Serial 7's—the counselor asks the client to start with 100 and subtract 7 and keep subtracting 7 as far as possible. This exercise indicates the person's ability to concentrate and shows the intelligence level.

Orientation to person, place, and time—the counselor asks the person the date as well as where and who he or she is. Poor responses indicate severe pathology.

Impulse control and judgment: The counselor attempts to assess how much control the client has of her or his behavior and **judgment**.

Insight: The counselor assesses the client's **insight** by asking him or her to describe how severe his or her problems are and why the problems exist.

When the beginning counselor interviews a new client, he or she should keep in mind these various categories of behaviors to be able to decide whether to refer the client to a medical doctor. Table 5.3 lists possible medical conditions that can be assessed from the Mental Status Exam.

SUBSTANCE ABUSE ISSUES

Checking for substance abuse on a regular basis is a good idea and is often part of the intake form in most agencies. Because clients involved with substance use and

TABLE 5.3 The Mental Status Exam

Observation	Normal	Pathological	Need Physician Referral / Possible Diagnosis
Appearance: Age, race, sex, height, weight, hygiene, clothing	21-year-old Hispanic, well groomed, clean, well dressed	1. 50-year-old man who looks older, has wrinkles and red nose	1. Alcoholic
		2. 27-year-old man, wears 3 layers of clothes; hair is poorly combed and greasy; man is unshaven; has body odor	2. Schizophrenic
		3. Client has missing teeth, open sores on face; has dirty clothes and hands; burn marks on arms	3. Crack cocaine addict
Attitude: Warmth, trust, cooperation, responsiveness	Friendly, open, cooperative, responsive	1. Overly playful or belligerent	1. Mania
		2. Euphoric, spacy	2. Drug intoxication
		3. Guarded, paranoid	3. Schizophrenia, dementia
Psychomotor Behavior: Alertness, gait, posture, facial expressions, eye contact	Alert, good eye contact, moderate movements, varied facial expressions, control of physical movement	1. Poor eye contact, slumped posture, hand-wringing	1. Depression
		2. Stiff posture, no movement, waxy flexibility	2. Catatonic schizophrenia

Psychomotor Behavior: (continued)		3. Rocking, head-banging rituals, rubbing 4. Constant movement, shaking, dropping things	3. Pervasive developmental disorder 4. Hyperactivity
Speech: Quantity, amplitude, impediments, speed	Moderate amount of content, no impediments, audible voice	1. Verbose, talkative, pressured speech 2. Slurring, mumbling 3. Poverty of content	1. Mania, speed intoxication 2. Alcohol, downers intoxication 3. Depression
Mood: Overall emotional tone and climate	Euthymic, pleasant, minimal anxiety, some sense of humor	1. Depressed appetite, disturbed sleep, social withdrawal, crying, lack of energy, loss of pleasure, helplessness, hopelessness, sense of worthlessness, suicidal ideation 2. Anxious, dizzy; has sweats, panic attacks, heart palpitations 3. Euphoric/irritable, has grandiose schemes; is overjoyous, angry	1. Depression 2. Panic disorder 3. Mania
Affect: Expression of feelings, emotional connection, display of emotions	Appropriate in direction and intensity	1. Blunted 2. Flat 3. Out of control 4. Labile	1. Psychosis 2. Depression 3. Mania, drug intoxication 4. Dissociative identity disorder (DID), histrionic *(Continued)*

TABLE 5.3 *Continued*

Observation	Normal	Need Physician Referral	
		Pathological	*Possible Diagnosis*
Thought Processes: Rate, form, content	Spontaneous, full, tight associations, realistic	1. Slow, retarded 2. Loose associations; tangential, incoherent thoughts; delusions of thought insertion, thought broadcasting, persecution, reference, jealousy, religion, grandiosity, sin	1. Depression 2. Psychosis
Sensory Perception: Hallucination: perceptions with no stimulus	None are normal	1. Auditory voices 2. Visual, tactile 3. Olfactory, gustatory 4. Derealization	1. Schizophrenia 2. Alcohol, tranquilizer withdrawal 3. Organic brain disorder 4. Lysergic acid (LSD) intoxication
Sensorium: Orientation, overall mental faculties; concentration, memory, general knowledge; ability to handle abstraction, serial 7's, proverbs	Oriented to place, person, time; good memory; sound knowledge of current events; ability to abstract and concentrate on tasks	1. Not oriented, poor memory 2. Bizarre proverbs 3. Amnesia, wandering 4. Poor knowledge and vocabulary	1. Organic brain disorder 2. Psychosis 3. DID 4. Mental retardation or lack of education

Impulse Control and Judgment:
Able to control behavior and aware of socially acceptable behaviors

Socially acceptable behaviors, moral conscience

1. Acts out sexually and violently; goes on gambling sprees, shopping sprees

1. Mania, DID, sociopathy, drug abuse

Insight:
The extent to which someone realizes she or he has problems

Awareness and acceptance of some problems

1. Denies any problems or blames others for them

1. Paranoia, drug abuse, mania

...en deny and minimize their use, the crisis worker will need to be ...rtive in gathering information about drug use. Following are some ...w to extract this information without offending clients:

...*ut your past and present drug and alcohol use.*

...ssumes that use exists/existed and is stated matter-of-factly, as if ...ocked to hear of it. If the person hasn't used drugs, he or she can ..ply say *none.*

How much alcohol do you use a week?

What other drugs besides cocaine do you use or have you used?

These questions do not seem to be as judgmental or grilling as the following do:

Do you use alcohol? Do you use cocaine? Do you smoke pot? Do you drink daily?

Using general, open-ended questions will save time and reduce defensiveness in clients.

The bulk of the session, and probably the most therapeutic, will be spent in identifying the client's beliefs and feelings, and then providing supportive statements, educational information, empowering statements, and reframing statements that will aid the client in coping. Of course, active listening skills remain important, but once these are mastered, the counselor is ready to use these more advanced skills, discussed next, to help clients improve their coping ability.

Support Statements   The counselor may, from time to time, tell clients that their feelings are normal, or suggest that there is hope that things will get better. In response to a woman who has just found out that her husband has been molesting their daughter and feels like the world has come to an end, a crisis worker might respond supportively by saying, "I know that right now you feel that everything is falling apart, but many people have gone through the same situation and have survived. You have every reason to believe you can survive, too."

Support statements are not necessarily false hopes or words like "It'll be OK," "Don't worry," or "Forget about it." These comments are typical of family and friends who mean well; however, they are not very useful. As crisis workers, we need to say things to people that others do *not* say. Also, because clients see counselors as experts in crisis situations, they will tend to take comfort in supportive comments from these helpers, often adopting a more optimistic attitude.

Educational Statements   Providing factual information, whether it be developmental or situational, is vital in every crisis. Often a client will be suffering merely because he or she lacks or has incorrect knowledge about the precipitating event and aspects associated with it. Thus, it is imperative for crisis workers to gather as much information as possible about each crisis situation. Whether this is done through formal academic courses, books, experience, or supervision, it will give counselors an edge in helping clients work through their issues.

Educational statements may include the psychological, social, and interpersonal dynamics involved or they may provide statistics or frequency of the problem. In any case, when a counselor helps a person in a crisis state increase his or her knowledge of facts, the client will have stronger coping skills for the current crisis and future crises.

Picture a woman who has been completely isolated from others while in an ongoing battering relationship. She will most likely perceive herself as abnormal and bizarre. When she learns that about 30% of women live in ongoing battering relationships, she may then feel differently about herself and the abnormality of the situation. Without this issue to deal with, the counseling is now freed up to process other issues.

Empowering Statements   Certain crisis situations in which clients feel violated and victimized respond well to **empowering statements**. Clients are presented with choices and are encouraged to take back personal power by making good choices.

Ample evidence shows that battered women, rape survivors, and survivors of child abuse suffer from learned helplessness; their perception gives them motivation only to survive rather than to escape. A useful strategy is to let these people know that they can make other choices. Also, the crisis worker can point out that they do not have to choose certain behaviors.

> **Example**   A rape victim might be told, "You didn't have a choice in being raped, but now you do have a choice of what to do. You can call the police, go to counseling, tell a friend, or *not* do any of these things. Let's talk about your feelings and thoughts on each of these choices."

Reframing Statements   In its simplest form, **reframing** is defining a situation differently from the way the client is defining it. It is a cognitive restructuring tactic that aims at changing the crisis from danger to opportunity. American clichés, such as "Every cloud has a silver lining" and "When life gives you lemons, make lemonade" convey this idea quite clearly.

Reframing may seem like rationalizing away a problem to some. However, it is probably one of the strongest healing skills available to the crisis worker and for people in general. It allows us to acknowledge that life is a struggle, that we aren't perfect, and that dwelling on our failings is not necessary or helpful. Instead, if we can believe that something positive or beneficial will be an outcome or result of the problem, we can usually integrate the difficult episode more easily. The crisis worker's responsibility is to be creative in finding the right reframe. This means actively searching for the positive. Reframing is an advanced technique that puts problems in a solvable form by changing the meanings of the behaviors and situations and providing a new perspective that opens up new possibilities for change.

> **Example**   Think of the woman whose rape case is rejected by the district attorney after she has hoped for a year that it would go to court. The rapist is free and her victimization has not been acknowledged because of a technicality. Now, the counselor and client can both throw up their hands, call the judicial system names, and seethe internally. Alternatively, the counselor can point out to the client that the rape prodded her to seek counseling that allowed her not only to work through the rape

issues but also to identify her co-dependency and its effects on her relationships. This knowledge led the way to better family relations and intimacy with her boyfriend. The reframe was that being raped was not completely awful because it set in motion self-understanding and growth.

Reframing is possible only if the counselor first understands fully the client's current frame of reference. Otherwise, the counselor would not know what should be reframed. Counselors can learn the client's frame of reference by asking direct questions: "How do you perceive the situation?" "What does it mean to you?" "What runs through your head about it?" Reframing is not a technique to be taken lightly and good supervision is necessary in learning its effective use.

Sometimes reframing is associated with a cold, strategic approach, but it can be done in an authentic, caring manner. The counselor does not deny the seriousness of the problem; instead, he or she offers a way out of a problem that allows the person to preserve the integrity of the self and often the family unit as well. Because reframes are usually offered with the person's self-identity in mind, shame is reduced and self-integrity is preserved. The example reframes provided in each of the following sections show this principle of self-preservation clearly.

In summary, the B section of the ABC model can be thought of as identifying issues one at a time, and providing various forms of feedback as the process moves forward to a place where the client can accept coping as viable behavior. Periodically, the crisis worker should summarize the precipitating events, the client's perceptions of them, the client's functioning in several areas of life, and any major symptoms of concern.

Key Terms for Study

delusion: A false thought that cannot be rationalized away. Such thoughts occur in people who are psychotic or organically impaired.

depression: A state of being in which the client is sad, low in energy, and suicidal; he or she feels worthless, helpless, and hopeless; the person lacks desire, is socially withdrawn, and is slowed in processes such as thinking and concentrating. This person should be referred to a physician for an evaluation.

educational statement: A type of therapeutic comment in which facts, statistics, and theories are presented to the client in an attempt to normalize his or her experience and change misconceptions.

empowering statement: A therapeutic comment that helps clients feel more in control and see choices they have. It is especially useful for clients who have been victimized.

hallucination: A false sensory perception. Auditory hallucinations are associated with schizophrenia, visual and tactile ones with substance abuse withdrawal, and gustatory and olfactory ones with organic brain disorders. Any hallucination is indicative of severe illness; when hallucinations are present, a doctor should be consulted.

manic state: A condition in which behavior is out of control, hyper, and grandiose. It indicates either a bipolar disorder or drug intoxication and requires the assistance of a physician.

Mental Status Exam: A process in which the counselor observes and questions the client to ascertain whether mental illness or organic illness is involved in the problems. The various categories of observation and evaluation include these:

>appearance
>
>psychomotor behavior
>
>attitude
>
>affect
>
>mood
>
>thought processes
>
>sensorium
>
>insight
>
>judgment

organic brain disorder: A condition due to a neurological disturbance, a genetic abnormality, or tumors.

reframing: A therapeutic restatement of a problem that helps the client see the situation differently, usually in a way that makes it easier to solve.

schizophrenia: A disorder usually requiring the attention of a psychiatrist and characterized by the following symptoms: hallucinations, delusions, loose associations, blunt affect, and poor appearance.

support statement: A therapeutic statement that makes the client feel validated and that the counselor truly understands and empathizes with his or her situation.

C: Exploring the Client's Coping Strategies

The last step of the ABC model is concerned with the client's coping behavior—past, present, and future. Past coping success can be built on to help the person weather the present and future difficulties.

EXPLORING THE CLIENT'S ATTEMPTS AT COPING

Toward the conclusion of an interview, the counselor should begin summing up the problem and moving the client into a coping mode. To do this, the crisis worker asks the client how she or he has managed crises in the past. All coping, whether it is helpful or not, should be examined. In this way, the client can make a mental list of what works and what does not.

If the client cannot think of any past coping behavior, the crisis worker should be very encouraging. The counselor might say, "Well, you must have done something or you would not have made it this far." Remember that even sleeping or social withdrawal are coping strategies and should be talked about as to their helpfulness/unhelpfulness in dealing with stressors. Eliciting unhealthy attempts at coping is especially helpful as it helps the client see what has not worked in the past. The client will generally be more open to alternatives once the ineffectiveness of his or her current behavior is made evident.

ENCOURAGING THE DEVELOPMENT OF NEW COPING BEHAVIORS

After current coping attempts have been discussed, the counselor can prod clients to ponder other possible ways of coping. The crisis worker can ask clients how they think they can proceed at this point to begin to get out of the crisis state. Remember that the client has already been presented with educational information, reframes, supportive comments, and empowerment statements. It is time for the person to do some of his or her own thinking.

Clients are more likely to follow through with a plan they have developed themselves than one suggested by the counselor. It is appropriate for a counselor to be challenging and persistent in getting clients to think of ways they could begin to cope better. This approach helps clients get in touch with their problem-solving abilities.

PRESENTING ALTERNATIVE COPING METHODS TO CLIENTS

Clients should be allowed first to propose their own methods for coping with their problems. When they have reached the end of the resources they know, however, the counselor should suggest other options. Many of these may be completely new to clients, offering them fresh insights.

Support Groups and 12-Step Groups   If **support systems** haven't already been discussed, now is a good time to identify some existing natural support, such as coworkers, supervisors, relatives, friends, schoolmates, or church members.

Clients may not have considered any of these in terms of helping them get through the crisis. With a little encouragement, they may be persuaded to reach out to others. This is not to suggest that crisis workers should avoid giving support to clients. However, it is often more comfortable for clients to receive help from natural support systems than to rely on mental health professionals during crises. As Caplan (1964) suggested earlier, effectively coping people actively invoke help from others, not necessarily mental health workers.

The idea of encouraging clients to help themselves parallels the adage of teaching a man to fish versus just giving him fish. Self-sufficiency is more economical in the long run. The author has often felt that as a crisis interventionist, her job is to put herself out of a job by encouraging her clients to function on their own and with the support of others in their lives. A crisis worker is merely a beacon shedding light on these resources.

Some clients may need referrals to 12-step groups such as Alcoholics Anonymous (AA), Al-Anon, Co-Dependents Anonymous, Cocaine Anonymous, or other groups. These mutual self-help groups are free and have no time limits for attendance; sessions can be found in every city at various hours of the day. The trend now is for insurance companies to pay for only 6 to 12 sessions of therapy, so the 12-step groups are a lifesaver for many people who cannot afford to pay for therapy out of their own pockets.

Long-term Therapy and/or Marital and Family Therapy   Sometimes clients' problems are so long standing that crisis intervention can't resolve them. Perhaps because of a personality disorder or other chronic emotional disorder, the client will need ongoing therapy with a trained professional. This might be in the form of individual therapy or marital or family therapy. Often, a crisis is an opportunity for the client to resolve long-term problems that have been hidden for many years.

Shelters and Other Agencies   To address other problems, crisis workers need to be very knowledgeable about community agencies and **resources**. Clients who are anxious and feeling overwhelmed are more likely to follow through with a referral when it is presented in written form with choices, addresses, phone numbers, and fees. Providing written information is much more effective than telling clients to look for certain services in the Yellow Pages.

Even if you are conducting a phone interview, having these resources in hand, separated by the type of crisis, will certainly aid in the expediency of referral. Also, crisis workers can be assured that the agency can actually service the client's needs at affordable rates if they have recently researched information about that agency and updated their listings.

At times, crisis workers may want to contact an agency and let someone there know about a referral. It is quite reasonable to ask for a follow-up call or note about whether the client used the resource. In other instances, a client may return to a crisis worker for another individual session and the crisis worker at that time can ask whether the client attended the support group or used the service recommended.

Medical and Legal Referrals   In some cases, **legal and/or medical referrals** will be necessary. Even if the crisis worker is considered a paraprofessional, he or she should have an understanding of the legal, political, and medical systems and how they will impact various crises.

For instance, workers should know the conditions under which a police officer may arrest a battering spouse. Also, they should have knowledge about restraining orders, which might be useful for a victim of abuse. How the court system generally deals with rape or child abuse is useful information as well. Though they are not expected to be lawyers, crisis workers need to keep abreast of recent laws that affect clients in crises.

Similarly, though not expected or allowed to be physicians, crisis workers need to be able to refer someone to a doctor for an evaluation when medication or other treatment might be useful. Learning to consult and work adjunctly with medical doctors is a skill worth developing. This is one reason for learning the Mental Status Exam at the paraprofessional level. Knowing when to make a referral to a physician is vital.

Bibliotherapy   Every crisis worker needs to have some knowledge of reading material for clients in a variety of crisis situations. Using these materials with clients is called **bibliotherapy**. Reading often provides a new way of looking at the crisis (reframing), information, and support—especially books written by a person who has gone through a similar crisis. For example, reading a book by a woman who was raped will help the recently raped woman see that her feelings are normal; this knowledge should have a calming effect. Also, reading helps people think rather than feel, encouraging more productive problem-solving activity. A commonality of all these types of coping referrals is that they all provide ways for the client to cope and think differently about the precipitating event.

COMMITMENT AND FOLLOW-UP

Part of making any referral or suggestion is **commitment and follow-up**—getting a commitment from clients that they will indeed follow through with the recommendation. This explains why it is best for clients to develop their own coping plans. They are more likely to follow through with a plan they formulated themselves.

In some cases, as with highly suicidal clients, a written contract may be prudent. The *no-suicide contract* is a popular and useful intervention and is discussed in the next chapter. Written contracts are often used with clients who need to control their impulses or with acting-out teenagers. Both the therapist and the client keep a copy of the contract and discuss it at the next session.

In summary, the C part of the ABC model first asks clients to explore current, past, and possible new coping strategies to deal with the crisis at hand. Then, the crisis worker offers alternative ideas, makes referrals, and asks clients for a commitment to follow through on the plan. The worker's hope is that clients will move from a dysfunctional state to a higher level of functioning and perceived control in regard to the precipitating event. At each visit, the crisis worker can verify and suggest connecting with these various coping aids. This gives clients something concrete to take home.

Key Terms for Study

bibliotherapy: The use of books as an alternative coping strategy.

commitment and follow-up: Verbal agreement given by client to crisis worker at the end of a crisis intervention session. Very specifically, it is what the client is going to do after leaving the session to deal with the crisis. It may include returning to see the same counselor or going elsewhere. Remember that the person in crisis is vulnerable and needs direction.

legal and/or medical referrals: Referrals made by the crisis worker if the client needs the services of other professionals. Legal and medical referrals are made when a person has been arrested, wants a restraining order, or has a severe mental or other illness.

resources: Sources of help in the community. A crisis worker must be knowledgeable about community resources to be able to connect a client in crisis with the appropriate support group or other service.

support systems: Networks of helping individuals and agencies. A crisis worker utilizes the client's natural support systems, such as family and friends, and also helps the client build new support systems.

To sum up the ABC model, a sample script is presented in Table 5.4. This gives readers an idea of the types of questions and statements a crisis worker might ask or make when using the ABC model. The steps of the model are repeated in the table. In each section, please note the specific words (italicized) that a counselor might say to a client.

TABLE 5.4 The ABC Model of Crisis Intervention

A: BASIC ATTENDING SKILLS

What brings you in today?
You seem to be having a little trouble getting started.

B: IDENTIFYING THE PROBLEM AND THERAPEUTIC INTERACTION

Identify the precipitating event.
What specifically brought you in today? Did something happen recently, something different?

Explore meanings, cognitions, and perceptions.
How do you think about it? What does it mean to you? What thoughts go through your mind when you picture the event? How do you put it together in your head? What is it like for you? What specifically do you mean? What are your perceptions about it (the precipitating event)?

Identify subjective distress (emotional distress).
How do you feel? What emotions are going on inside you? You seem sad, angry, ambivalent, in pain. How have you been feeling since (the precipitating event)?

Identify impairments in functioning in the following areas:

(Continued)

Table 5.4 Continued

1. behavioral
How have you been doing in your life? How are you sleeping? How is your appetite? Have you been carrying on with your normal activities?

2. social
How are your relationships with your friends and family? Have you been seeing anyone socially since (the precipitating event)? How do you feel or act around people?

3. academic
Are you going to school? How are your grades lately? Have you been able to study and concentrate in classes? How are you getting along with classmates?

4. occupational
How are you doing at work? Has your work performance changed since (the precipitating event)? Have you been able to function adequately at work?

Identify pre-crisis level of functioning in 1–4 above.
How has your ability to function socially, at school, and at work changed since (the precipitating event)? What was it like for you before (the precipitating event)? What/how were your relationships before (the precipitating event)?

Identify any ethical concerns:

1. suicide assessment
Have you been thinking about hurting yourself? Have you attempted to kill yourself? Do you want to commit suicide? Do you have a plan? Do you have the means? What is stopping you from killing yourself?

2. child abuse, elder abuse, homicide
Are your children in danger? Have you or your husband ever caused physical harm to your children? How hard do you hit your kids? How often do you leave your child alone? Have your kids gone without food for an entire day? Has your elderly parent been hurt by the retirement home? When did you first learn that your sister was stealing from your father? How often do you have thoughts about killing your wife? Have you ever hurt someone in the past? How strong are your feelings of murder?

3. organic or other medical concerns
Are you able to get up in the morning and feed yourself? How many hours do you sleep? Can you dress yourself every day? Do you ever hear voices? Does it ever feel like the phone wires are talking to you? Do you have special powers? Can people read your mind or put thoughts into your head? Do you think people are out to get you? Do you smell or taste things that are unusual?

Identify substance abuse issues.
What kinds of drugs have you used in the past? How much alcohol do you drink per week/month/day? What drugs do you use recreationally?

Use therapeutic interactions:

1. educational comments

Although you feel as though you are the only woman who stays in a battering relationship, it is estimated that about 30% of women in the United States live in ongoing battering relationships.

Going through a period of intense anger is quite normal and to be expected after the death of a loved one.

Actually, it is not uncommon to be raped by someone you know. Date rape is extremely common for women ages 15 to 24.

Studies to date do not show that one can catch HIV by shaking hands.

It is not uncommon for the spouse of an alcoholic to be highly anxious about the spouse's drinking.

2. empowerment statements

It is true that you did not have a choice about being raped, but you do have choices now, including whether to press charges, get a medical exam, or drop the whole matter.

Unfortunately, you cannot control your wife's drug use, but you can control your own behavior with her.

True, you are HIV infected and cannot change that. You can, however, choose how to live the rest of your life.

3. support statements

This is an extremely difficult situation, and I don't take it lightly. I can only imagine the pain you are going through. I am so sorry this happened to you. Please, let me be there for you; I care. It must feel pretty bad if you want to kill yourself. These kinds of traumas often make people feel like giving up.

4. Reframes

I think it takes a lot of strength to cry, and I don't see crying as a sign of weakness. Although you see suicide as a sign of strength, it is actually the easy way out of a life filled with difficulties for us all. Staying with a batterer for the sake of your children is evidence of your strength, not a sign of weakness. (Please see each chapter for more examples of reframing.)

C: COPING

Identify client's current coping attempts.
What have you done to try to feel better? What else have you done? Anything else?

Encourage client to think of other coping strategies.
What else can you think of to try to get through this? What have you done in the past to get through difficult times? What would you tell a friend to do in this case?

Present alternative coping ideas:

(Continued)

Table 5.4 Continued

1. refer to support groups, 12-step groups
You said you feel better when you talk to friends; how would you feel about attending a support group with other people in your situation? I know of a very special group where people going through what you are going through meet to learn ways to deal with it. Will you give it a try? You can go for as long as you need to and it is free.

2. refer to long-term therapy, family therapy
I believe you could benefit most by going to a family therapist/marital therapist. Would you consider this? It appears that your problems are long standing. I think longer-term therapy would be really good for you. I know several great counselors. I'll give you a list.

3. refer to medical doctor or psychiatrist
I would feel most comfortable if you see a physician. Your symptoms seem serious and you may need medication or a physical. Do you know of a doctor or shall I refer you to one that I really respect and work with on other cases?

4. refer to lawyer
I think you should get legal advice from an attorney. These matters are beyond my scope of expertise. Please go to the public defender today or tomorrow. Are you aware of restraining orders? You can find out about them at the district attorney's office.

5. refer to shelter, other agency
How would you feel about going to a battered woman's/homeless shelter? You will be safe there.

6. recommend books
Do you like to read? I know of some really good books that help explain more about what you are going through. Here is a list of books I recommend for you to read.

Obtain commitment; do follow-up.
When can you make another appointment with me? Call me when you set up your appointment with Dr. Jones. I am going to call you tomorrow. Will you promise not to hurt yourself until you at least speak to me first?

This concludes the sample ABC model. In the following chapters, the reader will find more specific questions and comments that apply to a particular crisis.

When Crisis Is a Danger

The responsibility of protecting society and its individuals from harm has been delegated to the mental health community when that harm is inflicted because someone suffers from a mental disorder. Although law enforcement agencies, such as police and sheriff departments, may be called on in such emergency situations, it is the mental health worker who must provide interventions to manage the life-threatening behavior. In this context, crises of emergency all involve life-threatening behavior, through which a person, because of a mental disorder, poses a danger to himself or herself or to others.

In fact, threatening suicide, posing a danger to others, and being gravely disabled (which is often a result of active, severe psychoses) are often grounds for involuntary hospitalization. The duty to protect clients and potential victims is legislated by each state. Guidelines are usually offered that inform practitioners of how to manage dangerous clients. Civil suits have been brought against therapists who have failed to prevent suicide or homicide. It is essential for crisis workers to be familiar with the laws of the state in which they practice (Corey, 1998).

Not all people who are suicidal, psychotic, or homicidal are detained in hospitals, however. Other interventions can be less costly and equally effective in managing these conditions. The first crisis we examine is suicide.

Suicide

Suicidal ideation is often a result of the client's feeling totally overwhelmed because of his or her perception of a variety of precipitating events, as discussed in Chapter 1. Understanding suicidal thinking and intervention strategies is essential for counselors working with all the situational crises to be presented in subsequent chapters. Although suicide is discussed as a separate issue in this chapter, the crisis worker must be aware that suicide assessment will be a part of all crisis intervention interviews, even if it is not the presenting problem. The possibility that a suicidal person will indeed kill himself or herself is quite high, and the threat must be taken seriously. Often, the media give more attention to homicide, but in actuality, more people die of suicide than of murder.

The burden caused by suicide and threats of it falls not only on the suicidal person and those closest to him or her. The effects spill over to the crisis worker, also. Responding to a suicidal client can be intimidating for a counselor and is often a source of personal stress. When dealing with this population, the crisis worker must seek and accept emotional support from colleagues, supervisors, and family.

An examination of numerical information about suicide from the National Center for Health Statistics is enlightening (Aguilera, 1990, pp. 169–170): Suicide ranks eighth as a cause of death in the United States. The rate of suicide in this country is 12.7 per 100,000 persons. The most common method of suicide is the ingestion of sedatives or hypnotic drugs. By age groups, the frequency of suicide occurs as shown here:

Years of Age	Frequency per 100,000 Population
15–24	12.8
25–34	14.8
35–44	19.9
45–54	15.5
55–64	17.8
65–74	19.9
75–84	29.2
85+	22.0

Stephen Wyman (1982), a medical doctor, offers additional statistics: (1) In the 15 to 19 age group, suicide is the second highest cause of death; car accidents are first. (2) Three males to one female successfully complete suicide attempts. (3) Three females to one male attempt but are not successful. (4) In terms of all professions, psychiatrists have the highest suicide rates and pediatricians the lowest.

In regard to psychiatric disorders, most suicides occur within the first three months of a patient's improvement following a depression. Of those diagnosed with affective disorders (major depression or bipolar disorder), 45% will attempt and 15% will die. Among schizophrenics, 25% will try; paranoids have the highest risk. Suicide will be tried by 25% of those diagnosed with dysthymic disorder; 12 of 100,000 will succeed. Among alcoholics, 25–30% will try (Wyman, 1982).

In her research on suicide, Steiner (1990) found that 1 million people attempted suicide in 1990 and the rate of suicide has quadrupled since 1950. In 1960, in Orange County, California, the rate of suicide was 4.49 per 100,000; in 1985, it was 13.8 per 100,000! Factors that are often associated with risk of suicide include unemployment, illness, impulsivity, rigid thinking (black and white, all or nothing), several stressful events, and release from hospitalization (Steiner, 1990).

SYMPTOMS AND CLUES

Suicide does not generally come without warning. Almost always, the person considering it shows symptoms or provides clues to his or her intent. It is important, however, for crisis workers to know how to read these, and to be able to distinguish between myths and reality. Let us begin by dispelling some common myths about suicide. How many of these have you believed?

1. If I discuss suicide with a client, she or he is more likely to do it.
   In reality, it will be a relief for this individual to talk about it with an accepting person. For thoughts about suicide to be eliminated, they must be discussed. If the person is not really suicidal, the conversation will not cause harm.

2. Suicide threats don't need to be taken seriously. If someone is going to do it, why would that person announce it?
   A large percentage of people who kill themselves have disclosed their intent to others.

3. Suicide is a completely irrational act.
   Suicide often makes sense when viewed from the perspective of the person doing it.

4. Only insane people commit suicide.
   Only a small percent of suicides are psychotic or crazy. Most are depressed normal people who are grieving, lonely, and hopeless.

5. Suicide is an inherited behavior.
   So far, there is no evidence to support a genetic tendency to suicide. However, it can be learned in a family, or be the result of an intolerable family life.

6. Once one ponders suicide, this thought never goes away.
   Many people contemplate suicide but recover from the painful feelings that lead to this.

7. Suicide is always impulsive.
   Some suicidal acts are very deliberate.

Suicidal individuals do not always tell the crisis worker their intent directly. Prudent workers learn to read between the lines when dealing with possible suicide risks in clients. Typical warning signs they can look for are these:

1. Giving things away

2. Putting things in order

3. Writing a will

4. Withdrawing from usual activities

5. Being preoccupied with death

6. Having experienced the recent death of a friend or relative

7. Feeling hopeless, helpless, worthless

8. Increasing drug and alcohol use

9. Displaying psychotic behavior

10. Giving verbal hints such as "I'm no use to anyone anymore"

11. Showing agitated depression

12. Living alone, isolated

   (Aguilera, 1990, p. 174; Gilliland & James, 1988, p. 81; Wyman, 1982)

A person displaying only one or two of these behaviors may not be suicidal. A crisis worker must take into consideration a number of factors. Remember, however, that you don't need to wait until you observe these clues before you assess for suicidality. No matter what the presenting problem, a crisis worker should always ask any client the following question in one way or another: "Do you have or have you ever had thoughts about hurting yourself?" If the answer is *yes,* the crisis worker must follow up with a detailed suicide risk assessment (Wyman, 1982).

SUICIDE ASSESSMENT

At the present time, there is no psychological test, such as the Minnesota Multiphasic Personality Inventory (MMPI), that can predict suicide in a particular client. **Suicide assessment** is largely a judgment call on the counselor's part (Wyman, 1982). Hence, being sensitive to risk factors and asking appropriate questions are vital strategies for any crisis worker. Depending on the client's responses to the questions, the worker can introduce various intervention strategies to reduce the risk of lethal behavior by the client.

Steiner has developed an outline for assessing a person's potential for suicide (1990):

1. *Ask if the person has thought of killing himself or herself.*
   How often?
   How badly does the person want to die (on a scale from 1 to 3)?
   Does he or she see suicide as a good solution or bad solution?
   Does the person perceive suicide as weak or strong?
   (At high risk is a person who thinks about suicide often, scores 3, sees it as a good solution, and perceives suicide as a strong act.)

2. *Ask family members if they are concerned that the person will commit suicide.*
   (If family members say they don't believe it would happen, that the person is just acting, this person is at high risk.)

3. *Check person's* **plan** *for suicide.*
   Is it detailed? General?
   Does the person have materials to carry it out?
   Does he or she intend to do it soon?
   Has the person given away possessions, said good-bye?

4. *Check person's mental status.*
   Is the person confused? Intoxicated? On drugs? Hallucinating?
   Is the person in control of his or her faculties? Impulsive? Clinically
   depressed? Emerging from clinical depression?

5. *Check the history of suicide in the person's life.*
   Has this person made other attempts?
   Does the person have friends or family who killed themselves?

6. *Find out what the individual's support system is like by asking these*
   questions.
   "What friends or relatives have you told about your intent?"
   "Who do you talk with when you are down?"
   "How does the family respond to your concerns?"

7. *How much control does the person have?*
   "Can anyone or anything stop you?"
   "What has been stopping you?"
   "What made you come for help?"

8. *Ask the person for a commitment to talk with you, to see you in two days,*
   to give up all rights to suicide for a set period of time. Have the person tell
   you how he or she will do that.

A PHENOMENOLOGICAL LOOK AT SUICIDE

Once an objective assessment of suicide risk is fairly well completed, the crisis worker needs to gain an understanding of the phenomenological aspects (the subjective, unique view) of the client's suicidal thoughts and behaviors, past and present. This, of course, is part of the B section in the ABC model of crisis intervention. Remember that the order of these assessments does not necessarily flow in linear fashion. Gathering objective information and exploring subjective perceptions of the client are usually done simultaneously. This approach is presented in outline only to make clear what information needs to be extracted in the B part.

Steiner (1990), who counsels largely in a phenomenological style within the strategic systems model, has presented case examples and several ideas that clearly demonstrate the value in taking this position. From reviewing certain statistics, she theorized that the reason teen suicide rates have increased is because perhaps teenagers' deaths in the past were ignored as suicide. It was too painful to admit that one's child killed himself. She suggested that nowadays there are fewer taboos in dealing with pain and family problems; therefore, more teen suicides are called what they are.

Based on interviews with adult suicidal clients, Steiner proposed that suicide might seem to some troubled individuals to be a more viable alternative in times when the economy is slow, making jobs harder to find and creating confused roles in the family and society. As she says, the American dream is not there any more for many people.

Two case examples presented by Steiner demonstrate her use of the systems model when teenagers' perceptions of their families led to suicidal ideation. In general, Steiner has found that many teens consider suicide because of chronic family fighting. The teen is often made to feel responsible for the arguments and tensions even though some conflict is inevitable with a teenager in the home. If this conflict is not dealt with well, the family could exist in a crisis state for five to eight years. Teenagers who believe they alone are responsible for these conflicts may just feel too overwhelmed by the constant stress and may perceive suicide as the best solution for everyone. This is especially likely when parents blatantly tell their adolescent that the family problems are all the teenager's fault! Of course, parents don't say this to encourage teens to kill themselves; the parents are in a crisis state and are ignorant about how to cope with the new demands of having an adolescent in the home.

Reframing a situation like this will often help everyone see the family differently and ease the tension. Some people need to be educated about the normal conflicts in families and to be shown that these are not one particular person's fault. Rather, they are the motivation that helps the family grow and adjust to the maturing child.

Example 1

A 16-year-old girl, as an English assignment, wrote a poem describing her thoughts of suicide. After reading it, the English teacher sent her to see Steiner for counseling. After interviewing the girl alone, Steiner asked the girl's mother to come to a counseling session. The mother complained about the daughter's disobedience and defiant behaviors. The parents were divorced and the mother had threatened to send the daughter to live with her father if she didn't change her behavior. The daughter, frightened of her father and interpreting this threat as complete rejection by her mother, had entertained thoughts of suicide as a response. Steiner saw the daughter's oppositional behavior as symbolic of the ongoing conflict between her parents.

Steiner's reframe was that this suicidal behavior was evidence of the daughter's love for her mother and fear of her father. The intervention used by Steiner was an agreement in which the mother would give up the right to send her daughter to her father.

Steiner is a firm believer in allowing clients to maintain their perspective that suicide is their right; she avoids the conflicts that can result from saying to client, "You have no right to kill yourself." She interprets Nietzche's words, "Suicide has saved many lives," as meaning that sometimes clients' only control over themselves and their lives is having the option of suicide. Simply having this option is often enough to reduce the pressure they feel to the point that it is bearable.

Example 2

A teenage boy felt lonely. People did not really know him and he did not express his feelings often. His parents had aspirations for him that he simply could not meet. They had filtered out his feelings of failure and had an unrealistic picture of what he could do. This boy was at high risk for suicide because his perceived view of his life looked very bleak and hopeless.

Including his parents in treatment was essential. Their expectations would have to be reframed as their own projections of what they expected of themselves, and the focus would be on them instead of the boy.

This shift in attention would help release the tension in the teenager. His feelings of failure could be reframed as his unconscious identification with his *parents'* feelings of failure. Family therapy could focus on each member's realistic hopes for himself or herself instead of projected and introjected expectations.

SUICIDE PREVENTION

Although most mental health professionals assume it is their duty to prevent suicide, Thomas Szasz (1986) believes differently. Before examining mainstream suicide interventions, let us look at Szasz's somewhat radical perspective on suicide. Common sense tells us that suicide is a mental health problem and that mental health practitioners have a duty to try to prevent it. Szasz (1986) challenges this perspective. He believes that each individual is ultimately responsible for herself or himself and that the nation's mental health policy on suicide "undermines the ethic of self-responsibility" (p. 806). Also, if this policy regarding duty to prevent suicide were changed, it would reduce the number of malpractice suits against mental health professionals, as failure to prevent suicide is one of the leading reasons for successful lawsuits against these individuals.

Another interesting point made by Szasz concerns the choice of words used to describe a mental health worker's duty with suicidal clients: *prevention*. He asserts that this term is synonymous with *coercion*; it implies a paternalistic attitude toward the client and gives certain people (mental health professionals) privileges and powers to protect the suicidal individual.

As an example, in California, suicide is one area that allows breach of confidentiality without client consent. Also, someone can be involuntarily detained in a psychiatric hospital for up to 72 hours if that person is deemed uncontrollably suicidal; the detention is to prevent the person from killing himself or herself. Szasz suggests that these acts of *prevention* undermine each individual's right to suicide. Szasz would not *encourage* suicide, but he believes that a person's decision *not* to do it is the person's responsibility, not the responsibility of the mental health worker.

Szasz (1986) concludes his message by comparing suicide with other moral decisions such as abortion or marriage. Why, he asks, are mental health professionals held liable for a successful suicide, but not for an abortion or divorce? Part of the reason has to do with the philosophy that suicide is an insane behavior, and if the mental disorder were treated, suicidality would cease to exist. In other words, suicide is never "desirable enough to justify it" (p. 811). This does not mean that Szasz accepts suicide as a legitimate option but only that mental health professionals should be allowed to "treat it as an act that they may approve or disapprove in general and may choose to counsel for or against in any particular case" (p. 811), as is often done in cases of abortion and divorce. This philosophy would eliminate making counselors responsible and greatly reduce lawsuits. Most important, it places responsibility back on the individual in this society where doctors seem to be viewed as having the wisdom of God.

There are many examples that demonstrate sane suicidality. Cases of painful disease, terminal illness (such as AIDS or cancer), and dishonor (in certain cultures) that make life not worth living point to suicide as a viable option. In fact, the Hemlock Society was created in support of such cases, when an individual is seen as having the right to choose her or his own death.

Szasz and the Hemlock Society are in the minority, however, when it comes to suicide prevention. Most crisis workers of all licenses and in most agencies would agree that it is their duty to prevent people from killing themselves. Szasz wonders about this, though, questioning whether this attitude would be so prevalent if suicide were not illegal and if a worker were not liable to be sued for failing to prevent a client from killing himself or herself.

With an opposing view, Steiner (1990), claims that although she sometimes can really understand how suicide might be better than living for some people, she would still try to prevent it. She states her overall attitude very clearly when she tells clients that she's in the business of helping people who will commit to being alive. These words tell clients that she opposes suicide and that she would not help them do it. When asked how she would deal with a dying AIDS patient who truly believed killing himself painlessly would be a better choice than dying in pain, Steiner suggested interesting questions to ask the patient: "What kind of example would you be for others who have AIDS or are just HIV positive? Can we find any meaning in your living it out until the end?" These questions might help the individual die in dignity knowing he or she had contributed positively to others. Certainly, Magic Johnson's attitude about his HIV infection is considered exemplary because he is basically saying that whatever short time a person has left on earth is valuable, and each person should make the balance of that life productive.

Steiner also suggests asking clients to think of reasons for *not* killing themselves. Usually, the most severely depressed person can think of one or two reasons to live. In my own practice, I worked with a very suicidal client who was ready to be hospitalized by her psychiatrist. When I asked her for reasons to continue living, she said she loved her four-year-old grandson and enjoyed taking him to the park. By exploring this with her, I was able to join her phenomenological world and use this knowledge to show her that suicide might not be her only option and certainly not the best one if she wanted to continue going to the park with her grandson.

INTERVENTIONS

After a client has been assessed as suicidal, the crisis worker must determine the likelihood that the client will actually kill himself or herself. Some clients can be treated as outpatients while they are dealing with active suicidal feelings. Others may need to be hospitalized until the risk is lowered. Whatever the risk level, the crisis interventionist must be willing to devote more energy and time than usual to a suicidal client. This extra attention is often what the hopeless client needs to feel cared about, and the crisis worker must give evidence of genuine caring. This means that keeping the client alive must be a priority for the helper.

Low-risk clients   Low-risk suicidal clients are those who have never tried suicide, have adequate support systems, and say things such as "I thought about it but I'm not sure. It scares me to have feelings like these and I need someone to talk to." These clients can usually be treated as outpatients and should be encouraged to make an appointment with a therapist if you cannot continue to see them (Wyman, 1982). They probably would respond well to educational interventions such as reading books by others who have attempted suicide. Also, providing reframes will be helpful. A crisis worker might tell the client, "The fact that you are here is evidence that you don't truly want to kill yourself. People who truly want to die usually don't go to a mental health worker because they know we have an obligation to prevent suicide."

An empowering supportive comment might go like this: "The part of you that sought help is obviously very strong, and you can take comfort in knowing you have this inner strength that helps you choose to cope with your problems actively."

A client might be comforted to know that pondering suicide when things look bleak or stressful is a common human experience; it has been written about by the greatest novelists and philosophers from ancient to modern times. A helper can point out that pondering one's own death is not the equivalent of creating it and that the client appears to be in good control of this. Such thoughts will usually be a relief to the low-risk suicidal client.

Cole (1993) describes another type of low-risk suicidal case. Elderly people often consider suicide after the death of their spouse. Cole does not deny that this is a sad situation, but if the client can be brought to the clinic and stabilized on medication or other resources can be mobilized, he or she can often be supported through outpatient services rather than hospitalization. Her goal is to empower clients and preserve their dignity by connecting them with medical services and other resources such as senior citizen centers or in-home support services provided by most county governments.

The counselor should try to get at least a verbal agreement from clients that they won't harm themselves without first speaking to the helper. This informal, no-suicide contract can be very effective psychologically with the low-risk client.

The Middle-Risk Client   The most common suicidal client a crisis worker will see is probably the **middle-risk suicidal client**. These individuals can still function at work but are not feeling well. They are often difficult to evaluate. They feel there is no way out of the situation they are in. Often, in the hearing of family members, they will threaten to kill themselves. Unfortunately, these threats are ignored or are not taken seriously. When this is the case, these clients may need to be seen every day or be hospitalized because they may carry out the threat just to get a reaction from the family.

Interventions common with middle-risk clients usually include a **no-suicide contract.** This is a pact to last for two to three days during which clients agree to give up the right to kill themselves while they see the crisis worker. An example of a pact follows.

Sample No-Suicide Contract

I _____ agree not to harm myself for the next week. I promise to contact
(client's name)

_____ when my suicidal feelings get too strong to control.
(crisis worker's name)

_____   _____   _____
(client's signature)   (Date)   (crisis worker's signature)

Shaking hands to seal the pact is a good idea. A no-suicide contract should not be trusted with a client who lives alone and has no support system. This person might not keep it. The client should be monitored with a daily phone call. Most clients appreciate this type of concern. If possible, enlist family members to conduct a **suicide watch** in which the family members accept a certain amount of responsibility for monitoring the suicidal person and commit to staying close by this family member. In this way, the family helps assume some of the responsibility for the client's well-being. This behavior can show clients that family members do care enough about them to invest some energy in helping them overcome their destructive feelings.

Hospitalizing the middle-risk client should be done only as a last resort. According to family systems theory, keeping the family involved makes more sense than reinforcing a family myth of an identified, sick patient. Suicide says much about the family, and the most effective treatment will include all the family. When a family member is hospitalized, that person loses credibility in the family, and the family members begin to treat her or him differently.

In a crisis intervention session, the crisis worker has several options for working with middle-risk clients. Besides a no-suicide contract and suicide watch, the counselor should ask clients to bring in and give her or him the planned **means** for committing suicide. The counselor must destroy or lock these away so no one can be injured with them.

A helpful strategy is to address yourself to the ambivalence of the client and focus on the part that wants to live. Try to elicit from the client ideas for future plans and explore the things that have happened to make life not worth living anymore.

The High-Risk Suicidal Client   **High-risk suicidal clients** say things such as "I'm going to kill myself and you can't stop me." They are usually very depressed and angry, have tried suicide before, and lack support from loved ones. If pressed, they will admit to having a viable plan and the means for killing themselves.

The crisis worker should be familiar with the laws in his or her state as they apply to the hospitalization of suicidal clients. If the client is hospitalized, the crisis worker must see that he or she is admitted to a psychiatric hospital rather than a general acute hospital, as staff are trained differently for psychiatric units (Wyman, 1982). If possible, the crisis worker should convince the client to admit herself or himself voluntarily to a hospital. This empowers the client and reduces conflict. At times, however, calling the local police or psychiatric emergency team (PET) to request **involuntary hospitalization** becomes necessary. Doing this often causes unpleasant scenes and can be embarrassing, but it must be done, according to mental health ethics, if it is legal in that particular state. When considering hospitalization for a high-risk suicidal client, the mental health worker should explore the benefits and drawbacks. Current economic trends do not encourage hospitalization if maintaining someone out of the hospital is at all possible. Partial hospitalization is becoming popular as it provides safety and economic efficiency. An example clarifies when the need for drastic intervention is immediate.

> **Example**   Cole (1993) received a call from the sister of a 22-year-old man who had doused himself with gasoline and was looking for matches. He wasn't doing well in college and couldn't get a job; his fiancee had broken up with him recently. In this case, the police and ambulance were called immediately and an involuntary, 72-hour hold was placed on this man so he could be cared for in a hospital.

Another instance requiring hospitalization would be for a schizophrenic client who is actively hearing voices telling the person to hurt himself or herself. In this case, the individual needs to be medicated to control the hallucinations; this action should have the effect of removing the suicidal tendency.

::::::::::::::::::::::::::::::::::

Exercises

In this section are several case vignettes with suggested references and other interventions. Practice the ABC model by role-playing these cases. Follow the outline in Table 5.2.

Case 1   A 19-year-old Asian boy received 2 D's on his college report card and feels he has shamed his family. He plans to kill himself by jumping off the highest building on campus because six other people have successfully ended their lives this way over the past 10 years.

> *Reframe:* Point out the shame the family will suffer if he kills himself in such a public display.

> *Support:* Tell him how proud he can make his family by improving his grades.

Focus on ways he can enhance his good qualities and point these out to his parents. Ask his parents to maintain a suicide watch. Have the client make a no-suicide pact that will obligate him not to harm himself.

Case 2   A 45-year-old woman is very depressed. Her children are all grown and married; she has been divorced for 20 years and is dissatisfied with her job. She sees no reason to live but has no specific plan to kill herself. She feels like a burden to her children.

>   *Reframe:* Show her that killing herself would be an even bigger burden on her children. Does she really want to traumatize them in this way?

>   *Support:* Help her think about her grandchildren who will need a grandmother.

Focus on volunteer work, adult education, and clubs. No suicide contract is needed here. Suggest that her children become more involved with their mother.

Case 3   A 68-year-old man whose wife died six months ago is very depressed and wants to shoot himself. He has a loaded gun at home. His dog has just died.

>   *Reframe:* Does he believe his wife will rest in peace if he kills himself?

>   *Support:* Let him know that you understand his loneliness and that there are groups and other involvements he can focus on now, though his life will probably never be the same.

This man probably needs to be hospitalized unless his children will take care of him. His gun needs to be confiscated; perhaps he can move in with his children temporarily.

Case 4   A 30-year-old woman feels hopeless and despondent. She thinks she is a bad mother and wife and can't manage her household. She has no appetite and can't sleep. She has little involvement with her children. She spends her days crying while they are left to look after themselves.

>   *Reframe:* A bad mother wouldn't care if her children weren't being cared for. This mother is not bad; she is just depressed.

>   *Support:* Let her know that being a mother is hard. Also, let her know that she feels this way because she is depressed; when the depression lifts, she won't be so miserable. There is hope!

Refer this woman to a medical doctor for possible antidepressants. She might also need hospitalization.

Managing a Client Who Is a Danger to Others

Periodically, a crisis worker may come across a person who is homicidal or somehow a threat to someone other than herself or himself. As mentioned earlier, the crisis worker has the *duty to warn* the intended victim when possible and to contact the police.

Sometimes a person may be a threat to the public because of a psychosis (as when an individual hears the voice of God telling him to pour poison into the town water supply). Other times, the individual may be angry and lacking in impulse control.

Following are some questions to pose in assessing someone's potential for harming others:

1. Is the subject actively or passively engaged in violent or dangerous behavior?

2. Does the subject state that he or she is going to carry out violent or dangerous behavior?

3. Does the subject have a plan to follow through with this behavior?

4. Does the subject have the means to follow through with this plan?

5. Does the subject have a background of violent or dangerous behavior?

6. Has the subject acted on plans for violence in the past?

Answers to these questions can be obtained from an interview with either the client or relatives of the client. Be as specific as possible about what the person has said or done and who the victims might be.

If the counselor believes the person is a threat and the therapist cannot comfortably end the session, she or he must call for assistance. If permissible in that state, involuntary hospitalization of the client must be instituted until such time as the person's violent impulses are contained, either by medication or other forms of therapy.

In less volatile situations, a crisis worker can try to help a person contain his or her violent urges by teaching the client ways to manage the anger or referring the person to a daily support group. If the client will agree to refrain from acting out and the intended victim is warned, the client can be treated on an outpatient basis as long as any psychotic symptoms are controlled.

Certain psychotic states (such as mania or paranoia) may require clients to spend several days in a hospital receiving medication to control the delusions that lead to dangerous behaviors. Once medicated and stabilized, these individuals can often function appropriately with just a few counseling sessions to help them make the transition from hospital to outpatient living.

Some clients who are a danger to others may not be manic or psychotic but may have an impulse control problem; examples are spouse batterers and child abusers. These people seem to function normally in the larger society but in close interpersonal relationships, they control through acting out violently.

Crisis workers have a legal obligation to report suspected child abuse to the proper authorities in most states. If the client hasn't already acted but tells the crisis worker he or she is on the verge of abusing a child, the crisis worker can suggest that the client call a child abuse hot line, go for a walk, count to 10, or temporarily move out of the house for a cooling-off period.

Telling the client that you are required by the laws of the state to report violence against a child can be helpful in deterring this behavior. Impulsive people often need external controls because they feel so out of control internally. This holds true for spouse batterers as well. Although crisis workers aren't mandated to report battering against another adult, if the batterer feels the police will be called in, this possibility will often act as a curb on the person's potentially violent behavior. Even so, the person may continue to use verbal and emotional abuse.

Some people are a danger to others because of antisocial tendencies and anger. In certain cases, the police should be involved, especially when the person has no history of being mentally ill. Cole (1993) tells of an ex-convict who came to a psychiatrist at the mental health clinic saying he was mentally disabled and needed medication. When the doctor evaluated him and took a history, he discovered that this patient had no history of mental health treatment and was not mentally ill, so he prescribed no medication. The man pulled out a knife, held it to the doctor's throat, and forced him to write a prescription. As soon as the man left, the police were called and he was arrested and put in jail rather than being hospitalized under provisions for involuntary commitment of the mentally ill.

Another example of danger to others is what Cole (1993) calls the "Fatal Attraction Case."

> **Example** A 23-year-old woman came to the mental health clinic complaining of being stressed out because her boyfriend had just broken up with her and was now with another woman. She was extremely angry and planned to wait until the man was in his house asleep, then to pour gasoline all around the house and set fire to it. In evaluating the reality of such a plan, the mental health worker asked the client if she had any history of another man breaking up with her and what had happened at that time. The woman said that when her last boyfriend broke up with her, his car was wired so that it blew up when he got into it. Additionally, she was discovered to have a history of mental health treatment going back 10 years. The worker also observed that she had a row of safety pins in her ear as earrings. By combining all this information, the worker decided that the woman was a danger to her former boyfriend. The client was involuntarily hospitalized, and the intended victim and the police were made aware of the situation.

Psychotic Breakdowns

Periodically, a crisis worker will come across a client suffering a **psychotic decompensation**. This has been referred to as a nervous breakdown by laypeople. In essence, it is a state of florid, active delusions and hallucinations in which the person is out of touch with reality. This condition causes extreme personality disorganization and heightened states of anxiety and the person cannot function in any way. People in this state cannot look after even their basic needs. They cannot provide themselves with food or water, or keep themselves clean. People in this condition need someone to take care of them.

The term **gravely disabled** applies here and may be grounds for involuntary hospitalization, depending on the laws of the state. Usually, while these clients are in the hospital, they will stabilize on medication and be able to function more realistically within a few days. For some, however, the stabilization period may take up to two weeks or six months, depending on the severity of the psychosocial stressor, the person's pre-morbid (before the breakdown) functioning, and the available support systems. Clients experiencing this type of distress can be diagnosed as schizophrenic, being in a paranoid state, or having an organic brain disorder such as Alzheimer's disease.

Example 1

A 17-year-old boy has become increasingly withdrawn and guarded at home. He no longer sees his friends and his grades have dropped over the past year. He seems distant and shows little emotion (blunted affect). His mother brings him in to a crisis counseling center because he has been suffering anxiety spells and believes extra-terrestrials are watching him at night. When he is interviewed, he tells the counselor that he's been pacing at night and is afraid to sleep because he hears a strange whisper saying, "We're watching you."

This is a typical case of an initial psychotic break. The young man will most likely be diagnosed as paranoid schizophrenic, hospitalized, and given antipsychotic medication that will reduce, if not eliminate, his symptoms. Unfortunately, he will probably have another breakdown at some time in the future.

Example 2

A man comes to counseling because his boss sent him. He had become belligerent on the job. During the interview, you find that he believes a white van is following him, tracking him with ultrared sonar equipment. He brought in a magazine with hi-tech weapons and electrical devices to show you. He is preoccupied with the information in the magazine and believes the equipment it describes is the type that is being used to spy on him. He seems connected to his family and friends and has a clear grasp on current events. He can still perform his job duties.

This man's condition may be diagnosed as a paranoid state; he might require hospitalization if it gets worse. Medication may or may not be effective in eliminating his delusions.

Example 3

A 70-year-old woman is brought to the mental health center by her 30-year-old granddaughter who found her sitting nude at home surrounded by newspapers and unopened Social Security checks. She hadn't eaten in several days because she believes the food is poisoned. She does not know what day it is, thinks she's still living in 1955, and believes that her granddaughter is her daughter.

The woman is probably suffering from Alzheimer's disease or senility. She is gravely disabled and needs someone to be her conservator (guardian of her finances).

Sometimes people's psychotic thoughts leave them both gravely disabled and a danger to themselves or others. Cole (1993) tells of a 25-year-old man who had been completely catatonic (immobile and mute) for three days. His legs were turning purple because of poor circulation from lack of activity and he was dehydrated. When he was informed by the mental health worker that he was going to be involuntarily hospitalized, he ran to the roof, threatening to jump off. Eventually someone was able to coax him off the roof and he was indeed hospitalized as both gravely disabled and a danger to himself.

In emergencies such as suicide and psychosis, family members need to be involved. In cases where there is no family, board and care homes and case managers serve as support systems for clients. The crisis worker must remain calm and not be afraid when working with these cases. As pointed out previously, the worker may have to be the client's **ego strength** until he or she returns to a realistic state of functioning.

Key Terms for Study

ego strength: A term that refers to the client's ability to understand reality clearly and take realistic action to meet his or her needs. Usually, when a client is psychotic or highly suicidal, ego strength is low and the crisis worker must provide some of these reality fulfillment functions for the client.

gravely disabled: Condition in which clients are psychotic or suffering from a severe organic brain disorder. People with such disorders are often incapable of meeting their basic needs such as food, shelter, and financial management. Being gravely disabled is often a reason a person can be hospitalized involuntarily.

high-risk suicidal client: A client has a plan, the means, and the intent for suicide; he or she cannot be talked out of harming himself or herself. Hospitalization is often indicated for this person.

involuntary hospitalization: Detaining clients against their will in a psychiatric facility for evaluation and observation when they have been assessed to be a danger to themselves or to others, or are gravely disabled because of a mental disorder.

low-risk suicidal client: A client who has pondered but never attempted suicide. This client has adequate support systems and can usually be treated as an out-patient. Therapy and educational interventions are encouraged.

means: The actual physical implement, pills, or action that a suicidal person uses to kill himself or herself.

middle-risk suicidal client: A client who has been thinking about suicide and feels depressed. This person probably still has some hope but he or she also might have a suicide plan. No suicide contract works as well for this person as a suicide watch. Crisis intervention should be intense and frequent.

no-suicide contract: A formal written contract or a verbal contract between the client and crisis worker in which the client makes a commitment to speak to the counselor before harming himself or herself. It is considered an effective intervention for low- and middle-risk clients.

plan: A blueprint for action the client has devised for killing himself or herself.

psychotic decompensation: A state in which the client is out of touch with reality and shows symptoms such as delusions and hallucinations. This often happens when a schizophrenic patient goes off medication or at the beginning of someone's first schizophrenic episodes. The state can also be associated with bipolar disorder and paranoid disorders. This person usually requires involuntary hospitalization.

suicide assessment: A process in which the crisis worker asks a series of directive questions to ascertain the seriousness of a client's suicidal intent and ideation. It includes identifying various risk factors, a means for suicide, a plan for suicide, and reasons for wanting to harm oneself.

suicidal ideation: The cognition component of suicide, the thinking involved.

suicide watch: Observation by family or friends of someone who is at middle risk of hurting himself or herself. Someone stays by the client's side 24 hours a day to ensure that the person does no harm to himself or herself. Suicide watches are also conducted in psychiatric facilities for high-risk clients.

CHAPTER SEVEN

Crises of Loss

On the topic of loss, Elisabeth Kübler-Ross's name is bound to be mentioned. She has provided an outline for understanding the different stages people go through in dealing with the **grief** of death and dying. Whether the grief is over a loss of a loved one to death or divorce, or over a loss of a body part or function, the crisis worker will be helping these clients work through similar issues of **bereavement**.

Death and Dying

Kübler-Ross's (1969) **five stages of death and dying** are presented as an introduction to the topic of loss. This chapter is an appropriate follow-up to suicidal crises that often bring up death and dying issues for the suicidal client and her or his significant others. If a suicide attempt is successful, grieving will undoubtedly be the focus of a crisis interview, and having an understanding of the stages of loss will be vital in helping a client through this process. Additionally, these stages can be generalized to other forms of loss.

On a related issue, loss often triggers suicidal thinking in a grieving person, especially after the denial and anger pass and depression sets in. This is one reason suicide was addressed in this book before crises of loss. Awareness of its possibility will help you assess for it with any client, no matter what the presenting crisis.

KÜBLER-ROSS'S FIVE STAGES OF DEATH AND DYING

After extensive work with terminally ill patients and a long study of the process of dying, Elisabeth Kübler-Ross identified five stages that seem to be universally involved in dying.

1. **Denial and isolation:** Denial and isolation comprise the first stage in the dying process as she defined it. Denial is both a healthy and familiar initial reaction. It cushions patients from the initial shock and allows them to deal with both their hope and their despair.

2. **Anger:** Anger frequently follows denial as patients begin to accept the real possibility of death. There may be rage, envy, resentment, and bitterness. This frequently includes the "why me?" question that so often has no answer.

3. **Bargaining:** The third stage is bargaining. Usually these bargains are secret pacts made with God, regardless of whether the patients have been religious earlier in life. When bargaining fails, the next stage develops.

4. **Depression:** When death is recognized as inevitable and the loss has become overwhelming, depression sets in. Depression often includes sadness, pessimism, gloominess, and feelings of guilt and worthlessness, along with heavy lethargy.

5. **Acceptance:** Eventually the depression lifts as patients work through mourning the loss of their lives or the life of a loved one and come to accept the inevitable. This stage is described as being almost void of feelings. At this point, individuals are in the process of disengaging from this life if they are dying or disengaging from a loved one if that person is dying or has died (Kübler-Ross, 1969, pp. 35–77).

The problem with Kübler-Ross's stages became apparent as her popularity increased. People were only too ready finally to talk about dying, death, grief, and mourning. Consequently, they frequently came to accept the stages as truth with a capital T. They tried to force all patients through the same sequence of emotions rather than understand that these were no more than generalizations. Not every patient goes through each stage and certainly not in a predictable, sequential order. Patients struggle back and forth, frequently experiencing other or similar emotions in varying degrees.

Although Kübler-Ross is often credited as the originator of the study and treatment of death and dying, others have dealt with this topic over the span of modern history. Some of the ideas from other theorists may help you offer greater empathy and more effective interventions when working with those who are terminally ill. Following is a historical outline that led to the development of Kübler-Ross's theories on death and dying.

Darwin: As early as 1872, Darwin (1965) commented that the separation reactions resulting from the loss of a loved one were innate. He observed similar body movements in grieving individuals, regardless of their cultural background.

Freud: Freud defined mourning as a period of the gradual withdrawal of libido from the now-missed loved object. He described the reactions as dejection, disinterest in the environment, and a detachment from others. He saw the process as self-limiting. The effects cease when the libido has completed its withdrawal from the loved object and is reinvested in a new object (Leick & Davidsen-Nielsen, 1991, p. 9).

Bowlby: John Bowlby (1980), noted theorist in the area of attachment and separation, proposed four phases of mourning: (1) numbing, (2) yearning and searching for the lost figure, (3) disorganization and despair, and (4) reorganization (p. 85).

Kübler-Ross: The most well-known name associated with death and dying, Elisabeth Kübler-Ross is a Swiss-born psychiatrist who began seminars on death and dying in the late 1960s. She had the courage to bring dying patients into the classroom and openly discuss with them their fears, concerns, and desires as part of the training process for psychiatrists. Until then, few doctors or medical schools openly discussed the need to deal honestly and openly with dying patients and their families (Kübler-Ross, 1969, pp. 35–36). From these courses, she extracted the five stages, described earlier, that she believed were experienced by people who knew they were dying; these emotions are also felt by those who are emotionally close to the dying individuals.

Since the beginnings of the study of death and dying issues, behavioral scientists have continued to develop their understanding of the various issues and intervention skills that are helpful with these clients. Let's take a look at some concepts that serve as an adjunct to Kübler-Ross's stages.

DEFINITIONS

As with any topic, understanding is predicated on shared definitions. In this book, the following are used.

> *Bereavement*: A state involving loss. To bereave means to take away from, to rob, to dispossess.
>
> *Grief:* The feelings of sorrow, anger, guilt, and confusion that arise when one experiences a loss. It is the affect that accompanies bereavement. One can be bereaved without grief, although full recovery seems to include some affective experience of the bereavement, usually in terms of grief.
>
> *Mourning:* The overt expression of grief and the usual response to bereavement. Frequently it is culturally modified and influenced. Whether one wears white or black, dances or cries, drinks or prays is often the result of cultural tradition.

TASKS OF MOURNING

Rather than think solely in terms of stages of grieving, the crisis worker can consider **tasks of mourning**. Task implies no time sequence. Tasks can be experienced as they come, rather than in any particular order. Additionally, task implies some action on the part of the bereaved. There is a need to do or experience something, to work toward a concrete goal.

Worden (1982) offers four tasks for the person working through the mourning process. These are delineated below.

Task I: Accepting the Reality of the Loss   As Kübler-Ross discovered, most people have difficulty accepting death. After a loved one dies (or a body part is amputated), the defense mechanism of denial is a typical coping strategy until the person can assimilate the knowledge that the loss is real.

Denial can take different forms. There can be a denial of the facts of the loss, denial of the meaning of the loss, or denial of the irreversibility of the loss. Denial can be a buffer, but it can become pathological if it continues indefinitely. The crisis worker can help by encouraging the client to release his or her denial slowly, accept the reality of the loss, and move toward expression of grief.

Task II: Experiencing the Pain of Grief   The broadest possible expression of pain is what needs to be experienced by the client. It may be more intense for some than others, but everyone needs to come to the point of experiencing the void that will be left in his or her life and the pain associated with that.

One way to avoid experiencing the pain is not to feel. Our society has been good at fostering this avoidance in a subtle way. We are not comfortable around people who are in pain; therefore, we give a subtle message to them not to express their grief. More directly, we give the message, "It's time to get over this" after the socially acceptable mourning period of four weeks has elapsed. However, as was pointed out by Caplan (1964) (see Chapter 1), mastering one's feelings is one of seven characteristics of people who cope effectively and should be encouraged by crisis counselors.

Task III: Adjusting to an Environment in Which the Deceased Is Missing   For many widows and widowers, realizing that they must cope on their own takes several months. Often, about three months after the loss comes the realization that they can in fact manage to live in this environment.

It is helpful for them to look at all the roles the deceased played in their life and to develop ways to cope with new demands and new roles that occur because of the loved one's absence. They often resist developing new skills at first, but eventually they reach a point of pride in their newfound abilities and the beginnings of a new self-esteem.

Task IV: Withdrawing Emotional Energy and Reinvesting It in Another Relationship   For many, the idea of withdrawing their emotional energy from the dead loved one is seen as betrayal; the guilt that comes with this must be overcome. Working through this task means acknowledging that there are others to love. It does not take away from the earlier relationship; it is simply different.

Mourning can be considered finished when the tasks of mourning are over. This certainly does not happen in four weeks. Mourning is individual; therefore, any attempt to set time limits is artificial and arbitrary. However, most literature supports the need for a year to pass before the loss is fully resolved.

Usually, at least that long is needed for a person to let go of old memories and to begin to build new ones, which will help facilitate the grief process. Holidays, seasons, and family events all must come and go during the mourning period before resolution is complete. That doesn't mean the expression of grief will be strong for the entire year, but the process of mourning continues and is experienced in all those events.

One indication that mourning may be finished is when the person is able to think and talk about the deceased without pain. The sadness at this point lacks the tearing quality of loss. Studies of widows in particular find that a year is frequently not enough time for them to recover. Often, they need three to four years to find stability in their lives again. One thing is clear: Mourning is a long-term process.

MANIFESTATIONS OF NORMAL GRIEF

Regardless of the period of time required for mourning, people who experience normal grief share common manifestations. The ones seen most often are listed here:

Feelings: Sadness, anger, guilt, and self-reproach; anxiety, including death awareness and phobia; loneliness, fatigue, helplessness; shock—particularly with sudden death; yearning and pining; emancipation, which can be a positive response; relief, particularly from suffering; and numbness

Physical Sensations: Hollowness in the stomach, tightness in the chest and throat, sense of depersonalization, breathlessness, weakness in the muscles

Cognitions: Disbelief, confusion, preoccupation, sense of presence, hallucination—usually transient

Behaviors: Sleep disturbances, such as early morning awakenings; appetite disturbances; absent-minded behaviors; social withdrawal—usually short lived; dreams of the deceased; restless overactivity; sighing, crying; fear of losing memories, treasuring objects

DETERMINANTS OF GRIEF

A person's response to loss will largely be influenced by several factors about the nature of the loss:

• Who the person was in terms of the relation to the survivor is important.

• The nature of the attachment—whether the deceased provided strength, security, or ambivalence in the relationship—will be influential.

• The mode of death will determine reactions. Natural death is easier to cope with than an accidental death or suicide or murder. At least one is somewhat prepared for the death of an 86-year-old grandfather, or a mother who has had breast cancer for two years. When a loved one is murdered or commits suicide, however, issues of blame and anger become very difficult to overcome.

• Prior grief experiences and mental health in general will also influence one's grief reactions.

• One's religious beliefs will affect the grieving process.

An individual may seek crisis intervention for grief issues at various points in the grieving process. While assessing the client's subjective distress, the counselor will determine the stage of the client's grief and therefore how to intervene.

Many crisis workers are emotionally taxed when dealing with death and dying. Counselors must come to terms with their own fears of death and their beliefs about death and grieving. If the crisis worker is in denial about death and mortality, she or he may inadvertently send messages to the client that grieving and connecting fully with one's pain is not necessary. The crisis worker must be able to handle the pain involved in mourning for the client to grieve as needed. To do this, the worker must be able to be both truly empathetic and objective and rational. The counselor then becomes a sort of *emotional tranquilizer* for the client in a bereaved state.

INTERVENTION

As with any crisis state, workers must be alert for symptoms that may require the attention of a physician. If the emotions are very strong and out of control, preventing clients from sleeping, working, eating, or taking care of themselves, medication might be necessary for a brief time. Remember that the counselor does not recommend medication; his or her responsibility is to refer the client to a physician if symptoms cause moderate to severe dysfunction (see the section on Major Depression in the Mental Status Exam in Chapter 5). If the client's symptoms seem to be typical grieving reactions, then counseling can assist the mourning process and help the client work through the normal expression of grief.

Before the client begins the process of grieving, she or he must be informed of the loss, be it a death or a serious or terminal illness. The person breaking this news might be a doctor, a lawyer, a police officer, or a friend or family member. How the loss is presented may affect the person's ability to accept it. It may even determine the person's emotional reactions.

In general, most people do not like to be lied to or patronized. Such behavior is disrespectful and may lead to feelings of resentment beyond that of the normal anger involved in grieving. A direct, honest approach is best. Empathy skills are most helpful at this time. Following are some specific ways that professionals or family members might break the news of a death or loss:

Physician: He didn't make it. I am very sorry for your loss. May I contact someone for you? Do you need some space to be alone?

Lawyer: I have been given the legal responsibility of informing you of some tragic news. Please accept my sympathy for the loss of your father, who has asked me to read you his will.

Police Officer: Mrs. Jones, I have come to you in person to ensure that you hear some tragic news with someone near you. Sadly, your child was fatally wounded in a car accident tonight. Please feel free to talk to me tonight about your grief. The loss of your child is a tragedy that no one else can understand but you, but I'd still like to assist you if I can.

Friend: Kathy, it's Jenny. I need to see you in person immediately. (After they meet.) Kathy, Margaret died today. We need to cry and talk together.

Family Member: Honey, your father became ill last night and didn't make it through the night. Please call your brother and sister for me. Let's all meet at my house as soon as possible.

If the person hearing the news loses control with grief, it is good to have another person available to help contain her or him. Emergency rooms are open 24 hours and medical personnel there could medicate someone who presents a danger to himself or herself or to others because of shock. However, people usually become numb on hearing news of a death and just need to have someone around for emotional **support** and to help take care of any legal or business details. Uncontrollable emotions might come during the funeral or weeks after, when the person has had time to accept the loss.

COUNSELING PRINCIPLES AND PROCEDURES

Counseling someone through a loss is difficult. However, knowing certain procedures and their underlying principles is helpful. The following list should be useful to workers counseling someone who is suffering a loss.

1.   Help survivors actualize the loss. Talk about the loss. What happened? Ask.

2.   Help them identify and express feelings. If they are dealing with anger, be indirect (what do you miss the most/least?). Four common difficult emotions are anger, guilt, anxiety, and helplessness.

3.   Help survivors in living without the deceased. The problem-solving approach works well for this. Discourage major life changes for a while.

4.   Facilitate emotional withdrawal from the deceased. Encourage survivors to go on.

5.   Provide time to grieve. Crucial times include three months, one year, anniversaries, and holidays. Help clients prepare in advance for these.

6.   Educate clients about customary grieving reactions of other individuals to help normalize the experience.

7.   Allow for individual differences. Be sensitive to individual styles.

8.   Provide for continuing support. Encourage clients to join support groups.

If a client's symptoms and grief reactions appear to be chronic—to last longer than one year—delayed, exaggerated, or masked, longer term therapy may be required. This individual may have underlying pathology. In this type of grief therapy, the person's defenses and coping styles would be assessed. Most likely, issues about loss and abandonment will surface. The counselor can best assist this type of client to get through the most recent loss by helping her or him grieve previous losses first. If the previous losses are great, therapy will probably be a two- to five-year process.

The two examples given next compare responses to crisis intervention and responses to grief therapy.

Example 1

A 45-year-old woman was referred to me for crisis intervention by the Victim Witness Assistance Program. Her 21-year-old daughter had been murdered horrifically four months earlier. She hadn't been able to work, continued to have nightmares, cried uncontrollably, and was having communication problems with her husband. Her grieving had continued to be strong and painful.

This client has a strong support system in her parents. They are still married, all her other family members are still living, her own 25-year marriage is a loving one, and she has two remaining daughters—17 and 11 years of age. She had a very stable and appropriate childhood.

She responded well to the ABC crisis intervention model. In the B section, she was helped to discuss what her daughter's death meant to her and how her life perspective has changed. Her functioning level was assessed for symptoms and behaviors each session.

In the C section, she was encouraged to consult with a physician because of a sleep disturbance. She was given medication to help her for about six months. She was referred to a support group for parents of murdered children.

This woman will do well with continuing crisis intervention that focuses on the current precipitating event—the death of her daughter. Her childhood does not have to be dealt with because she demonstrated excellent premorbid functioning. Her present symptoms can be assumed to be related strictly to the death of her daughter.

Example 2

A 35-year-old woman comes for counseling after the death of her older sister. Before we were able to process her grief over her sister, we had to discuss her childhood and young adulthood losses. This client's method of coping with trauma can best be described as a defensive style called denial. In her family, she was told not to be aware of her own feelings, that her mother and father knew her better than she knew herself. They beat her and degraded her, then abandoned her. Her only ally was the older sister who had just died.

Not only did this client need to grieve her sister's death; she also had to deal with abandonment by her parents. Being without her sister caused unbearable feelings of aloneness and emptiness for her. She was completely emotionally dependent on this sister, who had offered the only nurturing the client had experienced in her life after the complete deprivation of affection from her parents.

As you can see, the complexity in this case would require a longer term approach. The client would need to grieve her past losses and come to terms with her aloneness and her own death in addition to the grieving process triggered by the death of her sister.

WHEN THE LOSS IS ONE'S CHILD

Although the interventions discussed thus far can be used with all grieving clients, there are special considerations when dealing with parents whose child has died. As Nancy Ludt (1993) said in her presentation, "Losing a child has a different meaning than losing a parent. When you lose a parent you lose your past, but when you lose a child, you lose your future." It is this dream of the future that the crisis worker will need to discuss with the surviving parents.

If the parents are married at the time of the death, their relationship will usually be at risk when a child dies, especially if the death was unexpected, as in an accident. After such trauma, most parents have a lot of trouble getting along with each other, as well as with their other children. They no longer feel like the same people they were before the tragedy because their lives have been so drastically changed. The divorce rate of bereaved parents is 92% if the couple do not receive some form of help. However, receiving help can make a measurable difference in helping a couple survive the loss of a child. Ludt said that of the 1,500 people who had attended her support group over the last 16 years, only two couples later divorced. This is great incentive for crisis workers to recommend to bereaving parents that they attend support groups! In these groups, the couple can say things to each other they normally would not say at home. Also, the father has an opportunity to express his hurt as openly as the mother does in these groups. This is helpful, considering society's perpetuation of the traditional male stereotype of the strong man: He can't cry, but instead must be strong and go to work, even after the death of a child. It is obvious that if the father has a forum where he can communicate openly and express his feelings, the marital relationship has a greater chance to work.

Societal norms also affect parents regarding working after the loss of a child. Many places of employment allow only three days for bereavement. This is very inadequate, considering that the attention span of a grieving parent is about a minute and a half. Because of this, many parents may lose their jobs, further complicating their crisis state. It would be nice if people could grieve within tidy time frames, but this is not reality.

Crisis workers can ease the grieving parents' burden by *listening*. Because the parents' concentration is greatly affected, counselors should minimize their own talking, offering very brief educational and supportive comments. One reason that self-help groups are more popular than professional counseling groups is that parents feel they can just talk and be listened to, no matter what the topic. Structure will not be helpful as this population has changing needs—and these may shift from one minute to another. Guest speakers are usually not welcome because the members want to talk. If a grieving client comes to you on an individual basis, don't be a guest speaker. Let the client be the speaker. Other things a counselor can do for grieving parents is to help them feel normal and not to inhibit them if they want to talk about their children. Eventually, they need to remember the child's life, not the child's death.

Probably the best thing a crisis worker can do for parents whose child has died is to connect them to a support group. Here, they can feel and say whatever is on their minds and in their hearts and not fear ridicule or invalidation. Many times, parents will laugh when talking about the death. To many people, this behavior would appear insensitive. In a group with other grieving parents, it would be understood and shared.

Ludt (1993) presented 10 reasons that grieving parents prefer a support group—some for as long as 10 years after the loss of a child. She says that according to the members of her support group, the group serves these functions:

1.   **Is a place of safety where it is all right to say anything.** ("I'd trade my living son for my lost son.")

2.   **Fulfills the need to be with understanding people; even if we don't attend, we know it's available.** ("Feelings change over the years and although we don't need to come now, who knows when we will need to come?")

3.   **Is our child space.** ("We can talk about our child all night without any inhibitions. Often talking about memories hurts family members too much, but in group, our child is alive for two hours.")

4.   **Helps us to understand the death emotionally versus intellectually.** ("If we say he's dead enough times, we begin to believe it.")

5.   **Allows a hope for socialization in the future.** ("We often feel guilty when we have fun, but we learn here that we can have fun.")

6.   **Has no time frame on things.** ("He's dead forever, so it will hurt forever.")

7.   **Allows us to laugh or cry and not hurt anyone's feelings.**

8.   **Allows us to express our thoughts with no need to explain them.**

9.   **Can save our lives.** ("Suicidal thoughts are strong and group gives some hope and help.")

10. **Is a place where I know that you know that I know that you know.**

If the crisis worker cannot locate a group in the client's area, these ideas need to be implemented in the course of counseling.

Exercises

Conduct role-play interviews using some of the following ideas and case vignettes. Use the ABC model of crisis intervention.

First, here are a few things *not* to say. These are comments often made by well-wishers such as friends and family. They tend to discount the grief and seek to deny the experience.

"Cheer up."

"Don't be so depressed."

"Isn't it about time you got over this?"

"It'll get better."

"At least she's with God."

"Just think of the good things; don't dwell on it."

Now, here are some ideas that may be useful with the case vignettes and with your clients who are mourning.

During the B section of the ABC model, crisis interventionists can offer various therapeutic statements as they explore the client's belief system, knowledge, support systems, and self-esteem.

Reframes will help the client think about a disturbing event differently.

Rather than view yourself as weak and out of control when you cry, you might consider understanding this behavior as a sign of your love and part of the process it takes to learn to accept the loss strongly and boldly.

Educational statements will help normalize the client's experience and clear up confusions and misconceptions.

The grieving process usually takes a full year. Every holiday, birthday, and anniversary of her death will need to be experienced without the person you have lost.

Supportive comments do not mean taking away the person's pain. Rather, they let the client know that you understand her or his feelings.

I wish I could make the pain go away. But you and I both know that's impossible. I can be here to listen as you process your loss.

Empowerment comments will help show the client she or he has some control and choice despite not having control over the loss.

You don't have control over the reality that your wife will die of cancer, but you do have the choice of how you live your life with her until that time comes.

Be creative and look for clients' strengths. Having some knowledge about death and dying will help you work meaningfully with your clients. This is also a good chance for you to become aware of your own issues of loss and feelings about death.

Case 1 Your minister referred you to the crisis intervention center because you have just lost your husband. The minister is concerned because you and your two children have not cried since the death of your husband. You are still confused as to why you need to be coming in. You tell the counselor that you do not think about his death. When probed a little more, you begin to cry. You are left without any money and you have two children to feed. You were married for 10 years and they were good years. He died in an auto accident and the driver of the other car was drunk at the time.

Case 2 You are a daughter who lost her father. Your father died a year ago. You married 1 month after his death. You have never discussed his death with anyone.

You and your father were very close. He was the most supportive person you knew. Your marriage is not doing very well. You feel your husband is not as supportive as your father. Your work is beginning to suffer and you have been absent a lot lately. When questioned about your father's death, you talk as if he is not dead. Your mother was always jealous of your relationship with your father.

Case 3   You have been referred to the counselor by your doctor. You lost your son to cancer. You feel you cannot go on living. Life seems worthless and meaningless. He died when he was only 6 years old. Your husband does not understand your feelings.

Case 4   You are 64 years old and your dog of 16 years died two weeks ago. You have not eaten and have stopped going out. You feel lonely and your children live far away. Your spouse died 3 years ago.

Divorce and Separation

Relationship breakups are an extremely common presenting problem in crisis intervention centers. Reactions to separations, whether the partners are married or not, can create dysfunctional states in an otherwise normally functioning person. The reactions will range from severe depression to anxiety attacks. As with any situational crisis, how well the person copes with a breakup will depend on material, personal, and social resources. Why are relationship losses so devastating? Often a person's entire life and self-concept is based on being part of a couple. After a breakup, major adjustments will have to be made, sometimes even more so than when a spouse dies.

About 50% of all marriages end in divorce, and probably more nonmarriage relationships than that end at some point. Separations are usually experienced as a loss, even if they are desired and sought (Gilliland & James, 1988, p. 409). As the issues surrounding loss and mourning have been covered previously, these are not repeated here. Crisis workers should know that each partner will need to complete the tasks of mourning as he or she passes through each stage. In general, the longer the couple was together, the stronger will be the feelings of loss. If children are involved, the suffering will be increased and complicated. Parents often feel guilt and embarrassment when explaining divorce to the children. Rage and frustration are typical emotions that surface when parents are setting up custody arrangements. Crisis workers often step in to mediate these procedures. There will also be loss of financial status and social networks. Losing friendships and in-laws often increases the partners' feelings of depression and loneliness. Financial problems create anxieties and often lead to a lowered standard of living. Adjusting to these losses is another focus of crisis intervention in these cases.

The person who was "left" often seeks out crisis intervention and seems to suffer the most. This person may be a high suicide risk and may have the potential for increased drug and alcohol abuse. These possibilities must be assessed, appropriate contracts developed, and 12-step groups encouraged. This person in particular needs to rebuild a support system. Church, family, athletic organizations, and school ties can be helpful. Also, many excellent books are available that can give solace. The partner who "left" will have different issues to face. This person may alternate between feelings of grief and resentment. At one moment, he or she may still try to take care of the spouse; the next, this person may be reckless and irresponsible as he or she goes out "partying" and living the much-missed single life. Although at first this crazy, wild fun seems great, eventually depression usually sets in. It is hard to be single when one has been used to companionship, even though it was miserable.

INTERVENTION

The overall goal will be to help the client grieve. This individual needs encouragement to cry, write, read, pray, and go to divorce support groups. The crisis worker, as usual, needs to be soothing, comforting, and optimistic.

Letting the person know that many people survive divorce and breakups is helpful. The counselor should remind the client that although he or she may not believe it now, things will eventually be better. Completing mourning can take up to 5 years for some people. Educating clients about the grief process will help normalize their experience.

Other helpful educational statements that a counselor can offer deal with the client's concerns about children and in-laws. Most parents are concerned about the **effects of divorce on the children**; many believe that divorce will damage the children. A crisis worker can often point out that whether they are hurt depends on how the parents deal with the children and each other during the divorce. Civility and assurance that both still love the children helps them greatly. Unfortunately, as a result of the tremendous pain they are enduring because of the divorce, many parents use the children to vent their anger at the other partner. This places children in the dangerous middle.

Often a worried parent should be told that more damage may be done to the children when parents stay together than if they divorce, especially if the marital relationship was abusive and there was a lack of love and affection. This perspective allows them to reframe their perception that staying together *no matter what* is best. Another piece of information that may comfort a parent is that the average family is no longer a nuclear family, so their children need not feel weird or unusual compared to their friends.

In regard to in-laws, it is probably best not to tell them everything. What if the couple decides to get back together? A spouse may be able to forgive, but an in-law may not. Also, after a divorce, the children will still be involved with both in-laws; the less the grandparents know, the better. That way they will be free to be completely supportive and nurturing to their grandchildren.

Often, denial is very strong for the spouse being "left," and this partner must be helped gently to confront reality. The counselor can encourage this person to ask herself or himself if he or she truly wants someone who does not want her or him. Confronting such a question can give the "discarded" partners some control over whether they will retain any dignity. This is an example of *empowerment*.

In a final note regarding legalities, a good idea is to be familiar with legal clinics and divorce lawyers in your area. Clients may need referrals to these professionals to avoid being taken advantage of or to obtain a restraining order.

CRISES RELATED TO BLENDED FAMILIES

Many families come in with crises stemming from the joining of two families when divorced parents have married. The "Brady Bunch" system is not as fun as the old 1970s TV show portrayed it. Many of the conflicts in **blended families** arise because of the developmental stages of the children as well as the maturity level of each adult involved and the stage of grieving over the divorce either adult is working through.

It is rare to find a joining of two families in which each biological parent sets aside his or her own personal power struggles and resentments for the sake of the children. When dealing with four adults, at least one is bound to react dysfunctionally after the divorce and subsequent remarrying. Of course, sometimes one of the persons marrying into a family with children has not been married before or has no children from an earlier marriage. This circumstance may disentangle the web slightly, but it certainly does not assure complete cooperation and facility in adjustment.

> **Example** A 45-year-old man comes to counseling because his girlfriend moved in with him and his 13-year-old daughter after he had been separated from his wife for 5 months. He was very stressed because his girlfriend complained about how much time he devoted to his daughter and the girlfriend felt deprived. Subsequent couples counseling brought out the girlfriend's perception of being disliked by the daughter and her feelings that her boyfriend was too focused on his daughter.
>
> Crisis counseling focused on educating the girlfriend about parental attachment and responsibility. This helped alter her view of the "overly devoted father," normalizing his attention to his daughter. The daughter was brought in as well to explore the girlfriend's perception that the daughter disliked her. The daughter explained that she did not dislike her, but she felt awkward liking her considering that the woman was now in her mother's former role. Crisis intervention explored loyalty issues and allowed each to clarify her expectations of the other.

Loyalty issues are very common for children in cases where a stepparent becomes part of their home life. Children often feel guilty bonding with another adult for fear it will make their own parents angry or hurt.

If possible, the crisis worker may bring in the natural parent to tell the child it is acceptable to be nice to the stepparent. This will not be an easy task, however, if the parent is still grieving the divorce or has a serious personality disorder.

Incorporating the stepparent's rules and expectations into an existing system is another area in which a crisis worker may be needed. Here, a very brief, problem-solving approach is useful when everyone is encouraged to speak up and give suggestions and can perceive himself or herself as validated.

In conclusion, as with all people in crisis, clients divorcing and forming blended families will fare worse if they have low ego strength and maturity level. Although most people in this situation will suffer, not all will suffer the same.

Exercises

Practice role-playing with the following cases using the ABC model. Pay attention to all parts of the B section.

Case 1   You are feeling very confused and you cannot pinpoint the reason. You tell the interviewer that you wonder how she can possibly be of help to you. The counselor looks as though she has never experienced a separation. You basically need to build trust with this person. Two months ago your lover of 3 years left you suddenly and you have been waiting for him to return. Yesterday, you saw this person with another woman; they were holding hands and acting very much in love.
   Hint: Denial, supportive feedback, self-disclosure, and empathy.

Case 2   A friend has told you to come into this clinic. You have been yelling at everyone. You are not aware of how angry you feel. You tell the counselor that he looks like an inexperienced person and far too happy to be in touch with reality. The truth is you are very scared because for the first time in your life you feel alone. Your spouse of 7 years left you 3 months ago and so far you have been saying "Good riddance." The truth is that this is the first time you have ever been hurt by someone close to you.
   Hint: Check out current functioning in all areas, support systems.

Case 3   For the first time, you are feeling suicidal. You have been an even-tempered person most of your life and felt that you have been able to solve almost all your problems on your own. You are feeling very crazy and you are not sure what to do about it. You left your spouse because he was very cruel to you and you are amazed that you are having this reaction. You have not had a date and have kept pretty much to yourself for the year you have been alone.
   Hint: No suicide contract, support.

Case 4   You are very upset because your best girlfriend ran away with your spouse of 10 years. They have left you with two children, a house payment, and some debts. Fortunately, you have a job as a nurse and you were an A student in school—but you are not sure you can manage the bills. You do have a support system, your parents, who are both retired and live not far from you, but you have not wanted to bother them about your situation.

Key Terms for Study

bereavement: A state involving loss; a period of time when something has been taken away from someone

blended families: The joining of two previously separate families. This often means that children have stepparents, a situation that leads to many conflicts and requires adjustment to new rules.

effects of divorce on the children: Suffering often experienced by the children of divorcing parents because of the power struggles and immaturity of their parents. This does not have to occur; often counseling is necessary to ensure that parents don't act out their own feelings of anger and pain on their children.

grief: The feelings of sorrow and sadness that follow a loss

Kübler-Ross's five stages of death and dying: Five stages proposed by Kübler-Ross that she believes all people go through after the death of a loved one or while in the process of dying. They are as follows:

    denial and isolation: The person is in shock or in a state of nonacceptance about the death or dying.

    anger: The person becomes aware of feelings, especially of the unfairness of death, and feels rage and intense pain.

    bargaining: The person may try to make deals with God, the doctors, or with a loved one.

    depression: The person experiences true mourning and grief, feeling sad, nonenergetic, and despondent.

    acceptance: The person finally pulls out of the depression, accepts the death or loss, and is able to move on.

loyalty issues: Experienced in a blended family when the children sometimes feel guilty for loving or bonding with a stepparent. Their fear is that the natural parent will be angry or hurt. Unfortunately, it is often true. Crisis workers attempt to help both the children and natural parents come to terms with the reality of the blended family.

support: Help that is considered essential for clients experiencing a loss. Validation of such clients' feelings of pain is an important function of the crisis worker. Support groups have also been found to be helpful.

tasks of mourning: Four proposed tasks a person needs to complete to grieve a loss fully. They are as follows:

    Accepting the reality of the loss

    Experiencing the pain of grief

    Adjusting to an environment in which the deceased is missing

    Withdrawing emotional energy and reinvesting it in another relationship or activity

CHAPTER EIGHT

AIDS

Many of the issues and dynamics found in the previous chapter on death and dying will be useful in dealing with crises related to **AIDS (acquired immune deficiency syndrome)**. However, there are also many separate issues and facts that any crisis worker should be familiar with in dealing with these crises. If a counselor is working with someone with full-blown AIDS, death and dying interventions are applicable. However, when working with symptom-free clients infected with the AIDS virus, interventions will be different.

First, check your current knowledge about AIDS by answering T (true) or F (false) to the following items. The answers are at the end of the quiz.

____ 1. The AIDS antibody test will tell you if the AIDS virus is present in your body.

____ 2. Oral sex is the most common way that AIDS is transmitted.

____ 3. There is a difference between being "exposed" to the AIDS virus and being "infected" by the AIDS virus.

____ 4. There has not been a verified case of a man being infected with the AIDS virus through vaginal intercourse with a woman.

____ 5. Current estimates are that 25% to 50% of those exposed will go on to develop AIDS.

____ 6. The AIDS antibody test tells whether you will develop AIDS.

____ 7. It is possible to be infected with the AIDS virus without having a sexual encounter.

____ 8. In spite of the publicity, the incidence of diagnosed AIDS among heterosexuals has not changed in the past year.

____ 9. Condoms have been proven to protect against the sexual transmission of the AIDS virus.

____ 10. You can tell by looking whether a person has been infected by the AIDS virus.

___ 11. You can be safe in sexual contact with someone who has shown you his or her "negative" AIDS antibody test results.

___ 12. If you are in a relationship, you do not need to take any precautions against AIDS.

___ 13. Everyone who develops some symptoms of AIDS goes on to develop one or more of the opportunistic diseases that are usually fatal.

___ 14. White splotches on the tongue or throat are the first signs of AIDS.

___ 15. The most common opportunistic disease is a particular type of pneumonia.

___ 16. Any swelling of lymph nodes is an early sign of AIDS infection.

___ 17. Health care workers take considerable risk in treating AIDS patients.

___ 18. The average life expectancy of someone who has been formally diagnosed with AIDS is 18 months.

___ 19. A "positive" AIDS antibody test indicates the severity and extent of infection.

___ 20. If both partners in a relationship test positive on the AIDS antibody test, there is no value in practicing "safe sex."

___ 21. Dispensing disposable needles to intravenous drug users could solve the problem of AIDS virus transmission among that group.

___ 22. Oily (petroleum-based) lubricant is not recommended for sexual intercourse.

___ 23. Sexual intercourse (vaginal or anal) is safe if a proper spermicide is used before and after.

___ 24. A woman who is infected with the AIDS virus can pass it on to an unborn baby.

___ 25. Self-masturbation is safe only if a condom is used.

___ 26. Research indicates that some people have a natural immunity to the AIDS virus.

___ 27. When a vaccine is developed for the AIDS virus, it will not work on those who have already been exposed and tested positive.

___ 28. The AIDS virus can be absorbed through the outer layer of your skin into the bloodstream.

___ 29. Present estimates are that for every person who has a diagnosed case of AIDS, 8 to 10 more have symptoms of AIDS-related complex (ARC).

___ 30. The "incubation period" is the 2 to 8 weeks it takes to develop anti-bodies after exposure to the AIDS virus.

Answers: 1. T, 2. F, 3. T, 4. F, 5. T, 6. F, 7. T, 8. F, 9. F, 10. F, 11. F, 12. F, 13. F, 14. F, 15. T, 16. F, 17. F, 18. F, 19. F, 20. F, 21. F, 22. T, 23. F, 24. T, 25. F, 26. T, 27. T, 28. F, 29. T, 30. F. (Brown, 1990)

Basic Statistics about AIDS

This section provides some statistics about the human immunodeficiency virus and AIDS. The information is presented in outline and list form to make it easier to grasp and to emphasize its starkness. The section begins by explaining a few essential acronyms.

ACRONYMS/TERMS

AIDS virus: HIV (human immunodeficiency virus)

Asymptomatic infection: Without symptoms but still infected

ARC: AIDS-related complex

AIDS: Acquired immune deficiency syndrome

AIDS: A BRIEF OUTLINE HISTORY

1977–78	First cases of AIDS probably occur in the United States, Haiti, and Africa.
1979	Aggressive Kaposi's sarcoma and rare infections first seen in Europe and Africa.
1981	Kaposi's sarcoma and rare infections first reported in U.S. homosexual men; link with sexual transmission suspected.
1982	U.S. Center for Disease Control (CDC) establishes AIDS case definition; formal surveillance starts in United States and Europe. First education efforts started in United States by local homosexual groups. AIDS linked to blood transfusions, **intravenous (IV) drug use,** congenital infection.
1983	2,500 AIDS cases reported in United States. **HIV (human immunodeficiency virus)** identified in France and United States.
1984	First studies indicate AIDS is common among heterosexuals in Africa.
1985	Enzyme-linked immunosorbent assay (ELISA) blood test developed to detect HIV antibodies. United States begins screening donated blood. HIV is isolated in brain cells and cerebrospinal fluid.

First controlled clinical trials of anti-HIV drugs begin in United States.

1986   Estimated 5 to 10 million people are infected with HIV worldwide.

World Health Assembly recommends global strategy for AIDS control.

Some estimates indicate 1 to 3 million people infected in the United States. Estimate is reduced by the Reagan administration.

Several governments start national communication programs.

1987   The National Education Association (NEA) publishes "The Facts About AIDS" and joins the Health Information Network.

Education programs begin to expand; so does the number of AIDS cases.

1988   The Names Project creates the AIDS quilt, which helps publicize the epidemic.

1989   Over 100,000 AIDS cases in the United States.

1990   International AIDS conference is held in San Francisco. Many new treatments and potential vaccines are discussed.

The Federal Drug Administration (FDA) loosens regulations to allow people with AIDS access to experimental medication. (California Teacher's Association, 1989).

1996   Discovery of the "triple whammy"—doses of (1) the original antiretroviral drugs, such as AZT; (2) nonnucleoside reverse transcriptase inhibitors, such as nevirapine; and (3) the newest class of drugs, the protease inhibitors, such as invirase. The combination is expected to increase the life expectancy of those who are HIV positive as it has the ability to suppress the development of resistance to a drug type and to produce a rapid and sustained drop in viral load (Association for Continuing Education, 1997, p. 115).

Additional facts were reported by Bulnes (1989):

- In Africa, heterosexuals 25 to 40 years of age are most strongly affected.

- Since 1985, transmission of AIDS through blood transfusions has decreased greatly.

- The chance of spreading AIDS with needle sharing is close to 100%.

- Sexual intercourse may transmit HIV.

- Homosexual transmissions are going down while heterosexual, mom-infant, minority, and IV-drug user infections are going up.

Other statistics were collected by Slader (1992):

- Of women who are HIV positive, 50% are IV-drug users.

- Of men who are HIV positive, 24% are IV-drug users.

- In New York City, a higher proportion of HIV-infected individuals are IV-drug users than are homosexual.

The U.S. Department of Health and Human Services (Rouse, 1995) offers more current statistics regarding intravenous drug users and AIDS. According to its research about the U.S. population, intravenous drug use is presently the second most common route of HIV transmission, with homosexual sexual behavior first, and heterosexual sexual behavior third (p. 17). Regarding diagnosed AIDS cases through December 1994, for women, intravenous drug use was the primary mode of transmission—higher than heterosexual contact (p. 16).

The last set of statistics comes from the California Teachers' Association (1989). It has a special interest in AIDS as related to children.

AIDS and Adolescents

- Over one-fifth of people with AIDS are 20 to 29 years of age. Many of them were infected as teenagers.

- In the United States today, 11.5 million teenagers have had sexual intercourse. This number represents 5 million females (7 out of 10 by age 20) and 6.5 million males (8 out of every 10 by age 20).

- Nearly one-half of all people treated for sexually transmitted diseases are younger than 25.

- Of the young women who use contraception, only 22% use condoms; the remaining 78% use methods that are not as effective in preventing transmission of the AIDS virus.

- A conservative estimate is that 200,000 American teens have used IV drugs.

- An estimated 125,000 to 200,000 teenage men and women become involved in prostitution each year; approximately one-third of these are not runaways.

- A 1986 random survey of 16- to 19-year-olds indicated that sexually active adolescents are not protecting themselves against infection from the AIDS virus: of this group, 70% said they were sexually active; only 15% reported changing their sexual behavior to avoid contracting the AIDS virus. Only 20% of those who changed their behavior used effective methods.

AIDS and Education

- By 1991, one in five California teachers was expected to have a student with AIDS in the classroom.

- Two 1987 polls found that
  91% of adults approve of teaching about AIDS in public schools
  97% of teens believe that information about AIDS should be available

WHAT IS AIDS?

Acquired immune deficiency syndrome means that a virus has invaded the body and disrupted the immune system so that it can't protect the body from various deadly infections like cancer or pneumonia. AIDS is a life-threatening disease that sooner or later kills most everyone who has it. Once a person acquires AIDS, he or she could die within a few days or within up to a few years from the infections that attack the immune system. Most people die within six months to two years after a diagnosis of AIDS.

SYMPTOMS OF AIDS

There are some warning signs that may mean a person has AIDS, but some of these could be symptoms of other diseases. Most are signs that the person's immune system isn't working and may mean that he or she has **AIDS-related complex** if certain opportunistic infections are not yet apparent. If the person has the worst of these infections, like a certain kind of cancer or pneumonia, he or she is considered to have AIDS. Both ARC and AIDS can lead to death. Any of the following symptoms should be checked by a clinic or doctor:

- continuous fatigue

- fever and night sweats for more than a few weeks

- rapid, unexplained weight loss

- swollen glands in neck, armpit, or groin

- pink or purplish blotches or bumps on or under the skin, or in the mouth, nose, eyelids, or rectum

- long-lasting, dry (unproductive) coughing

- fuzzy white patches on tongue or in the mouth

- constant diarrhea

- loss of memory (Sequoia Y.M.C.A., 1987)

MISCONCEPTIONS

Misconceptions about AIDS are numerous and widespread. The following should help to dispel the most common of these.

Misconception 1: AIDS can be spread by kissing. New research suggests that saliva from healthy individuals actually inactivates the AIDS virus. Although HIV can be isolated from saliva, the concentration of the virus is so low that the likelihood of someone's becoming infected from kissing is very remote.

Misconception 2: AIDS can be spread by touching. HIV exists in sweat and tears; however, its concentration in these fluids is extremely low. Studies of health care workers who are in close contact with patients with AIDS have shown that the risk of infection through patient contact is remote (less than 1%). For persons coming into casual contact—hugging and shaking hands—the risk of HIV transmission is nonexistent.

Misconception 3: AIDS can be spread by sharing eating utensils. Again, HIV is present in saliva, but it cannot cause infection because the viral concentration is too low and saliva inactivates the virus.

Misconception 4: You can contract the disease by being near someone with AIDS. This is more a psychological response than a physical threat. People are generally repulsed by disease, especially diseases that are called "infectious" and are poorly understood. However, it is important to remember that HIV is not transmitted through the air like the influenza or cold viruses. HIV is spread solely through the exchange of bodily fluids, primarily semen and blood.

MODES OF TRANSMISSION

As important as it is to dispel the misconceptions about the ways HIV can be spread, it is equally important to know the ways the disease can be transmitted. The four common modes of HIV transmission are these:

1. Person-to-person transmission through sexual behavior that involves the exchange of body fluids

2. Use of HIV-contaminated injection equipment

3. Mother to infant during pregnancy, labor, delivery, or breast-feeding

4. Transfusion with infected blood or blood products (Association of Continuing Education, 1977, pp. 21–22)

Sometimes HIV will be spread through other modes, but these instances are much less common. It may be possible to catch HIV when kissing an infected person if both people have open sores in the mouth. Also, health care workers and police officers may become infected by inadvertent punctures from HIV-contaminated needles.

PROGRESSION OF HIV INFECTION TO AIDS

The development of AIDS can be thought of as a five-stage process:

1. *Acute infection:* The virus enters the body and replicates itself.
   The second stage can take one of two forms.
2a. *Acute HIV symptom illness (primary HIV infection):* Within the first 2 to 4 weeks, some people experience fever, weakness, sore throat, skin rashes, and lethargy; this stage can last 1 to 2 weeks.
2b. *Immune reaction against HIV:* The body begins to produce antibodies to fight infection. Within 2 months after infection, typical HIV-testing pro-

cedures can detect HIV, and for 95% of those infected, antibodies can be detected within 6 months.

3. *Asymptomatic HIV infection:* The HIV-infected person may show no symptoms for 6 months to 15 years or longer, depending on medical treatment.

4. *Chronic or symptomatic phase:* This stage was previously called AIDS-related complex (ARC) because AIDS was believed to follow these symptoms. Medical interventions have delayed the onset of AIDS in the last 10 years. Symptoms include fever, fatigue, diarrhea, skin conditions, thrush, and bacterial, fungal, and parasitic infections.

5. *AIDS:* The person develops one or more of the 26 AIDS-defining opportunistic infections or has a T-helper cell count below 200 cells in conjunction with HIV infection or T-helper cells that register less than 14% of total lymphocytes (Association for Continuing Education, 1997, pp. 10–14).

AIDS TESTING

There is an AIDS antibody test. A positive test result does not mean the person tested will develop AIDS. This test cannot predict whether the individual will eventually develop signs of illness related to the viral infection or if so, how serious the illness will be. A positive test result does indicate that the person has been infected by the AIDS virus and can transmit it to others.

TREATMENT

To date, there is no curative treatment for AIDS. There is not even a vaccine available despite many years of research for one. Many AIDS patients and HIV-positive patients take a variety of medications, AZT being the most popular, as it was the original medication for AIDS patients. The discovery of the previously described "triple whammy" can even bring the virus under enough control that it does not show up on a blood test in some people. The purpose of these medications is to block the deterioration of the immune system.

SOCIAL ASPECTS

Despite increased knowledge and education about the AIDS virus, a stigma continues to attach to people with AIDS. This stigma comes not only from the public but from professional health care workers as well. Much of the negative reaction toward AIDS patients stems from negative attitudes toward homosexuality and IV-drug users. The generally accepted view is that the spread of AIDS started with gay men and heroin addicts. For many, the lifestyle of these two groups is considered wrong, and extremists believe those afflicted are getting what they deserve because they are being punished by God. Because of these views, many AIDS patients have been isolated from family and friends who stay away because of fear and self-righteousness. Being a social outcast only worsens the trauma of AIDS.

Just as the general population discriminates against gays and IV-drug users because of their perceived immorality, many professionals also discriminate against these patients. Patients in these categories frequently don't comply with traditional medical model treatment plans. Some HIV-positive IV-drug users suffer from personality problems that don't respond to education and counseling. Because many people don't like heroin addicts, it is not uncommon for these individuals to be deprived of needed treatment. According to Slader (1992), the HIV-infected IV-drug user often feels entitled to use drugs and will manipulate people relentlessly to get a "fix." He asserts that many continue to share needles despite treatment and education. They behave as if they don't care about their health because that drug high is all-important to them. The treatment of the IV-drug user infected with HIV must be somewhat different from the treatment of others. The next section explores various approaches to crisis intervention in working with populations infected with HIV.

Intervention

According to Bulnes (1989), the crisis worker providing counseling in the area of AIDS should keep in mind various factors about the individual. Identification of these issues will further the worker's understanding of the subjective distress as well as help in determining coping alternatives. Following is a list of these factors:

1. Diagnosis—Whether the client has tested HIV positive, has developed ARC, or has full-blown AIDS

2. Inception—How the person became infected: homosexual, bisexual, or heterosexual contact; sharing needles; blood transfusion

3. Lifestyle—Was the homosexuality out in the open?

4. Marital status—Involvement of significant others?

5. Developmental stage (see Table 1.1 in Chapter 1)

6. Personality style—dependency issues, losses, narcissism

7. Cultural background

8. Social support network

Some issues have to do with the person's sense of loneliness and inability to relate to others, how to help a client relate to the disease and his or her body, self-worth, guilt, sex, emotions of love and hate, anger, depression, anxiety and control, and issues of survival and death.

Individuals diagnosed with AIDS as well as the precursor symptoms often suffer as much psychologically from the diagnosis as they do physically; therefore, psychological counseling is very appropriate for this population. With proper counseling, patients may be able to reduce their feelings of stress and depression, enabling them to enjoy a better quality of life. Counseling can also help the client address issues of death and dying and the denial, anger, and frustration associated with these. Isolation often compounds these emotions and is reinforced by the withdrawal of family and friends, once the AIDS diagnosis becomes known. Counseling must also focus on the psychosocial issues brought on by the stigma associated with the disease, homophobia, and loss of friends, work, housing, insurance, and other essentials of life (Baker, 1991, p. 66).

TREATMENT ISSUES

In 1991, the Ackerman Institute AIDS Project developed a training video dealing with crisis intervention for AIDS/HIV-infected patients and their families. This film is addressed to the **types of clients who may seek crisis intervention**. It offers some valuable insights into the psychological and interpersonal issues involved in the various stages of distress that clients will present to the crisis worker.

The first group the intervention worker should consider is also the largest number of clients. These can be called the *worried well*. Many of these individuals experience sexual guilt caused by fear of AIDS. They are often anxious about their own mortality and their children's future. They will present with ambivalence of whether to be tested or not to be tested for HIV. While waiting for their test results, they will often experience fear arising from their past sexual behaviors.

For example, if someone is gay but has been living as a heterosexual and may even be married, issues of disclosure about his homosexuality will often need to be discussed. As a reframe, the crisis worker might say, "This can be an opportunity to bring out past lies, which may help open up relationships and enhance communication."

Issues of suicide must be taken seriously. For example, a bisexual man may believe suicide would be preferable to disclosing his lifestyle to his wife and children. He may believe suicide would spare his family embarrassment. The crisis worker can reframe this issue by pointing out the burden to his family of losing him suddenly to suicide. After all, his wife can choose to leave or stay, and is it really his right to make that choice for her?

A second type of client a crisis worker may see is the one who is pondering *whether to be tested for the virus*. Issues of denial might be present, a sense that "it could never happen to me." Some people may even suspect they are infected but hold irrational thoughts such as, "If I find out, I may really die." Also, moral issues may exist such as, "If I don't get tested, I don't have any responsibility to tell any sexual partners."

Other people manifest a form of denial by just assuming they are positive and restricting their sexual behaviors. If they don't get medical help, however, they put themselves at risk. Therefore, denial really can be dangerous for others and the possibly infected person.

A crisis worker can offer information such as how the test can tell the person if he or she has the virus and can thereby expose others to it. Several reframes will also be useful. The worker can point out that even if the client tests positive, at least he or she can use the knowledge as an opportunity to live to the fullest and find new meanings in life. This is a common experience for people who have had near death experiences.

On the other hand, another reframe could ask, "Wouldn't it help you to know you aren't positive? At least then you can carry on life rather than be paralyzed with fear from day to day." Encourage the client to talk to others who have been tested to gain support and encouragement for completing this step.

A third group who will come to the crisis interventionist's attention are those clients who are *dealing with an HIV-positive test result*. Many issues must be explored during the time following the news of the result. A crisis worker can use Kübler-Ross's stages as a starting ground and help the client work through each stage.

Once the person is infected, he or she usually passes from a world of youthful and sexual activity to the world of the terminally ill, despite being asymptomatic. This means giving up any opportunity for childbearing, grieving a normal life with normal sexual freedoms, and feeling the burden of ostracism. In the beginning there may be a ceaseless vigil for symptoms, which wastes the person's valuable time and energy. Listening while the client expresses his or her pain and despair will be helpful to the client.

Two struggles to be aware of are disclosing the condition to partners and changing sexual practices. Denying the impact of a positive result—that it can lead to AIDS—can be useful in the beginning as the client works on these struggles and the impact of the infection on her or his relationships.

Some clients may struggle with losing their partners if they disclose the positive test result. The counselor will need to support both partners as they express fear, pain, anger, and sadness. When clients choose not to tell their partners, counselors must struggle with their own responsibility for the partners to know. Workers should encourage clients to explore any positive as well as negative reactions on disclosure.

Changing sexual practices is quite a private issue for most people. Sensitivity to cultural and family traditions will be vital because resistance to "safer sex" can often be understood better in these contexts. Some uninfected partners may feel guilty, so they will have unprotected sex to risk becoming infected as a form of punishment. Others may become suicidal at the thought of losing their infected partners to AIDS. In some marital situations, the woman may feel a need to protect her husband's masculinity by not requiring him to wear a condom.

Support groups that focus on optimism and education are an excellent resource for the HIV-positive client. Here, the clients can share common concerns and offer one another practical problem-solving advice that may not be well received from a non-HIV-positive, well-meaning counselor.

All the struggles of the HIV-positive client will be delicate and difficult to talk about openly. These issues need to be addressed by crisis workers in a nonjudgmental manner, behavior that is not easy. Stop and ask yourself how you are feeling at this point.

A fourth group who will need the help of a crisis worker is made up of those who first *start developing symptoms* (usually of precursor illnesses). With these clients, feeling dirty and contaminated is common. Fears of physical deterioration often lead to thoughts such as, "I just want to die because I know sooner or later ARC will turn into AIDS." Such clients may not allow themselves to get close to others because of their extreme fear of an imminent and painful death.

The counselor can help by working to restore a sense of hope. Whereas the typical attitude is that AIDS equals death, the counselor can begin to reframe the condition as a catalyst for a more meaningful life, in which the client learns to appreciate more fully what she or he has. Rather than creating distance from others, disclosure can rekindle relationships and create closeness.

Educational comments pointing out that family members are probably curious and afraid to ask about the diagnosis may encourage the client to open up to those who live with her or him. Once disclosures are made and an adjustment to changed sexual behavior is developed, the person's crisis state will be stabilized. Medical issues, of course, will continue to appear as will death and dying issues, once opportunistic diseases begin.

Since the scientific community began researching AIDS and HIV, the professional literature has been addressing the counseling of those afflicted. Education and support seem to be the prevalent modes of counseling for all levels of infected persons—from the asymptomatic to chronic pneumonia patients (Magallon, 1987; Price, Omizo, & Hammett, 1986; Slader, 1992). In his residential treatment house for HIV-positive IV-drug users, Slader focuses on teaching the clients skills to help them live healthy lives. Much of the focus for this particular population is educating them about how to prevent spreading the virus. In their case, eliminating needle sharing is the most effective prevention. Some would say that treatment should focus on complete sobriety; but stopping heroin use quickly is extremely difficult, so treatment may just have to concentrate on what is realistic. Many of these infected IV-drug users need to be told that they will die more quickly if they continue to use drugs because drug use damages an already deficient immune system. Pointing out that sharing needles could cause infections with other diseases, which deplete the immune system further, is an example of a useful educational comment. Support groups that deal with feelings and groups like Narcotics Anonymous can also be helpful with this population.

Magallon (1987) offers other information, particularly for women, regarding prevention of HIV infection. She suggests these behaviors:

- Avoiding sex with men who may be bisexual and/or men who may have had sex with a woman who has had sex with bisexual men

- Limiting sexual contacts preferably to one partner and avoiding sex with IV-drug users

- Using condoms in addition to normal birth control methods

- If infected, avoid becoming pregnant

A counselor may also want to reassure clients that their status is guarded by confidentiality ethics, though disclosure to partners will most likely be recommended by the physician. Magallon also encourages any counselor to point out that HIV infection does not equal having AIDS. The HIV-infected person is encouraged to avoid infecting others and stay in good physical condition rather than focus on preparing for full-blown AIDS.

Crisis workers will often give this additional information to HIV-positive clients:

How to reduce the risk of infecting others:

- Reduce the number of sex partners, preferably to one.

- Practice safe sex.

- Use condoms.

- Do use fondling, mutual masturbation, and other safe sexual practices for gratification.

- Clean up accidental spillage of body fluids, especially blood and semen, but also feces and vomitus. Fortunately, the AIDS virus is destroyed easily by alcohol, hydrogen peroxide, and bleach.

- Do not pass or receive body fluids, especially blood and semen.

- Do not engage in any form of sex that can cause injury to body tissues (such as rectal sex).

- Avoid poppers and other drugs that can cloud your thinking and reduce self-control.

- Avoid intravenous or other injectable drugs.

- Follow the rules of ordinary good personal hygiene. Give special attention to bathing before and after sex, and keeping your mouth, teeth, and tongue clean.

- Avoid sharing personal items, especially those that may be contaminated by a small amount of blood, such as razors and toothbrushes.

For patients with ARC, how to reduce the risk of developing AIDS:

- Maintain high nutritional standards; eat well.

- Keep your body strong through appropriate exercise, but do not exhaust yourself.

- Get adequate rest.

- Pay strict attention to ordinary personal hygiene, good health habits, and good housekeeping practices.

- Practice only "safe sex."

- Avoid anxiety and depression by reducing stress and getting regular counseling if necessary.

- Reduce the number of sexual partners to one person of the same HIV-antibody status.

- Avoid intravenous drug use and drug and alcohol abuse (Magallon, 1987)

For those already ill with AIDS, support groups are recommended. This participation will create a sense of family and reduce feelings of isolation. For the counselor, this is a time to model efforts to initiate and maintain contact with AIDS clients. These contacts will help reduce the client's feelings of dirtiness. Because brokering appropriate services is a vital part of any crisis intervention, knowledge of AIDS service centers in the area will be helpful for the crisis worker and her or his clients.

Exercises

Practice role-playing the following vignettes using the ABC model. Try to use some of the suggested reframes and educational knowledge presented to you in this section.

Case 1 A 32-year-old male comes to you after just having received results of his HIV test. He tested sero-positive. He has been living a "closet" gay life; his family and employer do not know he's gay. He does not have a current partner but has several buddies with whom he parties. He's depressed but feels good physically, so he's not very worried.

Case 2 A 50-year-old man comes to you on referral of the medical social worker at the hospital. His longtime companion of 20 years has contracted AIDS and is currently suffering from the opportunistic infection, pneumonia. He is drained and misses his friend's youthfulness and lively character.

Case 3 A 30-year-old man comes to you after finding that he is infected with the HIV virus. He found out at the public health department. He is married with no children yet. He thinks he contracted the disease from a prostitute. His wife does not know.

Case 4 A female heroin addict comes to you worried that she will get AIDS. She shares needles on a regular basis but feels uncomfortable asking whether the other users have been tested for HIV.

Key Terms for Study

AIDS—acquired immune deficiency syndrome: The disease that exists after HIV infection either when an opportunistic infection has invaded the body or when the T-cell count is very low.

ARC—AIDS-related complex: A term not used very much any more. It originally referred to the patient who showed symptoms, such as night sweats, thrush, and lesions, but who had not yet caught an opportunistic infection. It is a state between the dormant HIV infection and full-blown AIDS.

HIV—Human immunodeficiency virus: The virus that usually leads to AIDS. It depletes the body of T-cells, which fight off bacteria and viral infections.

How to reduce the risk of infecting others: Ways to reduce the spread of the disease. Crisis workers must be familiar with these. Safe sex includes the use of latex condoms, dry sex, mutual masturbation, and fantasy. Blood should not be exchanged in any way, including with needles, razors, or feces.

Intravenous (IV) drug use: Use of syringes by people to inject into themselves an illicit drug such as heroin. Such people have a high risk of spreading HIV to others when they share needles because of the direct transmission into the bloodstream.

Misconceptions about AIDS: Mistaken ideas about how the virus is transmitted. AIDS cannot be spread through casual contact, but people often feel worried about hugging and touching an HIV-infected person. HIV is spread through the bloodstream. Even kissing has not been shown as a likely way to spread HIV. Also, many people think only gay people or drug addicts get AIDS. Actually, the virus is well established in the heterosexual population and is appearing in more and more teenagers in the United States.

Types of clients who may seek crisis intervention: People who may seek help related to AIDS for a variety of reasons. Following are four typical types of clients:
worried well: People who feel guilty for their past risky behaviors and who are almost paranoid about being infected. They may over test themselves, even when test after test shows negative results.
The client pondering whether to be tested: The person who may have had unsafe sex or shared a needle; he or she may be in denial or just plain scared. The crisis worker can be a great support to this person by offering education and reframes.
The HIV-positive result: A test result indicating infection with the human immunodeficiency virus. Once a person tests positive, she or he may be in a crisis and is often suicidal. Education, support, and empowerment are needed to help this person through a very difficult time.
The beginning of symptoms: The move into the world of terminal illness. This person will be dealing with issues similar to Kübler-Ross's stages of dying. As with all persons dealing with HIV or AIDS crises, disclosure becomes necessary and is often very traumatic.

C H A P T E R N I N E

Substance Abuse

The media, celebrities, and politicians have all been campaigning against drug abuse since the "Just Say No" push of Nancy Reagan in the 1980s. In the 1960s and 1970s, by contrast, the slogans were "tune in," "trip out," "experience," "turn on," and "try it, you'll like it." Drug use was "in"; now, drug abuse is no longer a respectable recreation. Why, then, will so many families and individuals be severely affected by alcohol and drug abuse?

Any crisis interventionist will in time see a considerable number of substance abusers and/or their significant others. Substance abuse as used in this chapter means the use of alcohol and drugs when it affects a person's occupational, academic, family, social, emotional, or behavioral functioning.

Although some would include overeating, cigarette addiction, or caffeine use as substance abuse, these are not examined here. Before reading the information presented in this chapter, take a moment to complete the following quiz about drug use. The answers appear at the end of the quiz.

1. The most commonly abused drug in the United States is
   a. marijuana   b. alcohol   c. cocaine   d. heroin

2. People who are dependent on heroin keep taking it mostly to
   a. experience pleasure   b. avoid withdrawal   c. escape reality
   d. be accepted by peers

3. Which of these is not a narcotic?
   a. heroin   b. marijuana   c. morphine   d. methadone

4. Which age group has the highest percentage of drug abusers?
   a. 10–17   b. 18–25   c. 26–35   d.   36–60   e. 61 and over

5. Which drug does not cause physical dependence?
   a. alcohol   b. morphine   c. peyote   d. secobarbital   e. codeine

6. Most drug users make their first contact with illicit drugs
   a. through "pushers"   b. through their friends   c. accidentally
   d. through the media

7. What is the most unpredictable drug on the street today?
   a. PCP   b. heroin   c. LSD   d. alcohol

8. Which of the following is not a stimulant?
   a. amphetamine   b. caffeine   c. methaqualone   d. methamphetamine

9. The majority of inhalant abusers are
   a. men   b. children   c. women   d. the elderly

10. Which of the following poses the greatest health hazard to the most people in the United States?
    a. cigarettes   b. heroin   c. codeine   d. LSD   e. caffeine

11. Which of the following poses the highest immediate risk to users?
    a. marijuana   b. nicotine   c. LSD   d. inhalants

12. This drug was believed to be nonaddictive when it was developed in the 1800s as a substitute for morphine and codeine.
    a. LSD   b. heroin   c. horseradish   d. PCP

13. When does a person become hooked on heroin?
    a. first time   b. after 4–5 times   c. 20 times or more   d. different for each person

14. What sobers up a drunk person?
    a. a cold shower   b. black coffee   c. a traffic ticket   d. time   e. walking

15. Which of the following should never be mixed with alcohol?
    a. amphetamines   b. sedatives   c. cocaine   d. cigarettes

16. Medical help for drug problems is available without legal penalties
    a. if the patient is under 21   b. under the protection of federal law
    c. in certain states

17. Stopping drug abuse before it starts is called
    a. prevention   b. withdrawal   c. tolerance   d. education

18. How long does marijuana stay in the body after smoking?
    a. 1 day   b. 12 hours   c. up to a month   d. 1 hour

19. The use of drugs during pregnancy
    a. should be limited to tobacco and alcohol   b. may be harmful to the
    unborn child   c. should cease at 25 weeks

20. What makes marijuana especially harmful today?
    a. it is much stronger   b. it could affect physical and mental
    development   c. younger kids are using   d. all of these

How did you do? Here are the answers:
1. b   2. b   3. b   4. b   5. c   6. b   7. a   8. c   9. b   10. a   11. d   12. b   13. d   14. d   15. b
16. b   17. a   18. c   19. b   20. d

Recognizing Substance Dependence and Substance Abuse

If you scored high on the quiz, you have a good general knowledge about drugs and their use and abuse. As a crisis worker, however, you will need to combine this information with other, more specific data to be able to identify a person who is dependent on or abusing drugs. The following two sections set out criteria for helping you make these determinations.

CRITERIA FOR SUBSTANCE DEPENDENCE

In using the criteria for substance dependence, the mental health worker will need to specify which substance is being used. Essentially, however, the criteria fit most street drugs, prescribed medication, and alcohol. Note that the terms *alcoholic* and *drug addict* are not used in the formal nomenclature.

A maladaptive pattern of substance use, leading to clinically significant impairment or distress, as manifested by three (or more) of the following, occurring at any time in the same 12-month period:

1. tolerance, as defined by either of the following:
    a. a need for markedly increased amounts of the substance to achieve intoxication or desired effect
    b. markedly diminished effect with continued use of the same amount of the substance

2. withdrawal, as manifested by either of the following:
    a. the characteristic withdrawal syndrome for the substance
    b. the same (or closely related) substance is taken to relieve or avoid withdrawal symptoms

3. the substance is often taken in larger amounts or over a longer period than was intended

4. there is a persistent desire or unsuccessful efforts to cut down or control substance use

5. a great deal of time is spent in activities necessary to obtain the substance (e.g., visiting multiple doctors or driving long distances), use the substance (e.g., chain-smoking), or recover from its effects

6. important social, occupational, or recreational activities are given up or reduced because of substance use

7. the substance use is continued despite knowledge of having a persistent or recurrent physical or psychological problem that is likely to have been caused or exacerbated by the substance (e.g., current cocaine use despite recognition of cocaine-induced depression, or continued drinking despite recognition that an ulcer was made worse by alcohol consumption)

specify if:

With Physiological Dependence: evidence of tolerance or withdrawal (i.e., either Item 1 or 2 is present)

Without Physiological Dependence: no evidence of tolerance or withdrawal (i.e., neither Item 1 or 2 is present). (Reprinted with permission from the *Diagnostic and Statistical Manual of Mental Disorders*, 4th ed. Copyright 1994, American Psychiatric Association, p. 181)

If items 1 or 2 are present, the crisis worker needs to make sure that appropriate medical personnel are involved in the case. Withdrawal from certain substances such as alcohol, Valium, and barbiturates can have life-threatening consequences.

CRITERIA FOR SUBSTANCE ABUSE

There are similarities between the criteria for substance dependence and substance abuse. All are generally applicable to the most commonly abused substances.

A. A maladaptive pattern of substance use leading to clinically significant impairment or distress, as manifested by one (or more) of the following, occurring within a 12-month period:

1. recurrent substance use resulting in a failure to fulfill major role obligations at work, school, or home (e.g., repeated absences or poor work performance related to substance use; substance-related absences, suspensions, or expulsions from school; neglect of children or household)

2. recurrent substance use in situations in which it is physically hazardous (e.g., driving an automobile or operating a machine when impaired by substance use)

3. recurrent substance-related legal problems (e.g., arrests for substance-related disorderly conduct)

4. continued substance use despite having persistent or recurrent social or interpersonal problems caused or exacerbated by the effects of the substance (e.g., arguments with spouse about consequences of intoxication, physical fights)

B. The symptoms have never met the criteria for Substance Dependence for this class of substance. (Reprinted with permission from the *Diagnostic and Statistical Manual of Mental Disorders*, 4th ed. Copyright 1994, American Psychiatric Association, pp. 182–183)

Types of Drug Abuse Crises

When dealing with substance abuse problems, the crisis worker can be most effective when the person is really in crisis. A crisis condition is needed to confront the client successfully about the negative impact the drug is having on his or her functioning. Over time, crisis workers generally see four types of crises in relation to drug abuse. These will differ, depending on the substance being abused.

MEDICAL CRISES

Medical problems are most severe when alcohol or barbiturates are the substance of abuse. Seizures, heart attacks, strokes, and liver failure are some of the common reasons for hospitalization. For someone who is physiologically dependent on either of these two categories of drugs, a medical **detoxification** is necessary, as life-threatening complications can occur when a person tries to withdraw from the drug.

Despite the many stereotypes about heroin **withdrawal**, the medical risk of withdrawing from **heroin** is actually not serious. To the heroin addict, however, coming off the drug feels like a crisis of magnificent proportions. For several days, the heroin addict will experience flu-like symptoms that often prompt a visit to an emergency room. Although heroin addicts in withdrawal may feel as though they are dying, they are seldom in danger. Most medical facilities encourage abrupt and complete—or cold turkey—withdrawal. Some outpatient clinics provide an alternative to heroin called methadone. These clinics allow the heroin addict to withdraw from heroin slowly under the supervision of medical professionals while taking the substitute, methadone.

Medical crises will also be observed when the drug being abused is from the stimulant family, such as cocaine, crack, or crystal meth (methamphetamine). Sometimes the user will experience seizures or heart attacks and require emergency medical treatment. These occurrences can be life threatening, but they can also pave the way for the client to confront the addiction and do something about it.

LEGAL CRISES

Another reason that substance abusers and their families might seek crisis intervention would be because of an arrest or some type of court-ordered mandatory counseling. A common arrest for alcohol abusers is drunk driving or public drunkenness. Most states require not only a fine but also counseling and participation in Alcoholics Anonymous as part of the sentence for these crimes.

In addition to being arrested for being under the influence of alcohol or drugs, a person might be arrested for drug possession or sale of drugs. Because of overcrowding in jails and prisons, many diversion programs have been established to provide rehabilitation in lieu of incarceration in traditional correctional facilities. These programs almost always include counseling and education. Diversion programs are especially common for juveniles who are caught with drugs at school. They often lead to increased family involvement as well as cessation of the abuse by the teenager.

At times, a state's child protective agency may discover that parents are substance abusers and the workers will remove the children from the home. The agency may require the parents to enter counseling as a condition of having their children returned to them. The premise for this condition is that having one's children taken away should be a motivator for parents to stop the substance abuse; unfortunately, the desired result is not always obtained.

PSYCHOLOGICAL CRISES

Many people seek crisis counseling because of intense anxiety and depression associated with both the use of certain drugs and the *coming down* sensation after the drug effects wear off. Most of the drugs in the speed category create feelings of paranoia when too much is ingested or during the phase after a major binge. People who snort cocaine, smoke crack cocaine, snort or inject crystal meth, or take Ritalin experience a sense of unreality and often have delusions that they are being followed or are in danger. Additionally, a profound depression often follows several days of using and can precipitate suicide attempts or ideation.

Lysergic acid diethylamide (LSD) has long been associated with "bad trips," or adverse reactions to its ingestion. The affected person may be pseudopsychotic and delusional to the point of not being in control of his or her mind. People in this state need to have someone with them constantly to talk them through these derealized and depersonalized feelings. They need to be told continually that the bizarre sensations they are experiencing are all a result of the LSD and that in 8 to 12 hours, the trip will end.

SPIRITUAL CRISES

A spiritual crisis involves a parting from the normal sense of self. People in these crises realize that they are no longer who they once were. Such an individual may have a revelation after staying up all night smoking crack in a motel room with a prostitute. Perhaps the person looks in the mirror and sees a skeleton who hasn't slept or had a decent meal in months because of using speed. Maybe the person runs into an old buddy who is not a drug user and remembers a life before drugs. Whatever the spiritual awakening, the emotional result is often anxiety and depression; the person's self-esteem needs bolstering and his or her suicide liability needs to be assessed.

Whatever the crisis that brings a substance abuser into counseling, the crisis worker will be most helpful if the counselor can point out to the client how the person's current state of functioning is directly related to the substance use. The client must understand the consequences of substance use in clear and practical terms that are presented in a nonjudgmental manner.

Alcohol: The Leading Abused Drug

Although much media attention lately has focused on the use of speed and heroin, alcohol remains the number one most abused substance. Alcoholism affects an entire family, the alcoholic's job performance, and her or his health. It is extremely costly to the nation, and groups like MADD (Mothers Against Drunk Drivers) have lobbied for stricter drunk driving laws in an effort to reduce alcohol consumption and resulting deaths caused by drunk drivers. Other efforts to minimize alcohol use include an increase in sales tax on alcohol products and the reduction of alcohol consumption by characters on TV programs. Additionally, many television movies and soap operas have been portraying realistic alcoholic dynamics in both teens and adults.

Unfortunately, alcohol, like drugs, is big business; corporations and underworld drug lords are not likely to encourage consumers to *stop* using. However, certain television commercials have been promoting "responsible" drinking.

FACTS ON ALCOHOLISM AND ALCOHOL-RELATED PROBLEMS

Most of the facts and statistics in this section were compiled by the National Council on Alcoholism (1986). They offer a disturbing view of the pervasiveness of alcohol abuse and the destruction it causes.

• Alcoholism is a chronic, progressive, and potentially fatal disease characterized by **tolerance** and physical dependence or pathological organ changes, or both. All are the direct or indirect consequences of the alcohol ingested.

• Alcoholism and **alcohol abuse** occur in every socioeconomic group, although the problems may manifest themselves differently across groups.

• Alcohol is known to cause or contribute to other fatal illnesses including cardiac myopathy, hypertensive diseases, pneumonia, and several types of cancer.

• Alcohol is second only to Alzheimer's disease as a known cause of mental deterioration in adults. However, alcoholic mental deterioration is not progressive. If the patient stops drinking, the deterioration is arrested and substantial recovery can occur.

• Genetic influence is identifiable in at least 35% to 40% of alcoholics and alcohol abusers, and it affects both men and women. People with family histories involving parental alcohol abuse face increased risk. Furthermore, many types of alcohol abuse may exist, each with its own genetic predisposition interacting with a particular environment.

• Surveys conducted in the United States in the 1980s indicate that the first drinking experience usually occurs around age 12, in contrast to ages 13 to 14 in the 1940s and 1950s. It is no longer unusual for 10- to 12-year-olds to have serious alcohol abuse problems.

• Most youth begin to drink in adolescence. A recent study on adolescent alcohol abuse relevant to prevention efforts found that alcohol is the most widely used drug by youths between the ages of 12 and 17.

• About 30% of fourth-grade respondents to a 1983 *Weekly Reader* poll reported peer pressure to drink beer, wine, or liquor.

• Fetal alcohol syndrome (FAS) is the third leading cause of birth defects with accompanying mental retardation and the only preventable one among the top three. The incidence of FAS is approximately 1 in 750 live births or 4,800 babies per year in recent years; 36,000 newborns each year may be affected by a range of less severe alcohol-related effects.

•   Women frequently engage in the high-risk practice of abusing other drugs in combination with alcohol. In a 1983 Alcoholics Anonymous (AA) survey, 40% of female AA members reported addiction to another drug. The number increased to 64% for women aged 30 years and under.

•   About 65 out of every 100 persons in the United States will be in an alcohol-related crash in their lifetimes.

•   Alcohol-related highway deaths are the number one killer of 15- to 24-year-olds. The 1995 Public Health Services *Sourcebook* reports that 18 million people, 16 years old and older, had driven under the influence of alcohol or drugs (Rouse, 1995, p. 19).

•   Alcohol is a contributing factor in at least 15,000 fatal and 6 million nonfatal injuries in nonhighway settings.

•   Between 400 and 800 boating fatalities annually involve alcohol. Alcohol is implicated in 65% to 69% of all reported drownings.

•   Alcoholics are 10 times more likely to die from fires than are nonalcoholics, 5 to 13 times more likely to die from falls, and 6 to 15 times more likely to commit suicide than the general population.

•   Drinking is estimated to be involved in about 50% of spouse abuse cases and up to 38% of child abuse cases.

•   Among jail inmates convicted of violent crimes, 54% were drinking before they committed the offense; 62% of those convicted of assault had been drinking; 49% of those convicted of murder or attempted murder had been drinking.

•   Between 2% and 10% of people ages 65 and over experience some type of alcohol-related problem. Approximately 25% of the 65-plus population is on some form of medication. By most measures, older people consume more medication than any other age group, putting them at high risk for drug and alcohol interaction.

•   Alcohol is associated with attendance problems in the workplace (Rouse, 1995, p. 26).

THE ALCOHOLIC

The person with an alcohol problem may be called an **alcoholic**, problem drinker, or alcohol abuser. Many people working in the field of chemical dependency see alcoholism as a disease in which alcohol abuse covers up other underlying problems. Feelings such as shame, guilt, disgust, remorse, anger, and fear are denied by the alcoholic and anesthetized by alcohol consumption.

When alcoholics stop drinking they may exhibit symptoms of the *dry alcoholic* as they struggle with the emotions that used to be covered up by the effects of alcohol. Family members often complain about newly sober alcoholics because they often behave worse than when they were drinking. This phenomenon underscores the necessity of intervention with the entire family while the alcoholic is recovering.

Family involvement is one aspect of alcoholism that makes it different from other types of diseases. Another aspect is that alcoholics can control their own disease and accept full responsibility for the consequences of their actions. This assumption is one of the basic tenets of Alcoholics Anonymous (AA). However, this 12-step program suggests that the alcoholic participates in the program and accepts the support of a sponsor as part of assuming responsibility and controlling the disease.

Although **alcohol dependence** probably has some genetic and biological components, it is largely a psychological disorder in the beginning stages. In other words, a person experiences emotions and problems, or was socialized in an alcoholic home, and turns to a substance (alcohol) to deal with life stresses. Once used, alcohol helps the person cope with stress by denying and **minimizing** his or her feelings.

The criteria for determining substance dependence and abuse appeared earlier in this chapter and contain the formal terminology used in most mental health agencies, both profit and nonprofit. There are, however, other practical ways for a crisis intervention worker to understand the patterns and psychological processes of the substance abuser and the significant others. Tustin Community Hospital in California has developed a map of the progression and recovery of the alcoholic that appear as Table 9.1.

Gilliland and James (1988) offer some useful definitions of defense mechanisms often observed in alcoholics. Detecting and understanding these can aid the crisis worker in capturing the essence of the person's emotional concerns and needs.

1. *Denial*: Emotional refusal to acknowledge a person's situation, condition, or event the way it actually is. This is believed to be the favorite defense of alcoholics and all substance abusers and their families.

2. *Displacement*: The ventilation of hostility on a person or object, neither of whom deserves it. This allows the addict to shirk responsibility for her or his problems.

3. *Fantasy*: A state related to the euphoria brought on by alcohol intoxication. It allows the person to live in a world different from reality (which he or she perceives as intolerable otherwise).

4. *Projection*: The attribution of one's own motives and wishes to significant others. Because of alcoholics' low self-esteem and shame issues, they cannot cope with any flaws in themselves. This defense creates poor communication patterns as the alcoholic appears hostile, suspicious, and oversensitive.

5. *Rationalization*: Making excuses to support one's behaviors and drinking.

TABLE 9.1 The Progression and Recovery of the Alcoholic

Progression

Engages in occasional relief drinking

Engages in constant relief drinking

Alcohol tolerance increases

Memory blackouts begin

Crucial Phase

Has urgent need for first daily drinks

Has feelings of guilt

Has increasing dependence on alcohol

Memory blackouts increase

Cannot discuss problem

Bolsters drinking with excuses

Becomes less able to stop drinking
when others do so

Displays grandiose and aggressive
behavior

Experiences persistent remorse

Fails repeatedly in efforts to exercise
control

Can't keep promises and resolutions

Tries geographical escapes

Loses other interests

Avoids family and friends

Has work and money troubles

Loses ordinary willpower

Has unreasonable resentments

Chronic Phase

Has tremors and takes early morning
drinks

Neglects food

Alcohol tolerance decreases

Physical condition deteriorates

Lengthy intoxications begin

Moral deterioration begins

Thinking becomes impaired

Begins drinking with inferiors

Has indefinable fears

Is unable to initiate action

Has an obsession with drinking

Has vague spiritual desires

Exhausts all alibis

Admits complete defeat

Continues obsessive drinking

Rehabilitation

Has honest desire for help

Learns alcoholism is an illness

Is told addiction can be arrested

Stops taking alcohol

Meets normal and happy former
addicts

Takes stock of self

Begins to think logically

Examines spiritual needs

Has physical exam by doctor

Feels onset of new hope

Begins group therapy

Recovery

Appreciates possibilities of new way of
life

Feels diminishing fears of the
unknown

Takes regular nourishment

Begins realistic thinking

Sees return of self-esteem

Has natural rest and sleep

Loses desire to escape

Sees that family and friends
appreciate efforts

Makes adjustment to family needs

Makes new circle of stable friends

Develops new interests

(Continued)

Recovery (continued)

Faces facts with courage	Finds contentment in sobriety
Has rebirth of ideals	Recognizes rationalizations
Increases emotional control	Increases tolerance
Appreciates real values	Continues group therapy and
Makes first steps toward economic	mutual help
stability	Sees enlightened and interesting way
Gains confidence of employers	of life open up with road ahead
Takes care of personal appearance	to higher levels of functioning

Source: Adapted from handout produced by Tustin Community Hospital, 1987, Tustin, California.

6. *Minimizing*: Playing down the seriousness of one's addiction. Many alcoholics will say, "I only drink on weekends."

7. *Repression*: The practice of alcoholics in burying hurtful, threatening, and shameful events in the unconscious; when sober, often remembering nothing of their behavior while intoxicated. (pp. 285–287)

Addicts seem to have strong dependency needs and anger issues. Crisis workers need to be aware of these shame issues and build an environment of safety in which the client may express these emotions and still feel accepted by the counselor. **Denial** is great in these types of clients because most of them who come in for counseling are still capable of functioning on the job; therefore, they do not see themselves as addicts.

INTERVENTION

Treatment of the alcoholic ranges from education about the disease of alcoholism to psychodynamic characterological analysis, family therapy, behavior modification, and detoxification. The most popular approach is involvement in AA (Alcoholics Anonymous). Because AA (like all **12-step programs**) is not costly for the client, it is by far the most practical treatment approach on a long-term basis—which most would agree is necessary for an addict.

Before the long-term approaches in treating alcohol abuse are explored, some general techniques and suggestions need to be examined for dealing with the crisis state. Once the crisis is identified and the ABC model is applied, then the client can be referred to the most appropriate setting. Following is a list of actions for the worker in a crisis situation.

-   If the client is under the influence, ask questions that will let you know what he or she took and when it was ingested. Do not try to conduct any type of therapy if the person is intoxicated.

- Safety comes first—your safety, that is. Also, do not let an intoxicated client leave your office in a car. You may be held responsible should the client be involved in a car accident.

- Try not to be alone in a building or office with an addict or alcoholic, especially one who is under the influence of the drug.

- If the client is not currently intoxicated, find out the last time she or he used drugs and what types of substances were used. Remember, polysubstance abuse is very common.

- Check for lethal combinations.

- Find out pertinent medical information, including prescribed medications and illnesses.

- Inquire about possible genetic predispositions by asking whether any family members are drug or alcohol abusers.

- Get a picture of what the person's abuse is like: When does the client typically use? With whom? Under stress?

- Get as much information as possible about the client's functioning level and relationships.

- Find out what in the person's life might be falling apart now.

- Find out why he or she keeps using.

- Begin to confront the client on how the alcohol or drug use is tied into his or her overall problems once enough information has been gathered.

- Deal with the crisis presented.

- Never minimize the crisis or the abuse level.

- Deal with the family when possible.

- Encourage a crisis in the family when possible.

- Keep the focus on behavior that is a result of the abuse rather than focusing on the drinking or drug use itself.

Alcoholics Anonymous (AA)   Alcoholics Anonymous (AA) was created in 1935 by Bill Wilson, an alcoholic New York stockbroker, with the help of Robert Holbrook Smith. It has about 2 million members worldwide. Alcoholics Anonymous is a mutual self-help group that follows a holistic philosophy. During the meeting, the members focus on the person's physical, psychological, emotional, and spiritual aspects. The members are able to explore such issues as how they feel about themselves, their jobs, their families, and other interpersonal relationships and issues dealing with self-image and self-esteem.

There are also purely educational meetings that attempt to break through denial and other defense mechanisms as well as provide information. Many people convicted of drunk driving are ordered by the court to attend these types of meetings. This is evidence of the respect society holds for the AA program.

The basis of Alcoholics Anonymous is a 12-step program. Following is a list of the 12 steps.

1. We admitted we were powerless against alcohol, that our lives had become unmanageable.

2. Came to believe that a Power greater than ourselves could restore us to sanity.

3. Made a decision to turn our will and our lives over to the care of God, as we understood Him.

4. Made a searching and fearless moral inventory of ourselves.

5. Admitted to God, to ourselves, and to another human being the exact nature of our wrongs.

6. Were entirely ready to have God remove all these defects of character.

7. Humbly asked Him to remove our shortcomings.

8. Made a list of all persons we had harmed and became willing to make amends to them all.

9. Made direct amends to such people wherever possible, except when to do so would injure them or others.

10. Continued to take personal inventory, and when we were wrong, promptly admitted it.

11. Sought—through prayer and meditation—to improve our conscious contact with God, as we understood Him, praying only for knowledge of His will for us and the power to carry that out.

12. Having had a spiritual awakening as the result of these steps, we tried to carry this message to alcoholics and to practice these principles in all our affairs.

Family Intervention Another treatment model for alcoholism is to bring the family together and give the alcoholic a choice: Either go for her or his own treatment or move out of the family. The idea is that if the family system changes, the alcoholic can no longer live comfortably in it. To change requires much effort from family members, who are used to and comfortable with enabling behaviors and co-dependency (discussed later in the chapter).

Once the alcoholic is in treatment, family sessions can be conducted to explore new patterns of living for all family members. Sometimes, when the alcoholic sobers up, marriages end because the alcoholic decides he or she no longer wants the partner. Being intoxicated was often the only way the alcoholic could tolerate the spouse.

Example   An attractive, verbal, successful 44-year-old woman came to therapy very much in crisis because her husband, whom she described as an alcoholic, had become verbally abusive to her children (his stepchildren) and she couldn't cope with this behavior. She believed that if only he would stop drinking, everything would be all right.

The husband had been drinking since they had met, however, so there had never been any relationship based on sobriety. After a few individual sessions, she and the children confronted him and told him to stop drinking or they were moving.

The husband stopped drinking for about 1 month. During this time, marital sessions were conducted in which the husband decided that he didn't really want to be a part of this family emotionally. The wife found this unacceptable so they decided to divorce.

Medical Approaches   One of the most important aspects to consider in assessing the needs of a substance abuser is whether he or she needs medical intervention. Providing medical care is particularly vital when the abuser is physically addicted to alcohol, barbiturates, tranquilizers, or heroin. There will be many types of withdrawal symptoms from each of these drugs and some are life threatening.

Detoxification is a usually a 2- to 30-day period in which the person is in a hospital and provided with medical attention during the time of withdrawal. People undergoing withdrawal are given various alternative drugs, such as minor tranquilizers, to ease them through this very difficult time. These drugs must be given in some cases to prevent seizures and convulsions.

Heroin addicts can more readily be detoxified abruptly—or cold turkey— than other abusers, though this is not popular among this population of addicts. At times, they might receive a mild tranquilizer or begin a methadone program as a substitute for the heroin addiction.

Once the drug is out of the person's system safely, other psychological and social methods of intervention can then be instituted. During the hospital stay, clients will participate in many groups and activities such as occupational therapy, recreational therapy, assertion training, educational classes, and self-esteem–building groups. Often, an individual therapist will be assigned to provide psychological counseling as well. A psychiatrist may also be part of the team approach, and she or he may prescribe medications such as antidepressants or lithium.

Some hospitals that have alcohol/drug rehabilitation programs have designed partial hospitalization programs or day treatment programs. These offer the same groups and activities as provided by inpatient facilities but the client lives at home and goes to work during the day, attending the groups daily. This type of program has been widely accepted as more cost effective than residential treatment and is probably the way of the future. These hospitals offer a variety of therapies. They range from behavioral methods to social methods.

Behavior Modification Approaches   A number of behavior modification approaches are used with drug abusers. Two of them are discussed here.

Aversion Therapy. **Aversive conditioning** is based on Pavlov's classical conditioning model, which pairs noxious stimuli with the alcohol (or drugs). Schick Shadel started this treatment in 1935. Its popularity has lessened in recent years because its effects are not long lasting.

After patients have been detoxified physiologically with the aid of anti-depressants or mild tranquilizers, they are ready for this "throw-up" therapy. On an empty stomach, they drink two large glasses of salt water and take Emetine—a drug that makes them nauseous. A bottle of their favorite liquor is then placed in front of them. First, they sniff it, then gargle and swallow it. They immediately vomit. This is repeated several times.

The next day, patients are given the "Butterfly," a combination drink that smells like beer and continues the nausea. The third day, they are given a truth serum, sodium pentothal, and are asked if they want their favorite drink. If they say no, they are asked if they would like another kind of drink. If they say yes, the aversion process is repeated with that type of alcohol.

This same process is used on cocaine addicts with a substance that looks, tastes, and smells like cocaine. Treatment usually takes 10 days and costs about $11,000. After 30 and 60 days, the patient returns for 2-day follow-ups.

Synanon. Charles E. Dederich, a former alcoholic, developed a confrontational style of group therapy in 1958. He started **Synanon**, a self-help therapeutic community by this name based in a Venice, California, storefront and run by recovering addicts.

The basic goal of Synanon is for drug abusers to undergo a complete change in lifestyle; this includes abstaining from the drug, breaking patterns of criminal activity and learning job skills, developing self-reliance, and cultivating personal honesty. Counselors help residents confront their behavior problems, mainly in group therapy sessions. A resident usually singles out another resident and confronts that person with an issue. The discussion goes from there.

Although Synanon emphasizes rejection of life outside the community during the program, reentry into society is a major goal (*Orange County Register*, 1990, p. M3).

Most communities have a few of these recovery/residential/halfway houses, though the need far outweighs the availability. The Synanon approach is not practiced in its pure form in most homes, but the idea of change in social life is still a prominent component. Phoenix House is a popular example of one of these residential treatment facilities.

THE CO-DEPENDENT

In the last decade, many books have been written dealing with the psychological and behavioral dynamics of the spouses and children of alcoholics/drug abusers. The term **co-dependent** refers to the idea that this individual somehow fits into the picture of a person who is *dependent* on the substance. The co-dependent experiences many of the same emotions as the substance abuser such as guilt, resentment, fear, shame, and low self-esteem. The hallmark of so-called co-dependents is the need to be in control. In doing so, they don't allow users the dignity of living their own lives as they choose. Instead, co-dependents' lives center around the activities of the users, usually trying to get them to stop using or worrying about whether they are getting in trouble because of using.

Davis (1982) has designed an outline that describes various *enabling* behaviors of the co-dependent, shown in Table 9.2. These are defense mechanisms that maintain the alcoholic family system in its disease form.

TABLE 9.2   **Enabling Behaviors**

1. *Denying:* "He's not an alcoholic or other drug addict." As a result:
   a. expecting him to be rational
   b. expecting him to control his drinking
   c. accepting blame

2. *Drinking* with the alcoholic or *using* with the addict;

3. *Justifying* the use by agreeing with rationalization of the alcoholic or addict; for example, "Her job puts her under so much pressure."

4. *Keeping* feelings inside.

5. *Avoiding problems:* Keeping the peace, believing lack of conflict makes a good marriage.

6. *Minimizing:* "It's not so bad." "Things will get better when . . ."

7. *Protecting* the image of the alcoholic or user; protecting the alcoholic or user from pain or the co-dependent from pain.

8. *Avoiding* by numbing feelings with tranquilizers, food, or work.

9. *Blaming.* Criticizing; lecturing.

10. *Taking* over responsibilities.

11. *Feeling superior:* Treating the alcoholic or addict like a child.

12. *Controlling:* "Let's skip the office party this year."

13. *Enduring:* "This too shall pass."

14. *Waiting:* "God will take care of it."

Source: Davis, 1982.

Tustin Community Hospital (1987) has developed an outline of the progression and recovery of the significant other in the disease of alcoholism. This appears in an adapted form in Table 9.3.

TABLE 9.3 The Progression and Recovery of the Significant Other in the Disease of Alcoholism

Beginning Stages

Is embarrassed by other person's drinking behavior

Experiences dread and remorse before parties

Comments about other's "drinking too much"

Worries about what will happen

Attempts to control other's drinking

Fears the other's daily return home

Is constantly "smoothing the water"

Complains before and after parties

Denies any problem

Nees to "protect the children"

Is secretive about family problem

Engages in defensive drinking

Without Help

Makes nagging, critical comments

Increasingly takes over the household

Disposes of liquor in the house

Looks for the drinker

Expresses superiority/feelings of contetmpt

Makes excuses to family and friends

Believes the drinker's promises

Shows increased fear, helplessness, guilt, resignation, then rage

Is turned off sexually

Has depression, fatigue, nervousness

Calls workplace with excuses

Makes threats of divorce/separation

Feels trapped, resentful of children and job

Is bitter, self-pitying

Accepts or provokes violence

Has increased physical symptoms

Feels social and emotional isolation

Goes through flurry of activity then drops personal interests

Makes brief separations from drinker

Is totally obsessed with drinker

Bottoming Out

Chooses divorce/other negative relationships

Develops serious emotional/mental problems

Is driven to stress-related death/suicide

Beginnings of Recovery

Reaches out for help

Admits there is a problem

Learns of alcoholism as a family disease

Gains awareness of dependent relationship

Gains new perspective on the problem

Sees that others have found a way

Reduces isolation

(Continued)

TABLE 9.3 *Continued*

With Help

Physical/mental state improves

Constructive selfishness develops

Takes steps toward self-responsibility

Learns to detach

Begins to share thoughts/feelings

Develops new philosophy of living

Has increased concern for children

Increases self-esteem

Investigates own interests/skills

Is able to make decisions

Makes progress meeting emotionl/
  physical needs

Makes progress in self-acceptance/
  evaluation

Develops new skills in interpersonal
  relations

Increases ability to take risks

Increases independent behavior

Reduces fears

Plans and does new things

Has feelings of serenity and peace

Is able to manage own life

Source: Adapted from handout developed by Tustin Community Hospital, 1987, Tustin, California.

ADULT CHILDREN OF ALCOHOLICS

Adult children of alcoholics are often co-dependents and **enablers**. These people have been socialized in an alcoholic home. It is here they learned about finances, relationships, jobs, isolation, and self-esteem—the areas in which these people often develop problems because they did not learn realistic coping mechanisms for dealing with life's stresses. Instead, they learned how to use denial in dealing with their feelings.

TREATMENT FOR THE CO-DEPENDENT

Whereas about 40% of substance abusers come in for mental health treatment because of outside pressure, many more of the significant others of these abusers seek counseling voluntarily. These people are often in a crisis state, feeling very nervous and depressed because they can't control their spouse's, parent's, or child's drinking or abuse.

As with all people involved in alcoholism, the crisis worker must provide an atmosphere of warmth and safety, for these people have very little trust in the world. Many have had to grow up early because of parental irresponsibility. They feel as though they should be able to handle everything on their own, as they have always had to do so.

Education works well with this population. Most are willing to read books that describe their personality patterns and needs. Also, educating them about substance abuse is helpful.

Reframing can be useful as well. Co-dependents often perceive themselves as being "helpful" to the user. It is quite easy to reframe this thinking by suggesting that their help is actually *perpetuating* the abuse. Rather than treating the user like a mature responsible adult, the co-dependent has taken all the user's dignity and respect.

Co-dependent people may present as though they were in full control. However, it is easy to show them how controlled they are by their significant other. The crisis worker can empower these people by releasing them from the responsibility for "fixing" the abuser. They must be shown that they need to develop their own lives in a way that doesn't revolve around the addict if they are to regain self-control.

Davis (1982) offers empowering advice to those whose loved one is an alcoholic:

Don't regard this as a family disgrace. Recovery from alcoholism can come about as in any illness.

Don't nag, preach, or lecture to the alcoholic. Chances are he has already told himself everything you can tell him. He will take just so much and shut out the rest. You may only increase his need to lie or force him to make promises he cannot possibly keep.

Guard against the "holier than thou" or martyr-like attitude. It is possible to create this impression without saying a word. An alcoholic's sensitivity is such that he judges other people's attitudes toward him more by small things than outspoken words.

Don't use the "If you loved me" appeal. Since the alcoholic's drinking is compulsive and cannot be controlled by willpower, this approach only increases guilt.

Avoid any threat unless you think it through carefully and definitely intend to carry it out. There may be times, of course, when a specific action is necessary to protect the children. Idle threats only make the alcoholic feel you don't mean what you say.

Don't hide the liquor or dispose of it. Usually this only pushes the alcoholic into a state of depression. In the end, he will simply find new ways of getting more liquor.

Don't let the alcoholic persuade you to drink with him on the grounds that it will make him drink less. It rarely does. Besides, when you condone his drinking, he puts off doing something to get help.

Don't be jealous of the method of recovery the alcoholic chooses. The tendency is to think that love of home and family is enough incentive for seeking recovery. Frequently the motivation of regaining self-respect is more compelling for the alcoholic when he turns to other people for help in staying sober. You wouldn't be jealous of the doctor if someone needs medical care, would you?

Don't expect an immediate 100% recovery. In any illness there is a period of convalescence. There may be relapses and times of tension and resentment.

Don't try to protect the recovering alcoholic from drinking situations. It is one of the quickest ways to push him into a relapse. He must learn on his own to say "no" gracefully. If you warn people against serving him a drink, you stir up old feelings of resentment and inadequacy. (pp. 1–2)

As a crisis worker, you may want to offer these suggestions to your co-dependent clients.

TWELVE-STEP GROUPS

You may also recommend groups to co-dependent clients. There are several that have been created on the model of Alcoholics Anonymous. These use the 12-step, peer, mutual self-help pattern. Among them are Al-Anon, Co-Da, and ACA. Each of these is designed for a different population.

Al-Anon, Co-Dependents Anonymous (Co-Da), and Adult Children of Alcoholics Anonymous (ACA) have been created for the spouses, relatives, and children of alcohol abusers. Their purpose is to help these individuals cope with their feelings and unproductive behaviors associated with trying to control and change the alcoholic. At these mutual support, self-help meetings, the members receive support for nonenabling behaviors, and their feelings of isolation are reduced. Because these 12-step groups are free, widely available, and effective, the crisis worker should have knowledge about them in his or her community.

THE ROLE OF HOSPITALIZATION

Just as some alcoholics and drug addicts will undergo treatment in a hospital, some of the co-dependents will also benefit from hospitalization. If the person is extremely depressed and suicidal, hospital treatment may be indicated. There are even hospital wards specifically designed for this population.

In summation, alcohol abuse affects all family members, and crisis workers need to be sensitive to the needs of all. It is particularly important for them to be informed of community resources dealing with alcoholism because treatment is usually long term.

The next sections briefly examine other substance abuse issues. Most of what has been presented about alcoholism applies here also. The following parts should provide enough information about specific issues, however, that you will not be totally naive when you come in contact with drug abusers.

Cocaine, Crack Cocaine, and Speed (Amphetamines)

Every crisis worker should at least know the facts about cocaine. Health Communication, Inc. (n.d.) has developed pamphlets that describe cocaine and other drugs. They are updated regularly and can be ordered from the organization at this address: Health Communications, Inc., 2119-A Hollywood Blvd., Hollywood, Florida 33020.

One of the most pervasive of the illegal drugs in today's society is **cocaine**. The U.S. Public Health Service (Rouse, 1995) reports that there are 547 new cocaine users in the United States every year and overall in this country there are approximately 1.3 million users (p. 57). This is a central nervous system stimulant possessing both anesthetic and vasoconstricting properties. It produces a combination of amphetamine-like energy with the numbing (anesthetic) effect of some narcotics. It has been misclassified by the Drug Enforcement Administration for years as a narcotic. In recent years, cocaine use has seen a rapid increase, most notably in the educated, middle-class population.

Cocaine is derived from the coca bush. The leaves are approximately 1 to 4 inches in length and are harvested three times a year. The leaves are reduced to coca paste by the use of petroleum solvents. The result of this manufacturing process is a white powder.

Cocaine is rarely available in its pure form. Common additives are lactose, procaine, lidocaine, benzocaine, tetracaine, and amphetamines. The amphetamine enhances the high-energy effect and the other additives produce the anesthetic effect.

The drug is most frequently **snorted,** but it can be injected into the veins or muscles. **Freebase** smoking produces the most intense rush. This is discussed later in the section on crack.

Usually, after ingesting low doses of cocaine, users experience a short-lived (20–30 minutes) sense of exhilaration and euphoria. They tend to talk a lot and feel energetic and self-confident. The exhilaration of cocaine is very short lived. After the initial euphoria, psychological depression, nervousness, irritability, loss of temperature sensations, and muscle tightening or spasms may occur. To prevent these *coming down* effects, users must use the drug again every 20 minutes or so.

Another form of cocaine is **crack.** This is cocaine in smokeable (freebase) form. People have been smoking freebase for some time. Before crack was developed, however, they had to convert cocaine into freebase with highly flammable chemicals only users were foolish enough to risk handling. You may remember the case of comedian Richard Pryor, who nearly burned himself to death while converting cocaine to freebase.

Now, there is a safer way to convert cocaine into freebase, using ammonia or baking soda and water. The result is crack, so-called because of the crackling sound it makes when smoked. The crack looks like shavings or chips scraped from a bar of soap and is packaged in small plastic vials that sell for $10 to $20 each. Crack may be smoked through the stem of a specially designed glass pipe or sprinkled on tobacco or marijuana and smoked.

When it is smoked, crack triggers an explosive release of neurotransmitters in the brain and depletes the brain's supply of these natural substances, producing an intense craving for more stimulation. The user takes more and more crack to appease this craving that can never be satisfied.

Initially, the user will experience euphoria and excitement, but soon avoidance of coming down becomes the reason for using. Crack is almost instantly addicting. As the addiction takes hold, the user experiences memory problems, insomnia, fatigue, depression, paranoia, irritability, loss of sexual drive, suicide attempts, and violent behavior.

Soon, crack becomes the most important thing in the user's life and overpowers other needs such as eating, sex, family life, personal health, and career. In addition to these effects, there are physical dangers associated with crack use. About 64% of users report chest congestion, 40% have a chronic cough, and 7% say they have suffered brain seizures with loss of consciousness. Many others report chronic hoarseness; they produce black phlegm when they cough or suffer persistent bronchitis (National Council on Alcoholism of Orange County, 1986).

Another illegal drug is **crystal methamphetamine,** or "meth." Its popularity reflects its inexpensive cost and its strong potency in contrast to cocaine. It is a stimulant (speed) that is snorted, injected, or smoked as "ice." Its use can cause paranoia, weight loss, and disturbed sleep.

Crystal meth is highly addicting; the heavy addict will often need hospitalization to detoxify as well as participation in a 12-step program. The psychodynamics and treatment are very similar to those for cocaine addicts and abusers. The major difference between speed and cocaine is that speed lasts longer; therefore, the user doesn't spend all night trying to track down more to use, as does the cocaine user. Unfortunately, long-term use often leads to paranoia, violence, and serial arrests or psychological crises.

Methamphetamine is dangerous and can cause physical harm to the brain, heart, and general health. Users will often binge for several days before taking a break from using it. This practice takes a heavy toll on the body.

Another stimulant became popular in the mid-1990s: Ritalin. Historically, this drug has been used in the treatment of hyperactive children, as it has a paradoxical effect on them. Although a stimulant, Ritalin acts to calm these children. Many of their older brothers and sisters, however, have been using the drug as an upper, or stimulant, and this use has spread across high school campuses. Even pharmacists have been caught snorting Ritalin at work. This is a drug the crisis worker must know about and must inquire about when substance abuse is suspected. Table 9.4 contains information that will help the crisis worker understand the progression of and recovery from methamphetamine and cocaine/ crack abuse.

TABLE 9.4 Progression of and Recovery from Speed, Crack, and Cocaine Abuse

The Experimental User

Most friends are nonusers	Rarely has impairment of job duties
Uses only when drug is offered	Demonstrates little or no impact on finances from drug use
Has normal relationships	
Maintains average hygiene	Uses cocaine to enhance feelings
Rarely has sleep and nutritional losses	Uses to satisfy curiosity

The Compulsive User

More friends are users	Is regularly late to or misses work
Begins to buy cocaine	Has increased chance of toxic problems and polydrug problems
Fails to keep promises to friends	
Attempts to change self	Shows poor job performance and disciplinary problems
Shows increased social disruption and distance	Has a tendency to work alone
Has regular nutritional and sleep problems	Frequently overspends
	Accumulates unpaid debts
Shows tendency to use more coke	Uses to stop feelings, ward off depression and guilt, and mood swings

(Continued)

The Dysfunctional User

All friends use
User begins to deal cocaine
Increasingly lies, borrows, steals
Has possibility of violence and divorce
May use high doses in isolation
Has serious medical pathology
Is at risk of seizures
Has chronic sleep and nutritional
  problems
Looks terrible
Often has toxic psychosis, paranoia,
  delusions, hallucinations

Has serious polydrug problems
  including possibility of overdosing
Loses job, status, and professional license
In danger of embezzlement, theft of
  drugs, chronic overspending
  financial ruin
Uses to feel normal and cover guilt
Is totally preoccupied
Experiences compulsion, loss of control,
  inability to stop using despite adverse
  consequences

The User in Rehabilitation

Stops all psychoactive drug use
Is treated for medical complications
Has proper nutrition and sleep
Is educated about addictive disease
Is introduced to 12-step programs:
  AA, NA, CA

Learns addiction can be treated
Meets recovering addicts
Receives recovering addicts

The User in Recovery

Starts to think normally
Begins healthy, good relationships
Works 12-steps for spiritual needs
Develops increased psychological
  sophistication

Family and friends get recovery
  education
Explores returning to work
Grows spiritually and emotionally

Source: Adapted from the National Council on Alcoholism, Orange County, California, 1986.

Marijuana

People rarely seek crisis intervention for marijuana abuse; nonetheless, a crisis worker should be familiar with it. **Marijuana** is widely used and may impair a person's functioning and coping while in a crisis. Also, rather than use sober coping strategies, many people use marijuana to deal with stress. The U.S. Public Health Service (Rouse, 1995, p. 57) estimates that there are 9 million marijuana users in the United States. The average new user is 16 to 17 years old.

Marijuana is the unprocessed, dried leaves, flowers, stems, and seeds of the cannabis sativa plant. Delta-9-tetrahydrocannabinol (THC) is thought to be the primary psychoactive or mind-altering compound in this plant. The drug is usually rolled with cigarette papers into a *joint* or *reefer* and smoked like a cigarette. Hashish is the solidified resin of the cannabis sativa plant (Zimbardo,

1992, p. 129). It is usually smoked in a pipe as a brownish chunk. It is many times stronger than marijuana. Marijuana and hashish may also be baked and eaten in brownies.

The common street names of marijuana are *pot, weed, reefer, smoke, hooch,* and *dope.* Its effects are dependent on the potency of the particular plant, the experience of the user, and the user's expectations. Some marijuana users describe a subjective state of increased sensory awareness to music, touch, light, and social interaction. Other users experience anxiety, fear, and withdrawal from social interaction because of drug-induced paranoia.

Research by Health Communications, Inc. (n.d.) indicates that the following may be chronic effects of marijuana over long periods of time:

- *Respiratory System:* Bronchial problems, sore throats, coughing, susceptibility to bronchitis and pneumonia. Tar and cancer-causing agents in marijuana smoke are 5 to 10 times those amounts in a typical tobacco cigarette.

- *Immune System:* Reduced ability to fight infection from bacteria and viruses.

- *Endocrine System (maturational):* Possibly impeded physical, emotional, and mental development for 11- to 15-year-olds using marijuana.

- *Reproductive/Hormonal System:* Possible reduction in both male and female hormones. When this occurs, it can affect fertility, sperm reproduction, menstrual cycles, and ovulation. Sperm that are damaged and diminished in size have been reported. These hormone reductions are also related to the maturational processes, particularly in regard to secondary sex characteristics.

- *Intelligence and Behavior:* Decreased ability to store information, concentrate, make decisions, handle complex tasks, and communicate (Health Communications, Inc., n.d.).

Marijuana use is often regarded as soft drug abuse. However, the counselor should remember that it is illegal and that clients may find themselves in legal difficulties because of pot use. This may be the reason for their seeking intervention. Also, many companies are requiring drug screenings prior to employment or as grounds for continuing employment. A person may need help in staying off pot for this reason.

Pot Smokers Anonymous or Narcotics Anonymous may be helpful for marijuana users. These users typically need to develop a social network of non-using people with whom they can have fun and interact socially without drugs.

Denial will be a big part of the marijuana smoker's perception of her or his problem. This person will minimize the extent of use or the idea that it is a problem. The crisis interventionist may want to help him or her explore what life is like when the person is sober. Also, remember that the marijuana grown nowadays is very potent compared to that grown even 10 years ago.

LSD (Lysergic Acid Diethyamide)

LSD is also known as *acid* and is taken orally in tab form or licked off paper. A crisis worker may treat someone on a bad trip that has extreme panic associated with it. Many emergency room doctors and nurses as well as mental health workers have had to talk someone through a crisis state set off by LSD.

This drug distorts the person's sensory perception and sense of self. He or she may resemble a floridly psychotic person because of having hallucinations and delusions. The effect usually lasts 10 to 12 hours, and the person needs comfort, orange juice, and reassurance that the feelings are due to the acid.

LSD has made a major comeback in the 1990s, perhaps because teenagers are trying to imitate the perceived excitement of the 1960s teenager. The drug is frequently associated with underground "rave" parties. The location of these parties is unknown to parents and authorities. The music is loud, and teens and young adults engage in wild dancing. For young clients brought in from a party, a crisis worker should probe to discover the nature of the party.

Many teens use LSD daily or for an entire weekend. This drug can precipitate a psychotic reaction in otherwise normal kids. However, it is less prevalent than other drugs. About .5 million people in the United States are thought to use LSD (Rouse, 1995, p. 57).

Heroin

Heroin use is on the rise in the 1990s. The drug is usually injected and is highly addictive. A person withdrawing from heroin will experience flu-like symptoms and may do anything to get a **"fix"** of the drug. Methadone is often prescribed in oral-liquid form to help addicts withdraw from heroin. Sometimes an addict may be talked through an abrupt—or cold turkey—withdrawal.

Unfortunately, quitting permanently is very difficult because heroin covers up all pain and stress. When sober addicts must deal with normal life stresses, they are not prepared to cope; starting to use again is a strong temptation. Residential halfway house programs are somewhat effective for heroin addicts. As with all substance abusers, heroin users must make a complete lifestyle change to be cured.

By some estimates, two out of three men heroin users in their twenties will be dead, in jail, or still using by the time they're 50 years old. Unfortunately, heroin use is on the rise for middle-class men and women. They usually start out by snorting it, then move into mainlining—injecting the drug directly into a vein. After 3 or 4 days, the physical craving is so strong, they feel they have no choice but to use. At this point, they are using the drug to keep from getting sick. "Kicking the habit" is so named because users often go through miniconvulsions when withdrawing; they want to avoid this trauma at all costs (Turning Point, 1994).

Because of the high rate at which users return to heroin, and because the heroin user's life is completely wrapped up in how to get the next drug fix, this drug addiction needs a great deal of attention. Knowledge of how to work with this population will be beneficial for the crisis worker. Many mental health and medical health practitioners avoid working with heroin addicts because they are so difficult, but the impact on the community (crime, AIDS, welfare, and so on) is high and needs to be addressed.

A crisis worker can only point the way and give information about resources. The addict must do the rest. Give yourself a break and don't accept responsibility for substance abuse clients.

Exercises

Role-play the following vignettes using the ABC model. As the client, try to use some of the defense mechanisms that alcoholics, addicts, and co-dependents use.

Case 1   A 54-year-old woman comes to you. She is chronically depressed but is still able to work and is not suicidal. Her husband has been drinking beer for their entire marriage and she tries to control his drinking.

Hints: Try one or more of the following statements with this client.

Educational statements: People who live with alcoholics often try to control their drinking; this has been termed *co-dependency*.

Reframe: Although you think you are helping him by focusing on his behavior, you are really showing disrespect for him and taking away his dignity, which probably makes him feel the need to drink more.

Supportive statement: I can understand how hard it must be to have to be the only responsible person in the family.

Empowering Statement: Although you cannot control his drinking, you can control whether you focus on him or on your own needs in life.

Case 2   A 17-year-old boy is sent to you because his parents found a vial of cocaine in his bathroom. He tells you this was the only time he's used cocaine.

Case 3   A 30-year-old man comes to you because he has been missing work a lot lately. He drinks and smokes pot daily.

Case 4   A 28-year-old woman and her husband come to you because of financial difficulty. The wife has spent over $30,000 this past year on her cocaine habit.

Key Terms for Study

Alcoholic: A term often used by laypeople to mean anyone with a drinking problem.

Alcohol abuse: A formal term used in the *DSM-IV* which refers to the person who drinks when the drinking leads to impairment in functioning in one or more areas. This person may also be drinking for psychological comfort.

Alcohol dependence: Also a term from *DSM-IV*; it refers to the person who is physically addicted to alcohol and would suffer withdrawal symptoms if he or she were to quit drinking.

Aversive conditioning: A behavioral approach to help drug addicts and alcoholics quit by pairing the substance with a noxious stimulus such as emetine, electric shock, or dirty water. Formerly used frequently at Schick centers.

Cocaine: A white powder that is usually snorted; gives user a sense of being high and euphoric. Effect lasts 20 to 30 minutes and is highly addictive.

Co-dependent: A term that refers to the significant others involved with a substance abuser and the controlling and "helping" behaviors associated with this family member or friend.

Crack: A form of cocaine that is smoked. Crack is highly addictive and can have serious side effects such as heart failure, stroke, and brain cell destruction. A very popular drug in the 1980s.

Crystal methamphetamine: Commonly called crystal meth. A form of speed that is growing in popularity in the 1990s and can be made in home laboratories. It is cheap and highly addictive.

Detoxification: Cleaning a person's system of a drug. When a person is physically dependent on a substance, it usually takes three to five days for the substance to be flushed out of the body. Detoxification often needs to be done in a hospital setting under the care of a physician.

Denial: Considered to be the number one defense mechanism associated with substance abuse. The addict or family members simply refuse to see that a problem exists.

Enabler: The nonusing member in a family who encourages or helps the substance abuser continue to use.

Fix: A slang term for the dose or unit of consumption by a drug addict. Most commonly associated with heroin addicts.

Freebase: The procedure for changing cocaine to crack. To make crack, cocaine and certain chemicals have to be combined. The rock form of cocaine is smoked. Often, a large flame is needed for best results.

Heroin: A narcotic that is highly addicting. It is often first snorted, but soon the user injects it. The sensations are reported to be a strong euphoria.

LSD: Often called "acid." LSD is a hallucinogen. The user experiences distortions in sensory perception and feels either euphoric or paranoid if he or she experiences a "bad trip." LSD is not considered addictive.

Marijuana: A plant that contains THC, which creates a sense of euphoria in the user. It is smoked either in pipes, bongs, or joints.

Minimizing: Strategy by which substance abusers and enablers often admit that use exists but deny the extent of the problem.

Snorting: A way to use drugs by sniffing the powder up the nose with a straw.

Synanon: A type of treatment for addicts that relies on confrontation and a strong social support network to change the user's lifestyle.

Tolerance: Resistance to a drug. After prolonged use of drugs or alcohol, the body builds up resistance and needs more and more of the substance to feel its effects.

12-step programs: Considered to be the most effective model in treating substance abusers. These programs are based on the Alcoholics Anonymous model, which acknowledges that users need to seek out and trust a higher power in order to overcome their lifelong problem with the substance.

Withdrawal: Symptoms experienced when a user stops taking the drug. The user experiences various physical and psychological symptoms such as nausea, depression, paranoia, convulsions, and anxiety.

Crises of Victimization

Suicide and substance abuse issues were presented earlier because these issues will often be part of crises involving abuse victimization. Therefore, the crisis worker will need to assess for suicide and substance abuse as well as the other issues involved in being a victim.

Posttraumatic Stress Disorder (PTSD)

Posttraumatic stress disorder (PTSD) is a broad category that can apply to people who have been severely traumatized at one or more times in their lives; at present, they are not functioning effectively because they have not integrated the trauma and laid it to rest. Counselors first became aware of PTSD in dealing with war veterans, especially those of the Vietnam War. Often these were 19-year-old boys who were sent across the world lacking the coping skills to deal with seeing their buddies blown up and small children killed. The symptoms of the Vietnam veterans have been to reexperience the sounds of war, suffer from nightmares, and be unable to manage interpersonal relationships effectively. Support groups were set up to allow these veterans an opportunity to discuss their traumas and find ways to integrate this part of their lives into present-day functioning.

Posttraumatic stress disorder is also diagnosed in survivors of child abuse, battered women (when it is called battered woman syndrome), victims of rape (when it is known as rape trauma syndrome), and victims of other crimes such as robberies, and physical and sexual assaults. It is also seen in witnesses to murder. The symptoms of all these conditions are similar, and a crisis worker is bound to come into contact with clients who have not dealt with these traumas from the past. Something in the present may trigger a memory of the trauma, or the person's functioning may diminish to the point that he or she can't deal with society any more, so the person seeks the help of a mental health worker.

Other people exist in a chronic crisis state, never really functioning at all. They often go from one therapist to another or from hospital to jail to clinic looking for coping skills to deal with their current problems. Unfortunately, for many, until they deal with their past traumas, they cannot truly be effective in the present.

Posttraumatic stress disorder may also occur in victims of natural disasters such as severe floods, hurricanes, earthquakes, plane crashes, and car accidents. Recall from Chapter 2 that crisis work began with a man-made disaster: the Coconut Grove Fire. There have been many different disasters of this magnitude since then. A recent example was the bombing of the Oklahoma City federal building in April 1995. This was a monumental disaster in which over 200 people, including preschool children, were killed and many others were injured. Complete crisis intervention services were needed to help the survivors of the bombing and the people in the community deal with the trauma. When a disaster like this happens, it affects not only those directly involved but others who suddenly feel that their security is somehow threatened. Crisis response units were set up in many elementary schools to help children deal with beliefs that the community is no longer a safe place. The idea, "Something like this could happen to me and my family," was a common response for many. Crisis workers needed to help people think differently about the situation, showing the secondary victims through education and empowerment statements that they could cope with this situation.

To function during an emergency situation, an individual must put her or his feelings and normal human reactions aside. This state of denial allows the person to act in order to survive. If this initial shock did not exist, people would be so overwhelmed with feelings that they could not function at all. After the emergency is stabilized, those involved can come to terms at an appropriate pace with what has happened.

This process is referred to as a delayed reaction and is the basis for posttraumatic stress disorder. The tendency is for individuals who have been traumatized to seek resolution at some point in some way. This resolution takes a variety of forms and may occur at conscious as well as unconscious levels. For example, nightmares that replay the event are common in PTSD. It is as if the unconscious mind were trying to help the person bring closure to the trauma by creating stress at night so the person will be motivated to deal with the trauma in a wakeful, conscious state.

Once the individual has allowed the trauma to surface, a flood of feelings will be aroused. Professional help is then needed to channel these feelings into productive avenues for growth. As with all crisis situations, the person will need to see that some new meaning can be ascribed to even the most devastating trauma. Victor Frankl's work on logotherapy (meaning therapy) is a good example; it shows how he used his trauma as a Nazi concentration camp survivor to create growth in himself as a person. Despite the catastrophic nature of this experience, he found a way to see meaning in it. This ability no doubt helped him survive psychologically.

If a person does not receive help after a trauma, the posttraumatic symptoms get worse over time and he or she will learn to adjust to life in a less functional way. Such people will have less psychic energy available to deal with daily stress because the energy will be used to continue the denial of the feelings associated with the trauma. These people will most likely have difficulty in interpersonal relationships, which require feelings if the relationships are to be satisfying at all.

POSTTRAUMATIC STRESS DISORDER DEFINED

The *DSM-IV* (APA, 1994) defines posttraumatic stress disorder this way:

A. The person has been exposed to a traumatic event in which both of the following were present:

1. The person experienced, witnessed, or was confronted with an event or events that involved actual or threatened death or serious injury, or a threat to the physical integrity of self or others.

2. The person's response involved intense fear, helplessness, or horror. Note: In children, this may be expressed instead by disorganized or agitated behavior.

B. The traumatic event is persistently reexperienced in one (or more) of the following ways:

1. recurrent and intrusive distressing recollections of the event, including images, thoughts, or perceptions. Note: In young children, repetitive play may occur in which themes or aspects of the trauma are expressed.

2. recurrent distressing dreams of the event. Note: In children, there may be frightening dreams without recognizable content.

3. acting or feeling as if the traumatic event were recurring (includes a sense of reliving the experience, illusions, hallucinations, and dissociative flashback episodes, including those that occur on awakening or when intoxicated). Note: In young children, trauma-specific reenactment may occur.

4. intense psychological distress at exposure to internal or external cues that symbolize or resemble an aspect of the traumatic event.

5. physiological reactivity on exposure to internal or external cues that symbolize or resemble an aspect of the traumatic event.

C. Persistent avoidance of stimuli associated with the trauma and numbing of general responsiveness (not present before the trauma), as indicated by three (or more) of the following:

1. efforts to avoid thoughts, feelings, or conversations associated with the trauma

2. efforts to avoid activities, places, or people that arouse recollections of the trauma

3. inability to recall an important aspect of the trauma

4. markedly diminished interest or participation in significant activities

5. feeling of detachment or estrangement from others

6. restricted range of affect (e.g., unable to have loving feelings)

7. sense of foreshortened future (e.g., does not expect to have a career, marriage, children, or a normal life span)

D. Persistent symptoms of increased arousal (not present before the trauma), as indicated by two (or more) of the following:

1. difficulty falling or staying asleep

2.   irritability or outbursts of anger

3.   difficulty concentrating

4.   hypervigilance

5.   exaggerated startle response

E.   Duration of the disturbance (symptoms in Criteria B, C, D) is more than one month.

F.   The disturbance causes clinically significant distress or impairment in social, occupational, or other important areas of functioning.

(Reprinted with permission from the *Diagnostic and Statistical Manual of Mental Disorders* (4th ed.). Copyright 1994, American Psychiatric Association, pp. 427–429)

If the clinical symptoms do not meet these criteria exactly (e.g., the symptoms happen within one month of the stressor), the person may be suffering from acute stress disorder. The crisis worker should be particularly alert to this possibility. If intervention can be done within the first month, future problems can be prevented, as discussed in Chapter 1.

DIAGNOSTIC CRITERIA FOR ACUTE STRESS DISORDER

The *DSM-IV* also sets out criteria for acute stress disorder.

A.   The person has been exposed to a traumatic event in which both of the following were present:

1.   the person experienced, witnessed, or was confronted with an event or events that involved actual or threatened death or serious injury, or a threat to the physical integrity of self or others.

2.   the person's response involved intense fear, helplessness, or horror.

B.   Either while experiencing or after experiencing the distressing event, the individual has three (or more) of the following dissociative symptoms:

1.   a subjective sense of numbing, detachment, or absence of emotional responsiveness

2.   a reduction in awareness of his or her surroundings (e.g., "being in a daze")

3.   derealization

4.   depersonalization

5.   dissociative amnesia (i.e., inability to recall an important aspect of the trauma)

C.   The traumatic event is persistently reexperienced in at least one of the following ways: recurrent images, thoughts, dreams, illusions, flashback episodes, or a sense of reliving the experience; or distress on exposure to reminders of the traumatic event.

D.   Marked avoidance of stimuli that arouse recollections of the trauma (e.g., thoughts, feelings, conversations, activities, places, people).

E.   Marked symptoms of anxiety or increased arousal (e.g., difficulty sleeping, irritability, poor concentration, hypervigilance, exaggerated startle response, motor restlessness).

F.   The disturbance causes clinically significant distress or impairment in social, occupational, or other important areas of functioning or impairs the individual's ability to pursue some necessary task, such as obtaining necessary assistance or mobilizing personal resources by telling family members about the traumatic experience.

G.   The disturbance lasts for a minimum of 2 days and a maximum of 4 weeks and occurs within 4 weeks of the traumatic event.

H.   The disturbance is not due to the direct physiological effects of a substance (e.g., a drug of abuse, a medication) or a general medical condition, is not better accounted for by Brief Psychotic Disorder, and is not merely an exacerbation of a preexisting Axis I or Axis II disorder.

(Reprinted with permission from the *Diagnostic and Statistical Manual of Mental Disorders* (4th ed.). Copyright, 1994, American Psychiatric Association, pp. 431– 432).

Child Abuse

Child abuse may come to a crisis worker's attention in several ways. In each case, the person's feelings of shame, fear, guilt, and anger will exist and need to be identified so he or she can begin processing the family and/or individual dynamics that led to the abuse.

The National Center on Child Abuse Prevention Research, a program of the National Committee to Prevent Child Abuse, surveyed state child protection agencies in 1993 and found that there were 2,989,000 reported cases of child abuse and neglect nationwide. In 1992, the National Center on Child Abuse and Neglect surveyed 50 states, the District of Columbia, Guam, and the Virgin Islands. The survey findings indicated that 993,000 children were confirmed victims of child abuse (Tower, 1996, p. 65).

The discrepancy between reported cases and those considered actual cases of child abuse by the judicial system could be the result of a variety of factors, such as false reporting, inaccurate reporting, or a lack of evidence; also, children sometimes change their minds about reporting the abuse. Counselors must be aware of the emotional ramifications of all child abuse reports, whether substantiated or not. Even a false report could be a signal that a family is in crisis. The crisis worker can utilize the feelings and perceptions associated with both false and substantiated reports as a way to identify unmet needs and other problems in a family unit.

Sometimes the crisis interventionist will be called on to work with a child, her or his parents, or the entire family when a child is being abused by the parents. The abuse may or may not be the presenting problem. At times, a social worker will have referred the family for counseling after a teacher or doctor reported the case to the district's child protective agency. On the other hand, the crisis counselor may discover abuse to exist in a family that came in for other reasons. In these cases, the crisis worker will have to report the case to the state's **child protective agency**.

TYPES OF CHILD ABUSE

Child abuse can be categorized into four types. **Physical abuse** occurs when damage to tissues or bones is inflicted on a minor by other than accidental means. Whenever parental discipline causes marks on a child, this is typically considered abuse. **Sexual abuse** occurs when an adult or individual several years older than the minor engages in any sexual contact. This can include intercourse, oral sex, anal sex, exhibition, fondling, or kissing. When a family member sexually abuses the minor, the contact is considered incest and is reported to child protective services. When the sexual abuse is done by someone other than a family member, the offender is usually dealt with by law enforcement. **General neglect** occurs when the parents fail to provide for the minor's basic needs such as food, shelter, clothing, and proper medical care. Society and the law expect a child to be properly supervised, fed, and protected from bad weather by clothing and housing. **Emotional abuse** is the hardest to prove, but probably the most prevalent type of abuse. In this type, a minor is repeatedly criticized and demeaned, receives no love or nurturance, and is not allowed to develop a sense of self. This type of treatment is common in many cults, and the parents who treat their children this way are usually the most psychologically disturbed of all types of child abusers, except perhaps some sexual abusers.

HOW TO DETECT CHILD ABUSE

There are many clues for identifying child abuse and neglect. One sign alone may not necessarily indicate abuse. However, if a number are present, it is prudent to consider the possibility of abuse. Suspect abuse or neglect if a child exhibits any of the following:

- Is habitually away from school and constantly late; arrives at school very early and leaves very late because the child does not want to go home

- Is compliant, shy, withdrawn, passive, and uncommunicative

- Is nervous, hyperactive, aggressive, disruptive, or destructive

- Has an unexplained injury—a patch of hair missing, a burn, a limp, or bruises

- Has an inordinate number of "explained" injuries, such as bruises on arms and legs over a period of time

- Exhibits an injury that is not adequately explained

- Complains about numerous beatings

- Complains about the mother's boyfriend "doing things" when the mother is not at home

- Goes to the bathroom with difficulty

- Is inadequately dressed for inclement weather with, for example, only a sweater in winter for outerwear

- Wears a long-sleeved top or shirt during the summer months to cover bruises on the arms

- Has clothing that is soiled, tattered, or too small

- Is dirty and smells or has bad teeth, hair falling out, or lice

- Is thin, emaciated, and constantly tired, showing evidence of malnutrition and dehydration

- Is unusually fearful of other children and adults

- Has been given inappropriate food, drink, or drugs

Other signs may relate to the parents rather than the child. Some possible indicators are these:

- Parents show little concern for their child's problems.

- Parents take an unusual amount of time to seek health care for the child.

- Parents do not adequately explain an injury the child has suffered.

- Parents give different explanations for the same injury.

- Parents continue to complain about irrelevant problems unrelated to the injury.

- Parents suggest that the cause of the injury can be attributed to a third party.

- Parents are reluctant to share information about the child.

- Parents respond inappropriately to the seriousness of the problem.

- Parents are using alcohol or drugs.

- Parents have no friends, neighbors, or relatives to turn to in crises.

- Parents are very strict disciplinarians.

- Parents were themselves abused, neglected, or deprived as children.

- Parents have taken the child to different doctors, clinics, or hospitals for past injuries (doctor shopping).

- Parents are unusually antagonistic and hostile when talking about the child's health problems (Orange County Social Services Agency, 1982).

HOW TO DETECT SEXUAL ABUSE

Sexual abuse has several specific indicators. When one or more of these is present, abuse should be considered.

Presumptive Indicators of Sexual Abuse

1. Direct reports from children. False reports from young children are relatively rare; concealment is much more the rule. Adolescents may occasionally express authority conflicts through distorted or exaggerated complaints, but each such complaint should be sensitively and confidentially evaluated.

2. Pregnancy. Rule out premature but peer-appropriate sexual activity.

3. Preadolescent venereal disease.

4. Genital bruises or other injuries. Remember that most sexual abuse is seductive rather than coercive and that the approach to small children may be nongenital. The presence or absence of a hymen is nonspecific to sexual abuse.

Possible Indicators

1. Precocious sexual interest or preoccupation

2. Indiscreet masturbatory activity

3. Vaginal discharge; more often masturbatory or foreign body than abusive

4. Apparent pain in sitting or walking. Be alert for evasive or illogical explanations. Encourage physical examinations.

Behavioral Associations: Nonspecific

1. Social withdrawal and isolation

2. Fear and distrust of authorities

3. Identification with authorities. Too-willing acquiescence to adult demands may represent a conditioned response to parental intrusion

4. Distorted body image. Shame, sense of ugliness, disfigurement

5. Depression

6. Underachievement, distraction, and daydreaming

7. Low self-esteem, self-deprecation, self-punishment, passiveness

8. Normal, peer-appropriate behavior. Children may show no signs and carefully avoid risk of detection (Orange County Social Services Agency, 1982)

The San Francisco Child Abuse Council (1979) has identified specific indicators of physical abuse to watch for: bruises on any infant; bruises on the posterior side of a child's body; bruises in unusual patterns (belt buckle, loop from wire); human bite marks; clustered bruises; bruises in various stages of healing; burns from cigarettes or ropes; dry burns; lacerations of the lip, eyes, gum tissues, or genitals; possible fractures; absence of hair; bleeding beneath the scalp.

Infant Whiplash Syndrome   In the past few years, a newly recognized injury to children has been identified and described. This injury is known by several names, the most common of which is **infant whiplash syndrome.** This is a serious injury, and the results can be devastating.

Most of the time, infant whiplash syndrome occurs when adults, frustrated and angry with children, shake them. Most people are not aware how seriously this can hurt a child. Children have received whiplash injuries at other times also, such as at play and in car accidents. Such an injury can be sustained when anxious adults try to wake up a child who is unconscious after a fall or a convulsion.

Young infants have very weak neck muscles and only gradually develop the strength to control their heavy heads. If they are shaken, their heads wobble rapidly back and forth. The result can be somewhat like the whiplash an adult suffers in a car accident. Usually, however, the injury to the infant is much more severe. The back-and-forth vigorous movement of the head may cause damage to the spinal cord in the neck and bleeding in and on the surface of the brain. It is very important that parents and other adults know about this kind of injury and never shake an infant or child for any reason.

CHILD ABUSE IS ASSOCIATED WITH POSTTRAUMATIC STRESS DISORDER

If child abuse is not detected and brought to the attention of mental health workers for treatment, the abused individual grows up and often develops symptoms of posttraumatic stress disorder as an adult. The trauma of being abused will often affect a person's functioning in relationships—at work and personally. Often, adults who were sexually abused as children (**adults molested as children— AMACS**) may unwittingly repeat the abuse with their own children or perpetuate abuse on themselves. Suicide and substance abuse are commonly associated with these individuals as well. As children, denying the abuse helped in their daily survival, but as adults, this denial often works against their surviving daily stress.

The key for all child abuse is providing crisis intervention for abused children. If intervention comes early, many children can be prevented from experiencing delayed PTSD as adults.

REPORTING CHILD ABUSE

Mandated reporting of child abuse nationwide began after passage of the Child Abuse Prevention and Treatment Act in 1974. This federal legislation required every state to adopt specific procedures for identifying, treating, and preventing child abuse and to report the efficiency of these procedures to the Department of Health, Education, and Welfare.

Currently, all 50 states have **mandated reporting laws,** although who must report differs from state to state. Professionals who are involved with children, such as teachers, nurses, doctors, counselors, and day care workers, have become increasingly important in the detection and treatment of child abuse (Tower, 1996, pp. 13–14). Any professional who works with children must be knowledgeable about the mandated reporting laws in his or her state.

In most states, when a crisis worker suspects that abuse is occurring or has occurred, the worker must call the local child abuse registry or other welfare or law enforcement agency and report the information to a peace officer or social worker. Next, the worker usually submits a written report. Once the abuse is reported to the child protective services agency, a social worker will be responsible for investigating the case. Most reports are unsubstantiated; others are referred for crisis intervention. The goal is to remove the risk from the child rather than remove the child from the risk. When child abuse is reported, the parent enters a major crisis state and often needs intervention to get through the ensuing social services investigations, the judicial system process, and the reality of having a child taken out of the home. Most people are not prepared to deal with these things and need support and education to cope with them and to continue functioning. When a report is false, the crisis state is even worse and these parents are often in extreme distress. Many have a tremendous fear that their child will automatically be taken away when a report of suspected abuse is made, so the crisis worker needs to educate the parents on the probabilities of this *not* happening.

When the child was abused by someone other than family members, the police are to be notified. In most states, this type of abuse becomes a criminal case, and children are usually not taken from the home unless it is determined that the parents cannot protect the child.

INTERVENTIONS WITH AN ABUSED CHILD

When a crisis worker suspects that a child may be a victim of abuse, the worker must first, as gently as possible, confirm the abuse, and second, treat the problem. An abused child is not likely to come right out and confess to being abused. She or he has been taught not to tell. Colao and Hosansky (1983) propose eight reasons that children don't tell people they are being abused or sexually molested:

1. The child is physically, financially, or emotionally dependent on the abuser.

2. The abuser has threatened the child's safety or that of another family member.

3. The child blames herself or himself for what happened.

4. The child has been taught that the good are rewarded and the bad are punished and therefore assumes responsibility for the assault.

5. The child fears that no one will believe her or him, either because the abuser is a known and trusted adult or because the child has no proof.

6. The child has been given the message that sexual issues are never discussed.

7. The child does not have words to explain what happened, and adults in the child's environment aren't sensitive to what the child means.

8. The child totally blocks the incident from his or her memory, because of the trauma of the assault.

The crisis worker must provide a very safe atmosphere and assure the child that he or she will be protected by the counselor and other helpers who will be contacted. A helpful reframe is to point out that the child's parents just need guidance or help so they can learn better ways to discipline. If the child is being sexually abused, the counselor can point out that mommy or daddy is sick and needs professional help from a doctor to stop what he or she is doing. Another effective comment is to tell the child that many other children go through this, and when the helpers get involved, usually things start getting better. Some children fear for their parents; in these cases, it is quite valid to tell the child that the likelihood that the parent will go to jail is rare. Most judges want to keep families together and just want the parent to get help.

If the crisis worker believes that the parents, when they have the child alone, will coax him or her to deny the abuse, the worker should call the child protective agency and detain the child if possible. However, if the worker is going to continue working with the family, it is often helpful to reframe the reporting so it appears to be "for" rather than "against" the parents. To prevent outrage from parents, it is a good idea to have every client sign a form before treatment outlining the limits of confidentiality and mandatory reporting requirements. This can be used when informing them of a report.

Reframing for the abusing parents or spouse of a perpetrator can help reduce defensiveness also. A counselor can point out to the parents that they should be glad someone cares enough about their child to take the time and energy to protect her or him, even if the abuse doesn't really exist.

Educate the parent about the system; explain that the social services agency does not want to take their child if there is any other way to resolve the crisis. If however, the parents are guilty of severe abuse, they may remain hostile. In these cases, it is better to lose a client and get protection for the child.

Reporting child abuse to the state's protective agency can be reframed as opening a way the family can gain access to resources and services they might not otherwise get. Saying, "I need all the help I can get in serving you" will help reduce their defensiveness.

In cases of neglect, it is fairly easy to convince parents that the social services agency is there to teach or provide resources. In incest and severe physical abuse cases, parents are often more resistant, and they will need classes, groups, and marital and individual counseling.

Play Therapy   Abused children respond well to play therapy. Their concrete mental abilities prevent them from benefiting from insight-oriented verbal therapy. In play, they can work out their feelings symbolically and unconsciously. Coloring, painting, molding clay, telling stories, and playing with dolls can help clear up nightmares, acting-out behaviors, and withdrawal behaviors.

Family Therapy   Sometimes the child needs to confront her or his parents so she or he can hear an apology and acknowledgment of responsibility. These sessions can also be used to set up contracts between parents and children.

THE BATTERING PARENT

Counselors can work more easily with abusive parents if they have some idea of why the parents behave as they do. The Orange County Social Services Agency (1982) has developed an outline, adapted below, that attempts to explain **the battering parent**. Remembering this information may be helpful for the crisis workers trying to empathize with these clients, who often repulse them.

Battering parents often have these characteristics: They were violently or abusively treated physically and/or emotionally as children. They had insufficient food. They often lived with dirt and disease. As children, they suffered repeated fractures, burns, abrasions, and bruises. They commonly experienced overwhelming verbal onslaughts. They knew sexual abuse by molestation, incest, or aberrant sexual acting out. They engaged in little two-way communication. They tend to repeat the same behavior with their children.

As children, these parents developed a deep loss of worth and experienced intense, pervasive demands and criticism from their parents. They were convinced that regardless of what they did, it was not enough, not right, at the wrong time, or a source of irritation or disgrace to the parents. They never had the opportunity to work out their anger toward and forgiveness of the parents. These people tend to perpetuate those feelings into adulthood; they are often lonely and friendless whether living an active or lonely life.

When confronted with suspicions of battery, some parents display these behaviors:

- They show little concern, guilt, or remorse for the child's battered condition.

- They are fearful or angry at being asked for an explanation of the child's injuries.

- They make evasive or contradictory statements about the circumstances of the mistreatment, whether it be emotional or physical battery.

- They place blame on the child for any injuries.

- They criticize the child and say little that is positive about him or her.

- They see the worker's interest in the child's injuries or problems as an assault on themselves and their abilities.

- They refuse to participate in treatment.

- They cooperate out of fear for themselves rather than concern for the child while they try to conceal as much as possible.

- They don't touch or look at the child.

- They have unrealistic expectations of the child's capabilities and behavior, disregard for and minimization of the child's needs, and no perception of how a child can feel.

- They show overwhelming feelings of the child's worthlessness as well as their own worthlessness.

- They express guilt over and/or an expectation of another failure.

The family unit of which the battering parent is a part often has these characteristics:

- There is little communication and understanding among family members.

- The family unit is vulnerable to any and all stresses or ill winds.

- The family generally fails in problem solving.

- The family uses the child as a scapegoat for pent-up frustrations resulting from personal and marital conflicts.

- Parents demonstrate their frustrations by child abuse that is only rarely premeditated. (Orange County Social Services, 1982)

The crisis worker can reframe therapy to these people as an opportunity to correct their own behavior and do better for their children than was done to them. Providing parenting information and skills will be a part of crisis interventions. Many parents will for the first time be educated on how to talk, not yell; restrict rather than hit; and understand rather than discipline.

They will learn how to have a social relationship rather than a functional parent/object relationship. Giving them specific alternative behaviors to use when stressed with a child is useful. Here are some suggestions:

1. Call a friend or neighbor.

2. Put the child in a safe place and leave the room for a few minutes.

3. Take 10 deep breaths and 10 more.

4. Do something for yourself, such as play your favorite music, make a cup of tea or coffee, exercise, take a shower, read a magazine or book.

5. Change your activity into productive energy such as shaking a rug, doing dishes or laundry, scrubbing a floor, beating a pan or pillow, throwing away unwanted trash.

6. Sit down, close your eyes, think of a pleasant place in your memory. Do not move for several minutes.

INCEST

As mentioned earlier, many adults molested as children will seek crisis intervention. Incest is often repressed so well by children that it may not be detected even by skilled clinicians. When incest is chronic from early childhood and is accompanied by physical abuse, ritual abuse, or emotional abuse, the molested children may develop multiple personality disorder. This is the child's way to survive the traumas—by fragmenting each trauma into a different state or personality. Anyone so diagnosed needs long-term therapy, and the crisis worker needs to find a good resource. Crisis workers may be needed to provide short-term counseling for these people, to help them through the crisis of remembering and having to deal with their parents, knowing what they now know. This moment often has an emergency quality to it and suicide is to be watched for closely.

Other incest survivors can respond well to participating in support groups and reading books designed for them. Crisis workers are encouraged to become familiar with books about this topic and to refer them to clients.

The parent who commits incest needs a different intervention plan from the one for the battering parent. This father (mothers abuse also, but not so frequently) abdicates his responsibility for self, feels victimized by his family, and lashes out all at once. He must take full responsibility for his actions and work to reclaim the parts of himself that he has disowned (Caffaro, 1992). He seeks out his child as a substitute wife, caretaker, and sexual partner; this action lays on the child far more than her or his emotional capacity can handle.

Although controlling the incestuous behavior may be the initial goal of crisis intervention, at some point the offender will have to focus on the origins of his problem. According to Caffaro (1992), the incestuous behavior stems from his relationship with his own father. This relationship can be characterized as one of physical abuse, neglect, rejection, and abandonment.

Because his largely absent father did not display tender emotions toward him, the perpetrating father must learn to develop empathy in himself. Belonging to a men's group can be helpful. The members can serve as substitute fathers and can mirror the man's growing sense of self as well as demonstrate how to bond appropriately with others.

The crisis worker would do well to help this father express feelings of shame, fear, anger, and guilt in an accepting climate. Then, groups need to be created that focus on early childhood relationships with the man's father and his need to express his feelings and develop his sense of self.

::::::::::::::::::::::::::::::::

Exercises

Following are some vignettes to role-play. Using the ABC model outline, conduct a crisis interview. Practice reframing and educating.

Case 1   You are very upset. Your husband has threatened to kill your son, who is the son of another man. Your son is 4 years old. Last night your husband was drinking and your son was bothering him. He hit the boy and gave him a black eye. It is the first time he has hit your son. Usually, he takes his frustrations out on you. You tell your interviewer not to tell anyone because you are afraid of what your husband would do if he found out that he had been reported.

Case 2   You are 14 years old and you have come to this clinic because your mother believes something is wrong; your grades have been going downhill and she does not like the people you hang around with at school. Your father has been having a sexual relationship with you since you were 7 years old. You do not want to tell anyone because he threatened to throw you out of the house if you told. Your mother appears to be happy with him.

Case 3   You are an elder in your church. You run your own business, which is very successful. You live in a high-class neighborhood and everyone believes you are an ideal citizen and parent. You are raising three children on your own because your wife died two years ago. You have come in because you have for the last year been taking out your frustrations on your oldest child, who is 9 years old. You have broken his arms twice and have hit him with a board on several occasions. You realize you need help.

Case 4   You have brought your family in because you and your spouse were reported for child neglect. You tell the interviewer that you are very upset by the false statement. You are a very religious person and your children are very well taken care of. They eat at specific times and are not allowed to snack. During the interview, the children are going through the wastepaper baskets looking for food. The mother tells you that they missed breakfast this morning and will have to miss another meal because good children do not miss meals.

(**Hint:** Maintain a nonjudgmental attitude)

Spousal Abuse

It is now against the law to batter one's spouse. Sounds crazy, but this is a fairly recent law, and it is still sometimes difficult to press charges and secure justice in even severe cases of spousal abuse. In 1989, police officers were given the right to press charges if they observed spousal abuse, even if the battered spouse didn't press charges. This change of attitude is partially because of recent acknowledgment of the battered woman syndrome (a type of PTSD), which often inhibits the battered partner from pressing charges. In 1994, a new bill was passed in California requiring health practitioners who are employed in a health care facility, clinic, or doctor's office and who have knowledge of a woman being battered by a partner to report this behavior to a law enforcment officer. The reason for external control is the relatively new idea that a battered woman cannot adequately make the decision to get out of the dangerous situation if she suffers from battered woman syndrome. An additional bill was also passed in California that requires applicants for several professional licenses to show that they have completed course work in spousal abuse.

Since the murder of Nicole Brown-Simpson in June of 1994, the entire nation has been alerted to the reality of spousal abuse. The famous O. J. Simpson trial has probably been the primary reason for the abundance of spousal abuse movies, talk show topics, and legislative proposals that came in the mid-1990s. A major change this case has led to has been a focus on providing counseling services for the batterer. The obvious flaws in the judicial system have been looked at, and funding is now available to help prevent rebattering by requiring the batterer go to diversion groups instead of simply ignoring his behavior, as in years past.

Although battering of a male partner by a woman occurs, this is not discussed in this chapter. Typically, the dynamics of posttraumatic stress disorder don't exist in these cases as they do when a woman is being battered. Examine the current literature on abuse of males by their female partners to learn more about this phenomenon. About 97% of partner abuse cases are male to female battering, so it makes sense to focus on these.

DOMESTIC VIOLENCE STATISTICS

The extent of battering of women is astonishingly high. The statistics presented here indicate the severity of the problem.

- A woman is battered every 15 seconds.

- Four thousand women die each year as a result of beatings.

- Eventually, 60% of battered women leave their abusive partners.

- Beating someone is assault; assault is a crime.

- Violent families are found in every income category, ethnic background, racial group, educational level, and profession.

- Boys who grow up in violent homes are more likely to be abusive partners as adults.

- In 60% of violent homes where the female partner is beaten, so are the children.

- More children are served in battered women's shelters than are adults.

- In cases of domestic violence, 97% involve women abused by men.

- Nearly one-third of female homicide victims are killed by their husbands or boyfriends.

- Battering is the single major cause of injury to women in the United States.

- Over one-half of marriages in the United States involve at least one incident of battering.

- Absenteeism relating to spousal assaults results in an economic loss to the country of $3 million to $5 million per year plus another $100 million in medical bills.

- Of all hospital emergency room visits by women, 20% are attributed to wife beating.

- Battered wives account for 70% of all emergency room assault cases.

- Of the men in prison, 90% came from violent homes.

- Battered women have twice as many miscarriages as nonbattered women. (Woods, 1992)

COMMON MYTHS

A surprising number of misconceptions exist about domestic violence. Here are some of the most common myths.

1. Battering happens only to minorities and in lower socioeconomic families.

2. Women are masochistic and achieve unconscious satisfaction in being beaten.

3. The battered woman has a dependent personality disorder.

4. Battering is caused by alcohol and drug abuse.

5. Batterers are mentally ill. (Woods, 1992)

A HISTORICAL PERSPECTIVE

Many feminists have examined the beginnings of wife abuse in an attempt to understand this social problem. As part of a grassroots movement in the 1970s, women began to propose an alternative causality model for wife battering than was offered by traditional psychiatric theories. It became viewed as a social illness rather than the result of a man's or woman's individual pathology. Women, according to these pioneer feminists, have always been portrayed as subservient in the media and have been trained to be so by parents and men alike since ancient times.

As far back as 750 B.C.E., laws were written that sanctioned wife abuse, making a woman property and the husband responsible for her. A "rule of thumb" law existed until 1864. This law stated that a "man was allowed to beat his wife as long as the stick he used was no wider than a thumb" (Fenoglio, 1989).

In 1974, the first battered women's shelter was created in Minnesota. Since that time, about 700 such shelters have been established throughout the United States. This is not enough, but at least it is a start. Feminists are now proposing that more emphasis be placed on making the man leave the home as he's the one with the problem, rather than sending the wife and children out to a shelter for safety (Woods, 1992).

Women in Western industrialized nations are more fortunate than those in certain South American countries where wife battering is legally sanctioned. In a recent case, a Brazilian man was acquitted of murdering his wife using a defense of *machismo*. The blow to his honor of having to live with the fact that she had committed adultery was more than a man should have to bear, according to the rules of this male-dominated society.

WHY DO THE WOMEN STAY?

You can probably make some guesses as to why a woman would stay with a man who verbally, emotionally, physically, or sexually abuses her. How many of the following had you thought of?

- She is afraid that he'll kill her, the pets, her children, her family. He often threatens to do this.

- Her religious beliefs forbid her leaving ('til death do us part).

- She is influenced by the profamily society (stay together at all costs).

- She is economically dependent on the man. He often has forced her to quit school or her job, or never allowed her to work or know about their finances.

- She has no resources (no place to go, no transportation, no money).

- The children need a father.

- She gets no support from her family; many of these women are told to stick it out.

- She hopes he'll change—because she loves him when he's not abusive.

- She believes him when he says it is her fault he beats her.

- She sees no other options.

- She feels insecure and unable to take care of herself (psychological dependence).

It will be helpful for the crisis worker to have an understanding of the characteristics of both the batterer and the battered woman (Table 10.1). These traits are offered as a general guideline to aid you in empathizing with your clients and to help identify when battering exists. Denial can be so strong in these relationships that the battering may not be mentioned unless you inquire about it. This is not to say a counselor should question the partners in a harsh, judgmental

TABLE 10.1 Characteristics of a Batterer, a Battered Wife, Their Children

Batterer	Battered Wife	Children
Shows poor impulse control, is explosive	Sees self as suffering, being a martyr; endures frustration	Show limited tolerance; have poor impulse control and high frustration levels
Suffers from stress and psychosomatic disorders; masks dysfunction well, depending on social and educational sophistication	Has depressive and hysterical complaints, psychosomatic complaints	Show depression, stress; have school absences, delinquent behavior
Is emotionally dependent	Is economically and emotionally dependent	
Has secret depressions known to family	May be secret user of drugs and alcohol	May be at high risk for alcohol and drug abuse, sexual acting out, running away, isolation, loneliness, fear
Has limited capacity for delayed reinforcement	Shows unlimited patience; travels far on tiny bits of reinforcement	Have both poor impulse control and hope for improvement
Shows insatiable ego needs and narcissism	Is unsure of own ego needs; defines self in terms of family	Have shaky definition of themselves, grapple with childlike parents
Presents self at times as having potential for change and improvement	Has unrealistic hope that change is imminent; believes the man's promises	Display mixture of hope and depression
Has poor definition of self in parenting role; has low self-esteem and high self-disappointment	Has low self-esteem; hopes mate will get lucky break	Have low self-esteem; see themselves with few options to succeed

(continued)

TABLE 10.1 *Continued*

Batterer	Battered Wife	Children
Sees self as having poor social skills; is closer to mate than other people	Is aware of increasing social isolation, loss of contact with family	Show either social isolation or total identification with peers
Makes accusations against mate; is jealous, afraid of being abandoned or cheated	Is unable to convince partner of her loyalty	Use bargaining behavior with parents
Uses many methods to contain mate; uses spy tactics; cleverness depends on level of sophistication	Allows containment/confinement and restriction by mate; interprets it as a sign that partner cares	Practice deception, lying; make excuses for outings; steal and cheat
Has no sense of violating others' personal boundaries; accepts no blame for failures or violence	Loses sight of personal boundaries for self and children; accepts all blame for domestic situation	Have poor definition of personal boundaries
Believes his forcible behavior is aimed at securing the family nucleus	Believes that transient acceptance of violence leads to resolution of family problems	Have little or no understanding of dynamics of violence; assume it is normal
Apparently feels no guilt on emotional level, even after intellectual recognition	Accepts guilt for mate's behavior; thinks mate can't help it	Feel self-blame for family feuding, separation, and divorce
Has generational history of family violence	Has generational history of family violence	Will probably continue pattern of family violence in own adulthood
Participates in pecking order battering	Participates in pecking order battering	Kill animals, batter younger siblings and sometimes parents in later years

(continued)

Batterer	Battered Wife	Children
Has assaultive skills that improve with age and experience, accompanied by a rise in danger potential and lethality risks	Learns which behavioral events will divert or precipitate mate's violence, but level of carelessness increases, judgment of lethality potential deteriorates over time	Use violence as problem-solving technique in school, with peers, and with family
Is demanding and often assaultive in sexual activities; sometimes punishes with abstinence; at times experiences impotence	Has poor sexual self-image; assumes that role is to accept partner's sexual behavior totally	Have poor sexual image, uncertainty about appropriate behavior, immaturity with peers
Increases assaultive behavior when mate is pregnant; pregnancy often marks first assault	Is at high risk for assault during pregnancy	Are at higher risk for battering during mother's pregnancy

Source: Adapted from Boyd & Klingbell, 1979.

manner, but if evidence begins to show itself, the counselor should consider abuse a possibility.

THE BATTERING CYCLE

Spousal abuse can be understood as a recurrent three-phase pattern. According to Woods (1992), **the battering cycle** usually starts out in the honeymoon phase.

Honeymoon Phase The man may show jealousy, which makes the woman feel special and important at first. They feel love and often dependency on one another. Mutuality, which is often a part of healthy intimacy, is not present, however.

Tension Building Phase At this point there may be minor incidents such as criticizing, yelling, and blaming. The woman often walks on eggshells because she believes it may be her fault that he's upset. He says it's her fault, and she spends her time trying to figure out how she can prevent any violence from happening. The batterer may still feel in control of himself at this point. He may see that he has a problem, and if intervention could be given at this point, there might be a window of opportunity for preventing the next stage. Unfortunately, the tension usually escalates into a violent episode.

Explosive Phase   The tension will be released in a variety of ways, depending on the history of violence in the relationship. Typically, it gets worse over time. At this point, the batterer is out of control. He may terrorize his wife for hours, break things, hit, spit, push, choke, burn, tie up, rape, or kick her. She will often survive this stage with bruises and broken bones and may end up in a hospital. Sometimes the police will be called at this stage.

It is after this violent episode that the window of opportunity exists for the woman before denial sets in. However, in most situations, denial does set in for both, and there is a return to an adapted honeymoon stage.

Honeymoon Stage—Again   Now, the batterer apologizes and begs her to believe the violence won't happen again. She can't believe it actually happened and is in shock. This leaves her vulnerable to accepting his apologies and flowers. After all, she loves him and has hope that it won't happen again. There is a false resolution based on denial and minimization, and life goes on. He may encourage her to go shopping or throw a party; he treats her well for awhile. Then, as is normal in any relationship, tension develops, and without appropriate stress management and communication skills, the cycle continues. Sadly, the honeymoon stage is the first to be eliminated and battering relationships end up being a tension-violence cycle.

THE BATTERED WOMAN SYNDROME

After this pattern has been experienced for more than a couple of cycles, the woman often develops the **battered woman syndrome**. This is a type of posttraumatic stress disorder that needs to be addressed and treated by the crisis counselor.

Three components of battered woman syndrome can be identified:

1. The Posttraumatic Stress Disorder Symptoms   Because of the traumatic effects of victimization by violence, various symptoms develop, as this violence is outside the range of normal human experience. The woman may reexperience the trauma in dreams, avoid stimuli associated with the trauma, avoid feelings, and experience a numbing of general responsiveness. She may be detached, experience loss of interest, show increased arousal and anxiety, and have difficulty sleeping.

2. Learned Helplessness   A state of learned helplessness develops after she attempts to leave or get help and meets with no success, because of system failure or other factors. She defends against this frustration by learning to survive rather than escape the battering.

3. Self-Destructive Coping Responses to Violence   As she may perceive that her only choice is to stay (she may fear getting killed or has no place to go), she often uses drugs and alcohol to escape or may attempt suicide; at least, electing to die would be her choice (Fenoglio, 1989).

After determining that a client is a battered woman, a counselor must attempt to understand the phenomenological view of the woman without judging her. It may be helpful for you to have an idea of some of the beliefs these women have, based on previous cases of counselors working at battered women's centers and shelters. Woods (1992) says that many of these women were brought up to take care of men, and believe it is their role to nurture their partner when he's hurt.

Also, the woman may have been convinced by books, the media, or other mental health professionals that she is a co-dependent and is the sick one for deciding to stay. Rather than acknowledging that women in our society are socialized to be dependent, she may be judging herself and calling herself weak for staying.

Other women may not even be aware they are in an abusive relationship, and you may have to ease the client into accepting this idea and giving up denial. The Southern California Coalition on Battered Women (SCCBW) (1989) offers some useful questions to ask a woman who may be unsure of whether her relationship is truly abusive:

How many of these things has your partner done to you?

- Ignored your feelings

- Ridiculed or insulted women as a group

- Ridiculed or insulted your most valued beliefs, your religion, race, heritage, or class

- Withheld approval, appreciation, or affection as punishment

- Continually criticized you, called you names, shouted at you

- Humiliated you in private or public

- Refused to socialize with you

- Kept you from working, controlled your money, made all decisions

- Refused to work or share money

- Took car keys or money away from you

- Regularly threatened to leave or told you to leave

- Threatened to hurt you or your family

- Punished or deprived the children when angry at you

- Threatened to kidnap the children if you left

- Abused, tortured, or killed pets to hurt you

- Harassed you about affairs he imagined you were having

- Manipulated you with lies and contradictions

- Destroyed furniture, punched holes in walls, broken appliances

- Wielded a gun in a threatening way

Other questions that may help the woman decide if she is in an abusive relationship might be these:

> Do you often doubt your judgment or wonder if you are crazy?

> Are you often afraid of your partner and do you express your opinion less and less freely?

> Have you developed fears of other people and tend to see others less often?

> Do you spend a lot of time watching for your partner's bad and not so bad moods before bringing up a subject?

> Do you ask your partner's permission to spend money, take classes, or socialize with friends?

If she answers yes to many of these questions, the woman has probably been abused and has changed as a result of being abused (Southern California Coalition on Battered Women, 1989).

You may also need to educate her on common behaviors that indicate a battering relationship by informing her that she may be a battered woman if these statements fit her:

- Is frightened of her partner's temper

- Is often compliant because she is afraid to hurt her partner's feelings or is afraid of her partner's anger

- Has the urge to rescue her partner when or because her partner is troubled

- Finds herself apologizing to herself or to others for her partner's behavior when she is treated badly

- Has been hit, kicked, shoved, or had things thrown at her by her partner when he was jealous or angry

- Makes decisions about activities and friends according to what her partner wants or how her partner will react

- Drinks or uses drugs (Southern California Coalition on Battered Women, 1989)

INTERVENING

The purpose of intervention with a battered woman is to encourage her to act for her own well-being and safety. The goals of intervention with a battered woman are these:

1. Let her know help is available.

2. Give her specific information about resources.

3. Document the battering with accurate medical records.

4. Acknowledge her experiences in a supportive manner.

5. Respect her fight to make her own decisions.

While you are helping her identify the battering and her perspective, you will also be offering her your knowledge of battering and reframing some of her ideas. Additionally, the crisis worker will offer empowering and supportive comments as well as suggest resources such as books, shelters, or groups.

Woods (1992) believes it is also important to give the woman various facts about battering—presented at the beginning of this section. This will help her see she is not alone. Additionally, she needs to be told that the violence usually increases in intensity and frequency and that her batterer needs professional help if he is ever to change.

Reframes Woods (1992), like most feminists working in the battered women's movement, believes that someone needs to tell the woman that the batterer has the problem and nothing she can do will prevent the next battering episode. This goes against her belief that if she only had dinner ready, had the kids quiet, made the bed, and so on, he wouldn't get upset. Pointing out to her that he is sick and needs help from a professional may be accepted by her.

Another reframe has to do with her belief that she is weak for staying and for using drugs and alcohol. The crisis worker might reframe these behaviors as evidence of strength. Her behavior can be equated to that of a prisoner of war who learns how to get what he or she needs to survive. Her weakness is now strength. This new perspective can often turn her around into believing she has strength to take new action with the crisis worker's support.

Cusick (1992) also agrees that the "therapist must show the client that she has orchestrated her own survival and has the skills to continue to do so" (p. 48).

Empowerment and Support The last thing the battered woman needs is for someone else to decide for her what she should do. Avoiding doing so can be very stressful for the crisis worker because often the battered woman client will choose to stay with her batterer and be abused again.

Typically, she has had every decision made for her by the batterer, so the best thing the counselor can do is provide her with choices and support them. The counselor can give her names, phone numbers, and suggestions. Her main concern will often be "How am I going to be safe?" The counselor may let her know she is at most risk when she leaves her batterer but that if she wishes, a plan can be made that will assure her safety.

Helping her explore her own resources, such as family, friends, or church, is a good idea before you offer your own ideas. Battered women's shelters are usually free and should be used as a last resort. They are not like resort hotels, and a considerable amount of freedom is lost in a shelter. However, if there is nowhere else to go and/or no funds, the shelter is a great resource.

Following is an outline presented by Judy Bambas, volunteer coordinator at the Women's Transitional Living Center, on how to provide effective support for a battered woman:

1. Let her know you believe her.
"Many women have been beaten by their partners."
"I'm glad you've told me about the abuse."

2. Let her express her feelings. She has a right to be angry, scared, etc. This may be the first time she is feeling safe enough to express anger over the abuse.
"You seem very afraid of your partner."
"You seem nervous talking about being abused."
"You seem very angry about being abused."

3. Express your concern for her safety and the safety of her children. She may deny that abuse occurs or deny the level of danger to herself or her children.
"This injury shows you are in great danger. You have a right to be safe."
"Your safety is important. I'm very concerned about you and your children."

4. Let her know that help is available. Keep information at hand to share with her about helplines, shelters, counseling, and other resources. Ask her if she wants to report the abuse to the police. Explain slowly and carefully the choices available to her. She may need time and a safe place before she makes any decisions.
"I have information that can help you."
"There are many people in the community who can help you."

5. Reinforce the idea that nobody deserves to be beaten. She tends to believe some of the myths about domestic violence even though they may contradict her own reality. Remind her that she is not the cause of the beatings.
"No one deserves to be hit."
"You aren't the reason he hits you."

6. Realize that she may be embarrassed and humiliated about the abuse. She may worry that those who have offered to help in the past (family, friends, etc.) will be too burned out to help this time. Support her desire for help now.
"You may feel embarrassed, but there are many women who have told me they are abused."

7. Be aware of the effects of isolation and control through fear. The woman may be physically and/or socially isolated due to location, language, intimidation, economic dependence, etc. Remind her that she is not alone. Connecting with others, through services such as support groups, can help break the isolation battered women experience. Support her efforts to reach out to others.
"You are not alone. Others can help and understand. I have information that may help you."

8. Assure her that you will not betray her trust.
"What you share with me is confidential. My concern is for your safety."

9. Document the battering with specific information in her medical record. Her medical records may be used as evidence if she decides to press charges against the batterer. Be specific in description and sites of injuries. If patient presents abuse as the source of injuries, note "Patient stated . . .," then continue statement with who injured whom with what. If patient refers to an instrument or weapon used by the abuser, note that in her record. If the injuries are inconsistent with the patient's explanation, make a note of it. If you suspect battering but the patient denies it, note "suspected abuse" in her record. Your notes may help identify her as battered on a future visit.

10. Remember that she may have other problems that demand immediate intervention. She may lack food or housing, be unable to care for her children or herself. Make appropriate referrals. If she is staying in a hospital, she may fear that the batterer will visit her. She may want her location to be kept confidential.
"It seems you have a concern about housing. I have information about other resources."

THE BATTERER

Is there ever hope for a batterer? Can he be cured? Can marriage counseling help? The answers to these questions are tricky because they depend on the man and his motivation. According to Woods (1992), there is only a 1% success rate for batterer treatment programs. Despite this very low estimate, some studies do show that court-ordered counseling may help.

A 1990 outcome study compared 120 court-referred abusers with a comparison group of 101 nonreferred abusers. Results indicated that 75% of court-referred men who attended court-sponsored counseling reduced their recidivism rate. Another 1990 study found that after counseling, abusive men had been violence free for one year. Based on these studies, the Family Service Center of the Marine Corps in San Diego established a model program to combat domestic violence (Barnett & LaViolette, 1993, pp. 126–127).

More and more battered women's shelters are including batterers' programs in their facilities. Many more therapists are offering groups for this population, who really need the help. Judges are mandating counseling instead of jail time when a man is charged and convicted of battering his partner. This trend demonstrates a greater focus on the man's part in the problem.

A PHENOMENOLOGICAL VIEW OF THE BATTERER

It is possible that crisis workers will on occasion interview a batterer. This man may or may not see himself as a batterer, may or may not have chosen to seek help, and may or may not be amenable to intervention depending on his personal and social resources.

Recently, a batterer was brought in to counseling by his wife of two years after he hit her with a broomstick. He didn't perceive himself as a "wife beater," but was willing to accept whatever the counselor told him. The therapist proceeded to suggest to him that he might be a batterer if the following behaviors fit him:

- You are very jealous.
- You sulk silently when upset.
- You have an explosive temper.
- You criticize and put down your partner a lot.
- You have difficulty expressing your feelings.
- You drink or use drugs.
- You believe that it is the male role to be in charge and/or have contempt for women.
- You are protective of your partner to the point of being controlling.
- You are controlling of your partner's behavior, of money, of decisions.
- You have broken things, thrown things at your partner, hit, shoved, or kicked your partner when angry.
- You were physically or emotionally abused by a parent.

After realizing how many of these behaviors described him, the man began to define himself as a wife beater and realized he needed help to change. As with many batterers, he had a history of poor role modeling by his own father and was in fact abused as a child.

INTERVENTION

With his wife present, the therapist began to educate the man about the dynamics of power and control typically found in abusive relationships. The client agreed that most of these were present in their relationship.

Woods (1992) offers an outline of the patterns the husband used to maintain power and control. They have general application to many batterers.

Intimidation: Putting her in fear by using looks, actions, gestures, loud voice, smashing things, destroying her property.

Isolation: Controlling what she does, who she sees and talks to, where she goes.

Emotional abuse: Putting her down or making her feel bad about herself, calling her names, making her think she's crazy, using mind games.

Economic abuse: Trying to keep her from getting or keeping a job. Making her ask for money, giving her an allowance, taking her money.

Sexual abuse: Making her do sexual things against her will. Physically attacking the sexual parts of her body. Treating her like a sex object.

Using children: Making her feel guilty about the children, using the children to give messages, using visitation as a way to harass her.

Threats: Making and/or carrying out threats to do something to hurt her emotionally, threatening to take the children away, threatening to commit suicide, threatening to report her to welfare.

Using male privilege: Treating her like a servant, making all the big decisions, acting like the master of the castle.

Physical abuse: Twisting, biting, tripping, pushing, shoving, hitting, slapping, choking, pushing down, punching, kicking, using a weapon, beating, grabbing.

After educating this man on the destructive patterns he was using, the therapist attempted marital counseling and contracted for 12 crisis intervention sessions. They worked on communication skills and compromise as is done with other couples. An odd thing was occurring, though. Nothing ever satisfied the man, and he was still angry. His wife, he said, wouldn't give him sex, didn't spend enough time with him, spent money wrong, and was sick too much. It soon became apparent that his needs were not being met by anyone. After two months, he reoffended. He told his wife this was how he was and would always be! She then decided she would have to divorce him. (Later she changed her mind, and they continue to try to work things out with periodic marriage counseling sessions.)

Despite the education and many attempts by others to empathize with his needs, he still was not "cured." Why? Most feminists and clinicians who work in the field of domestic violence believe that traditional family therapy is not an appropriate intervention in domestic violence cases (Segel-Evans, 1991). They believe that the batterer is completely responsible for the violence, and that he should be the one in therapy to work on his violence problem. Marriage counseling gives him the message that his wife has a part in creating the violence, thereby exonerating him from accepting full responsibility for his sickness. With this perception, the recommended treatment for domestic violence cases is twofold. First, the woman should be assessed for safety and given choices and support. It should be emphasized to her that her symptoms evolved only after the trauma of being abused. Second, the man should be the one to leave and attend groups for battering men and/or enter individual therapy to work on his violence. He must accept responsibility and learn more appropriate ways to communicate, deal with stress, conquer his insecurities, and learn to meet his own needs.

Not all clinicians would agree with this perspective. Kugler (1992) agrees with many of the ideas, but believes the battered woman is not the passive helpless victim she is often portrayed to be. He holds the victim accountable for her own violence toward the husband, which may provoke his violence. Also, he believes therapists need to point out to the woman that the abuse won't stop unless she makes the man accountable, legally and morally. He suggests that mental health workers help empower the woman by assisting her to "realistically evaluate the situation and understand the interactional dynamics of the relationship" (p. 45). Then she can learn to alter her behavior, which may help alter his behaviors.

Kugler feels that too many women get weakened by well-meaning counselors who set the boundaries for them. This, he says, doesn't help the woman in the long run, for she is likely to enter another abusive relationship without having learned effective limit-setting behaviors.

Kugler does not believe that the woman gets blamed for the battering simply by understanding the abusive behavior in the context of the violence. He says that those who dogmatically say that couples counseling is never an appropriate crisis intervention modality greatly limit help, especially for the woman who truly believes she has a part in the abuse and wants to work on changing her behavior.

As with all crisis work, crisis workers must keep in mind all this information as they interact with each client, using what will be helpful and putting aside parts that are not relevant.

Exercise

Try role-playing these vignettes. Notice your own feelings. Frustration? Powerlessness? Anger?

Case 1   Jamie is 35 years old. She has been married for 13 years. Her husband is a college professor who makes a good salary. She is a college graduate who has never worked outside the home. Jamie has two children, ages 10 and 8. She came to the counseling center complaining of depressed feelings. She is concerned for the welfare of her children. She doesn't feel capable or good enough. She feels helpless.

Case 2   A 27-year-old nurse comes to you. She is working to put her husband through medical school. She is complaining about being unassertive. She sits uneasily in the chair. When she moves, she sometimes grimaces in pain. She loves her husband and wants to please him but does not think she can. Due to her lack of sexual responsiveness, he sometimes gets extremely angry and "does things."

Case 3   A 65-year-old woman comes to you. She lives in a retirement trailer village with her husband who is a retired salesman. She comes to the session crying. Her mouth is cut and her right eye is swollen and bruised. She expresses anger and hatred toward all men. Her husband beat her last night because there was too much grease on his plate. She wants to leave but is afraid. He has threatened to kill her if she tries to leave.

Sexual Assault

Rape is the common term used when discussing sexual assault. It is a frequent oc-currence in our society. In the last few years, there have been several rape trials publicized in the media, and talk shows are exploring date and acquaintance rape.

Some of the clients who seek crisis intervention will have just recently been raped. Others will have been raped many years ago but were triggered to come for help by a current event (e.g., watching the Tyson trial brought out the anger of a 69-year-old woman who was raped by her fiancee 40 years ago—Heller, 1992). Despite the time difference, victims of rape often go through similar stages called **rape trauma syndrome** (another type of PTSD). This syndrome is recognized in California courts as a condition that occurs following a rape. The crisis worker must help the rape victim proceed through these stages, to be discussed later.

COMMON MYTHS AND FACTS ABOUT RAPE

Like so many other common topics, rape has generated its own set of myths. Wesley (1989), a rape crisis counselor with the Orange County Sexual Assault Network, presented the following typical myths and the facts during a presenta-tion to a crisis intervention class at California State University, Fullerton.

1. *Myth:* Rape is rare and will never happen to me.
   Fact: Every 6 minutes a rape takes place. The FBI estimates that one in four women and one in ten men will be sexually assaulted in their lifetimes. Most rapes are not even reported.

2. *Myth:* Rape is about sexual desire.
   Fact: Sex has little to do with it. Sex becomes the weapon, the vehicle to accomplish the desired end result, which is to overwhelm, overpower, embarrass, and humiliate another person. Also, looking at typical rape victims shows clearly that this crime is not about sex: 90% of disabled women will be raped. Children and the elderly are also at high risk of being raped because of their vulnerability. An attacker can easily overpower these victims.

3. *Myth:* Rape only happens by strangers. Forced sex among acquaintances is not rape.
   Fact: Between 60% and 80% of all rapes are between a victim and an assailant who know each other. Additionally, for raped women from 15 to 25 years of age, 70% of the assaults are date rape. The woman is vulnerable at these ages because she is starting to have sexual feelings, set limits, and pursue inti-mate relationships.

4. *Myth:* Rapists are psychotic or sick men.
   Fact: Less than 5% of convicted rapists are clinically diagnosed as psychotic. The media presents these cases to the public because of the bizarre nature of the rapes, but the rapist can be anyone.

5. *Myth:* Women who get raped are asking for it.

Fact: Women who try to look attractive and sexy are asking for attention, approval, and acceptance—not victimization. Babies in diapers and fully clothed grandmothers are evidence that rape is not caused by sexy clothes.

6. *Myth:* He can't help it; once he's turned on, he can't stop.

Fact: Could he stop if his mother walked in? Humans can control their sexual behaviors. (Adapted from Wesley, 1989)

WHAT IS RAPE?

Rape is a sexual act against one's will; it is sexual violence. It might be intercourse, oral sex, anal sex, or penetration with any foreign object. Rape is a felony that carries a sentence of 1 to 16 years for each count. Most rapists don't go to prison because most rapes aren't reported. About 95% of rapists are men. Almost none of the men who are raped report it because of the homosexual aspect of male-to-male rape. This is unfortunate because male rape victims underutilize crisis services, leaving a population of men who will be struggling emotionally with feelings of humiliation and loss of masculinity.

RAPE TRAUMA SYNDROME

Rape victims often experience three identifiable stages after the assault. Together, these are referred to as rape trauma syndrome. A crisis worker is well advised to understand these so as to better join with the client at any given point in the crisis.

Stage 1: Immediate Crisis Reaction   During this, the acute phase, which lasts two to six weeks, the victim experiences emotional pain, specific physical pain, and general soreness. As with posttraumatic stress disorder, sleep disturbances are common as the person often feels vulnerable when asleep or is weary of nightmares. Eating disturbances will also be seen, evidenced by nausea and loss of appetite. Emotional reactions will encompass hysteria, fear, anxiety, humiliation, shame, embarrassment, guilt, anger, and an acute sense of vulnerability. How the victim copes has a lot to do with previous coping style.

Stage 2: Reorganization   As the initial feelings start to subside, the victim realizes she may get through it. She may tell herself she needs to get back to normal, and she just can't keep dwelling on the attack. This type of thinking leads to a state of denial whereby the experience is minimized or blocked altogether.

If she doesn't get professional help, she may stay stuck in this phase. She may be able to function somewhat, but it will be at a lower level than before the rape. Mood swings, depression, psychosomatic illnesses, substance abuse, phobias, failed relationships, sexual dysfunctions, suicide attempts, and revictimizations may exist. The crisis worker is likely to encounter a woman who has been stuck in this phase for several years because she just can't function any more.

As discussed in Chapter 1, it is easier to work with a victim in Stage 1 because she hasn't invested energy in denial yet. The longer she waits, the longer the intervention will have to be.

Stage 3: Reintegration   In reintegration, the client moves from being a victim to being a survivor. With proper crisis intervention, she can emerge as a stronger, more assertive person, more aware of herself and with increased self-esteem. After all, she has survived an extremely traumatic experience. That is evidence of her strength (Wesley, 1989).

INTERVENTION

Much of the material about how to work with rape victims comes from literature from the Orange County Sexual Assault Network. In addition, the ABC model presented in this book has been incorporated into its working model with its clients.

If a rape victim happens to contact a crisis worker immediately after the rape, she or he will likely be confused about what steps to take. The person may feel guilty and not think about being a victim who has the right to medical attention and police assistance (Heller, 1992). A counselor can help the survivor decide what to do by giving her information and resources. Overall, an **empowerment model** is suggested with this population. It encompasses the steps described next.

A: Achieving Contact   During the first five minutes or so, the survivor will probably be sizing up the crisis worker, thinking, "Can this counselor handle what I've got to say?" It is important for the helper to be calm, clear, and trustworthy—somehow giving the message, "I'm not going to be shocked."

During this early contact, reassure and validate the client for seeking help. Ask questions to get a clear picture of what happened; doing this will help get the interview moving and will calm down the client. At this point, it isn't important to attain a full graphic picture of every detail. Reflecting, paraphrasing, and asking open-ended questions are excellent strategies for this stage.

Assessing for symptoms is also important in case the client needs help from a physician. Sometimes a client will be severely depressed and will need medication to function at even a minimum level.

B: Boiling Down the Problem to Basics   At this point, it is appropriate to identify how the client is feeling now, keeping her in the present. To understand what makes the rape a crisis for her, a good question is this: "What is the hardest part for you?" Her answer will give the counselor a place to begin, a focus for reframing, educating, empowering, and supporting the client. The statements following are models of the types you might find helpful at this time.

Supportive Statements. Every rape victim needs to be believed and her experience legitimized. People rarely make up stories about being raped. Use of statements like the ones shown here will help restore the woman's dignity and reduce her sense of embarrassment.

"It must have been frightening."

"It wasn't your fault; you did not ask for this to happen and you deserve to be taken care of and treated with dignity and respect."

"It is difficult to scream when you're frightened."

"Sure you were hitchhiking, but not to get raped."

Educational Statements. The client can benefit from learning about rape trauma syndrome. This information will help normalize her experience so she doesn't think she's reacting unnaturally. She will also benefit from knowing that rape is not about sex but about power. The rapist just happened to use sexual behavior as the weapon of assault.

Empowering Statements. Constantly help the client focus on being in control of her decisions.

"You weren't in control during the assault, but now you are in control. You've already chosen to seek help from me. Let's look at some other options so you can make more choices."

Reframing. The crisis worker can offer a different way of interpreting the victim's behavior while being raped. She can help the client see that in no way should she consider herself stupid for not resisting the rapist.

"It sounds like you were very wise to keep still and quiet rather than risk further injury by fighting."

C: Coping By exploring the ways the client has coped with other crisis situations, you can activate her strengths and further empower her. Encourage her to think of other ways to cope. Perhaps she can make use of her current support systems and reach out to new systems such as support groups.

After the client has presented all the ways of coping she can think of, the crisis worker can then suggest other resources and brainstorm additional ways. The worker might recommend literature, taking a self-defense course, or calling a hot line; she also might offer to accompany the client to the police station or doctor's office. As long as the client makes the decision, many options are possible for the crisis worker.

Recently, there has been a lot of attention on date rape. This is a situation in which a woman voluntarily goes out with a man and may even engage in some form of sexual conduct; at some point, however, the relationship becomes involuntary. This is very common among the 15- to 24-year-old age group. It brings up some especially difficult issues because the woman is confused. At a certain point, she wanted to be with this person. However, when the situation gets out of control, she often does not know what to do.

Steiner (1994), the clinical supervisor at Mariposa Women's Center in Orange, California, offers some valuable thoughts on how to educate and support women who are survivors of date rape or any woman at risk of date rape:

First, no one can predict how [she] will react in a threatening situation. Nor can she blame herself for not reacting differently. Too much of a survivor's recovery is spent on trying to redo what has already happened. We all can only change our futures, not our pasts. Don't be afraid to be seen as rude or paranoid. If he gives you a hard time or humiliates you because you don't want to go in his room, or to his apartment or for a drive, he is exhibiting a behavior common to date rapists—no respect for your feelings.

Go ahead, wreck his stereo, or anything else you can reach if he doesn't stop when you say "no." When it's all over, he'll have a hard time saying, "You know you wanted it and no one would believe you anyway" if his room is in a shambles. If somehow you were wrong about him, a new stereo is a lot cheaper than a year of recovery from rape.

When you don't report it and you don't tell your close friends, you increase the damage inflicted by the rape by isolating and blaming yourself. If your friends don't react the way you had hoped, don't blame yourself. Remember that what happened to you is bad and they are afraid to believe it could happen to them. They need help in facing it.

Everybody needs help in recovering from traumatic events. Ask for what you need from friends, family, rape support centers, and others trained to help. People do recover from rape, and they are never the same. They can be stronger, more compassionate of others, and more respectful of themselves.

Exercise

Conduct an interview using the following case vignettes, but—instead of what you *should* do—try to be judgmental, nonsupportive, and nonempowering. Discuss the effects these behaviors had on the client and counselor. Then conduct new interviews using the ABC model and compare the results.

Case 1   You have recently been raped by an old friend. You went to a party, had a few drinks, and on the way to your car this friend of yours forced you into your car and raped you. You have told no one. Your biggest problem is that this friend works for the same company you do.

Case 2   You are a male and were raped by two men. You are feeling a great deal of shame because you feel you are the only male this has ever happened to. You are also very angry because you were unable to do anything to stop this incident. One of the men had a gun. You are afraid no one will believe your story.

Case 3   You were walking across campus and four men forced you into their van and raped you. There were other people around when it happened and no one did anything to stop the event. When you told your parents, they became upset with you and believed you were to blame. Your father told you that if you would just stop wearing such sexy clothes these things would not happen. You are confused and feel unable to study and have thought about suicide.

Key Terms for Study:

AMACS (adults molested as children): Adults who often manifest posttraumatic stress disorder because of the unresolved emotional residue of childhood sexual abuse. Support groups for this population are increasing.

Battering cycle: The events leading to, through, and away from domestic violence. The cycle begins in the honeymoon period when both partners are in love and feel happy. The tension builds and eventually an explosion happens, either verbally or physically. After the explosion, the batterer feels relieved and seeks forgiveness and the honeymoon begins again. Eventually, the honeymoon period goes away and the couple oscillates between tension and violence.

Battering parent: Parent who beats a child—as a disciplinary action, out of frustration, or for other reasons. This parent was probably abused as a child and lacks skills to properly communicate with and discipline a child. The parent's anger is out of control and he or she is using the child to relieve stress.

Battered woman syndrome: A form of posttraumatic stress disorder frequently manifested by women who are continually beaten by their domestic partners. Often, the woman develops a sense of helplessness and hopelessness. She does not consider leaving her abuser; rather, she focuses on surviving the abuse. She is often in a daze.

Child abuse: One type of trauma that can cause posttraumatic stress disorder (too prevalent in our society). The four most common kinds of child abuse are these:

> **Physical abuse:** Indicated by tissue damage, broken bones, or organ damage from nonaccidental means. Burns, welts, bruises, and other marks are also indications.
> **Sexual abuse:** Occurs when an adult gratifies himself or herself sexually with a minor. Abuse ranges from fondling, to voyeurism, to intercourse.
> **General neglect:** Indicated when parent or guardian fails to provide for a child's basic needs such as food, shelter, clothing, and medical care.
> **Emotional abuse:** Difficult to prove. Occurs when a child is continually humiliated, criticized, and deprived of love. Usually leads to severe psychiatric symptoms.

Child protective agency: A county or state agency established to protect children from abuse by investigating reports of child abuse and intervening when necessary.

Empowerment model: An intervention model for clients in crisis that helps to restore the person's sense of control. When working with survivors of rape, crisis interventionists use this type of approach when issues of power and feelings of helplessness are discussed. The survivor is presented with alternative ideas that help him or her feel more in control and powerful. The worker may want to point out choices and decisions that are still under the person's control, even though the sexual assault may not have been.

Infant whiplash syndrome: A very serious form of child abuse that results when a baby is shaken. The shaking causes the brain to roll around in the skull cavity. This abuse can lead to brain damage or death.

Mandated reporting laws: Laws requiring professionals such as counselors, teachers, and medical personnel who work with children to report any suspicions of child abuse to either a child protective agency or a law enforcement agency. Exactly who is required by law to report and the procedures for reporting vary from state to state.

Posttraumatic Stress Disorder (PTSD):   A state in which the person reexperiences a traumatic event as flashbacks or in nightmares, feels anxious and hypervigilant, and has impaired functioning.

Rape trauma syndrome: A form of posttraumatic stress disorder commonly found in women and men after a sexual assault. First, there is the immediate crisis reaction with all the symptoms of anxiety one would expect. Then, the rape survivor attempts to reorganize. Without help, the survivor reorganizes by using ego defense mechanisms. With help, the survivor learns to cope with her or his feelings and works through the trauma to move to the third phase, reintegration. Finally, the survivor comes to terms with the assault and integrates it into her or his life.

CHAPTER ELEVEN

Selected Situational Crises of Adolescence, Adulthood, and Old Age

A number of situations that can become crises are unique to specific periods of life. In this chapter, several of these situations are examined and discussed.

Crises of Adolescence

Adolescence is a stormy period in which the teenager is struggling for independence, yet still needing guidance and emotional support. When a family system does not allow for both **autonomy** and nurturance, the teenager may engage in various self-destructive behaviors largely in an effort to meet either or both of these needs. Although individual and group therapy are very effective with this population and are used widely in teen shelters and group homes, a look at the family structure and intervention with the family is vital for permanent resolution of the problems. For this reason, most adolescent treatment programs require family involvement.

TEEN PREGNANCY

The United States has the highest teen pregnancy rate in the industrialized world, and California has the highest rate in the country. When pregnant teens are compared to those who did not become pregnant as teenagers, a number of social factors emerge. Teen pregnancy is linked to other social problems such as high school dropout rates, dependence on welfare, drug and alcohol abuse, domestic violence, child abuse, and unemployment (Simpson, Pruitt, Blackwell, & Swearingen, 1997).

Simpson, Pruitt, Blackwell, and Swearingen (1997) have identified several common risk factors for adolescent pregnancy: being the daughter of a teen parent, poverty, poor academic achievement, low self-esteem, dating at an early age, dating boys or men five or six years older than the girl, and minority status. In addition to these individual risk factors, others have suggested that certain family characteristics can also contribute to teen pregnancy. Jacobs (1994) proposes that teenagers' developmental needs of autonomy and attachment seem to be a factor in their desire to be sexually active; this behavior is perceived by the teen as a defiant act of **differentiation**. In many families in which a daughter acts out sexually, the parents were noncommunicative about sexual matters and put excessive restrictions on her. In these families, adolescents do not feel that they can talk to the parents, increasing their secrecy about their social activities.

In addition to seeking autonomy, the majority of the girls also seek a closeness that they do not have with their parents. Some choose to keep their babies instead of offering them for adoption because of the misguided notion that a baby will provide them with the nurturing that was lacking at home.

Many clinics and shelters have been set up to address the problems particular to this group of teenagers. For example, pregnant teen girls can often be cared for in a home for unwed mothers, go to school, and learn how to parent after the baby is born. The crisis worker should be aware of the availability of such homes in the area. Often, parents are willing to help out, and the crisis worker must help the entire family adjust to the pregnancy and the baby. This often means that the girl must drop out of school. More important, her social life will change. If the girl does not wish to keep the baby, the crisis counselor must have knowledge of adoption agencies and abortion facilities and present these options to the girl and her parents.

GANGS

The issue of teenagers involved in gangs is an extremely difficult problem for a crisis worker. Local police usually have gang units that can help in counseling these youths and their families. Other options include helping the family move out of the area or helping the youth develop new friends and an improved social attitude. Such complete shifts are difficult to bring about, and cultural sensitivity is of utmost importance.

In trying to understand what makes some teens join gangs, a worker should look at both family structure and societal and cultural conditions. Much informative demographic data related to gangs has been produced by research studies. These data are helpful in refuting many of the myths that have sprung up around gangs, such as the following:

1. Gangs consist only of males in urban areas.

2. Only minorities are in gangs.

3. Gang activity is limited to low-income youths.

4. Gangs are concerned about the safety of the gang member's family.

5. Gang leaders care about each member.

6. Gangs are made up of a group of loyal friends.

7. Gangs do not put the members' lives in danger.

8. Gangs are strictly an American problem.

Most research findings do not support these myths. Kenner (1996) reports that gangs exist in most cities and towns in the United States. Additionally, surveys show that in 175 cities with populations between 50,000 and 250,000, 84% had gang problems. Statistics indicate that there has been a 640% increase in U.S cities reporting gang problems from 1970 to 1995. That is extreme.

Another finding is that gang activity is not limited to low-income youth, but that middle- and upper-class youths are also involved in it. The acts of vandalism, robbery, and drug dealing attributed to these groups are often thought of as the result of boredom or alienation from families and peers, not poverty.

The factors associated with gang involvement can generally be grouped as (1) family dynamics, (2) self-concept, and (3) societal stresses. Drass (1993) further categorized these as parental neglect, abandonment, and dysfunctional families; lack of a sense of self-esteem, absence of personal safety and adult guidance, social alienation, and boredom; and the lack of job opportunities and presence of socioeconomic stresses.

Children who join gangs are likely to grow up in a family that has little verbal communication. Often, there is only one parent, and he or she has minimal interaction with the children. Lack of family structure and no sense of belonging are also associated with gang involvement. The child seems to be seeking a place to belong—a place with some type of structure, albeit a dangerous and illegal one.

It is not uncommon for gang involvement to be transferred down from one generation to another; parents who have been in gangs often encourage gang membership in their children. This process occurs in Asian, African-American, Caucasian, and Hispanic cultures. For first-generation gang involvement, the family of origin is usually disengaged, with the children receiving very little nurturance and guidance. Because of this **disengagement**, it is easy for the child to become **enmeshed** in a gang.

Prevention tactics are much more effective than intervention strategies used after the child has joined a gang. Once the child is a member, getting him or her out of the gang is extremely difficult. People are often hesitant to talk about gang activity. It may be easier to ignore gang behavior than report it. The old cliché, "Don't get involved," applies to this problem because of the reality of retribution by gangs against anyone who testifies against a gang member. As a society, however, we can't extinguish gang activity if we do not talk about it. Gathering accurate information about gangs is a first step. Learning how to manage tension and conflict in interpersonal relations is the next step. Be sure that when gang activity is reported or if a parent confronts a child about gang involvement, conflict will follow. Many parents ignore the way their children dress or the people with whom they associate, because they want to avoid conflict. If parents can set limits before the child is a full-fledged gang member, they have a greater chance of preventing gang involvement. Parents need to know what gang members wear and how they behave to be able to watch for early signs of gang involvement among their children—much like being aware of beginning stages of alcohol or drug use. Then, parents need the courage to speak up and assert their parental authority and support.

Intervention tactics include both involving the community (as in neighborhood watch programs) and increasing the gang member's exposure to positive social activities. These may include counseling, sports programs, mentoring programs, and educational or occupational programs. The most effective interventions will address issues of racism, poverty, and family dysfunction and attempt to create opportunities for the gang member, with the aim of showing him or her other avenues that will appear more attractive than gang membership. When possible, family involvement should be encouraged.

RUNAWAYS

Like teenagers experiencing other crises of adolescence, the teen who runs away from home is also trying to meet his or her needs for both differentiation and nurturance. If a family prohibits **individuation**, the teen is unable to establish a mature identity and develop the capacity for intimacy that is needed to assume adult roles and responsibilities. Without the love and acceptance of their families, teens face much anxiety during this most stressful stage of development. Running away from home is one way to achieve autonomy and independence, but it can be very dangerous. Runaway teens may be drawn into prostitution, pornography, and drug use. Teens are susceptible to the influence of others when they are runaways because of the sense of aloneness they feel. Often, they feel abandoned by their parents and seek the acceptance of anyone.

More and more nonprofit agencies have been created to house teen runaways to prevent them from being preyed on while trying to live on the streets. These teen shelters usually provide brief crisis intervention and family counseling either to find a permanent residence away from the family or to reunite the family. If the teen is abused, this will be reported and attempts will be made to help the teen find a safe place to live with the assistance of the state's social services department.

In intervention, families are taught more effective communication skills and the counselor attempts to address the needs of the teen for autonomy and support. Cultural differences must be recognized and the counselor must be sensitive to parents' rights and values. This is not an easy task. A good idea is to seek consultation from others who have worked with adolescents and clients from other cultures.

Once the crisis intervention is completed, most agencies offer ongoing support groups, continuing family therapy, and follow-up services. The stress in these families must be changed for the teen to return home and not act out again.

Crises of Adulthood

HOMELESSNESS, UNEMPLOYMENT, AND OTHER FINANCIAL CRISES

In spite of low unemployment and a booming economy, there are always people who, for various reasons, are homeless, unemployed, or are unable to manage their financial obligations and therefore experience a crisis state. Most of us have observed homeless people standing on street corners with signs asking for food or money. Many of these are untreated mentally ill people or drug and alcohol addicts. These types of homeless people would probably not seek out a crisis interventionist because they prefer their lifestyle to accepting the responsibilities that would be required in taking government assistance. Another type of homeless person, however, may experience a crisis state. An example might be a man who recently lost his job because of downsizing, lost his home in a fire, and has no family. Once his unemployment reimbursements run out, he may be forced to sleep in shelters or his car. Because he had not been used to this lifestyle, he may suffer depression and anxiety—different from a crack addict who becomes used to the homeless mode of survival and even prefers it to a traditional job.

Even if unemployment does not lead to homelessness, losing a job can create devastating feelings in a person whose self-esteem is largely maintained by the productivity and status of a career. Crisis intervention is helpful for this type of client when the counselor offers optimism and support regarding the person's acquiring another job soon. Often, the loss of a job can be reframed as an opportunity to start over in a career that is more fulfilling than the previous one. For some clients, the crisis worker can suggest that they research what local colleges have to offer in the way of career development. Most community colleges are relatively inexpensive and financial aid is available if someone needs assistance to attend college. Those clients who are not college oriented may be educated on how to look for a job, write a resumé, and interview successfully. The counselor may help the person deal with feelings of deprivation at not having money to buy nice things and how to adapt to a different standard of living.

Other clients may also have to change their standard of living when a financial crisis hits. Because so many people use credit to purchase items, it is easy to become overextended financially. People with good-paying jobs often experience depression and anxiety because they cannot pay their bills. These clients need referrals to credit or financial counselors; often they need to learn to communicate with their spouses more openly about the financial situation at home. The counselor may even suggest practical assignments to help clients learn how to set up a budget, the importance of letting creditors know when payments will be late, or how to manage time and save money.

In true crisis intervention form, this type of client is best served if he or she seeks help soon after the precipitating event. The counselor can encourage the client to take action and move toward a solution rather than slowly sink into depression.

THE HOMOSEXUAL *COMING OUT* CRISIS

Although many people do not think of being gay or lesbian as negative, the unfortunate reality is that many people in society perceive this population as troublesome. Discrimination against them is not uncommon. Adults who present themselves to the world as gay open themselves to criticism and rejection by family, friends, and co-workers.

However, keeping one's homosexuality hidden can also lead to mental health problems such as anxiety and depression. The **closet gay** person must always worry about keeping his or true sexual orientation concealed. Often these people must lie to those they care about, and this duplicity leads to negative feelings.

Crisis hot lines and centers have been established to help this population live as homosexuals, disclose their orientation to others, and learn how to handle rejection from society. A counselor must be sensitive to the special issues faced by both the closet gay and the openly gay person. It is best to find out how each individual perceives his or her situation and continue with the interview following the ABC model. Knowing community resources is a big help. Many of the situational crises this group faces have been dealt with in previous chapters, as many involve relationship difficulties and financial stresses.

Crises of Old Age

ALZHEIMER'S DISEASE

An estimated 4 million Americans are afflicted with **Alzheimer's disease.** It is the fourth leading cause of death among American adults. Because the population is aging, an estimated 14 million will have the disease by the year 2050. Ten percent of those over age 65 and almost half of those over age 85 have the disease. These statistics tell us that we need to be aware of the problem and its effects on the significant others. It is the caretaker who will often use crisis intervention services because of the emotional drain the Alzheimer's patient puts on him or her. Although there is no cure for Alzheimer's, the caretaker can be supported and referred to groups to vent her or his frustrations and ambivalent feelings. The crisis worker should be knowledgeable about the available services for these families.

This disease is particularly difficult because of the pervasive impairments it brings in cognitive, emotional, and physical functioning. The patient is often depressed, paranoid, incontinent, and psychotic. It is very sad for people to see their parents deteriorate to the point of not recognizing their own children. The caretaker needs much empathy and education about the disorder.

ELDER ABUSE

According to the National Center on Elder Abuse (1994), this abuse can be categorized as **domestic elder abuse, institutional elder abuse,** and **self-neglect** or self-abuse. Domestic elder abuse refers to mistreatment by someone who has a special relationship with the elder; it includes physical abuse, sexual abuse, emotional abuse, neglect, and financial or materal exploitation. Most states collect data on these types of abuse and have mandatory reporting laws. Institutional abuse refers to the same types of abuse when they occur in residential facilities for elders, such as nursing homes and board and care homes. Self-neglect refers to elders' abuse or neglect of themselves that threatens their health or safety, often because of mental impairment.

One of every 20 older Americans may be victims of abuse each year; nearly 1.57 million older people became victims of domestic elder abuse during 1991 (National Center on Elder Abuse, 1994). A survey of 30 states in 1991 reported the following types of elder abuse, with percentages of occurrence: physical abuse, 19.1%; sexual abuse, 0.6%; emotional abuse, 13.8%; neglect, 45.2%; financial exploitation, 17.1%; other types, 4.0% (National Center on Elder Abuse, 1994).

The crisis worker needs to understand why some caretakers abuse the elderly. Crisis intervention may focus not only on helping the victim but also on helping the abuser, who is probably a caregiver.

Stress in the caregiver is often a cause of abuse. Dealing with elderly people who are mentally impaired is frustrating, especially for caregivers without proper equipment or skills. If this is the case, the crisis counselor may refer the caregiver to a support group, offer education about mental impairments, or help the caregiver find low-cost medical equipment. Respite care may be very useful for this caregiver. It gives caregivers a break, allowing them to have a vacation from caregiving while a paid caregiver comes to the residence and cares for the elderly person. In some facilities, the elderly can be kept for the entire day. The crisis counselor often helps the caregiver work through guilt feelings caused by the sense of abandoning the elderly relative. A useful reframe is to suggest that without getting a break, the caretaker is abandoning the elder in other ways, such as emotionally. A really loving husband, wife, or child would take a break in order to be refreshed and offer appropriate caregiving.

Remember that caregivers have other life stressors to deal with, and they may be taking out their frustrations on the elder because she or he is an easy target. If this is the case, the crisis worker can help the caregiver cope better with life problems. These issues should be addressed as part of crisis counseling.

In cases of physical abuse, some suggest that the cycle of violence theory holds, in that the children of the elderly parents were abused by them when they were children. They then act out their anger on the dependent elder parent because the use of violence has become a normal way to resolve conflict in their family. The crisis worker must help the adult child caregiver address his or her own past history of child abuse to stop the cycle.

In some cases, the abuser has personal problems, such as substance abuse, financial problems, emotional disorders, or other addictions. Adult children with such problems are dependent on their elderly parents to support them and live with them. This situation increases the likelihood of conflict and abuse.

Many states provide training for caregivers. Some hospitals have support groups for caregivers. The state's adult protective agency may offer support services for caregivers. The crisis worker needs to be aware of what is available in the community.

INTERVENTION WITH THE ABUSED ELDERLY

Dealing with elder abuse is a multifaceted process. It includes interventions by physicians, social workers, nurses, psychiatrists, psychologists, and other professionals and paraprofessionals, all working together to protect and heal the damage done to the elderly person. The crisis worker must be knowledgeable about community support groups for abused elders and the array of support and protective services that are available. **Public guardianship** programs and financial planning and transportation are just a few services available to help the elderly be more autonomous and be taken care of by people who are closely monitored.

Mental health providers can also use an empowerment model with the elderly, teaching them assertiveness skills and **self-advocacy**. The crisis worker can encourage the elder abuse victim to join with others in educating the public and elders on the prevalence of the problem so the elderly won't feel shame and guilt in coming forward with reports of abuse. As with all forms of abuse, the crisis counseling must be supportive as the person speaks, always validating the shame and pain of abuse, but always later focusing on the survival aspect that allows the person to move forward.

Family counseling may be an option, especially if the abuser and the abused will continue living together after the abuse has been reported. This counseling may focus on airing and resolving resentments, improving communication, and defining roles and expectations.

Key Terms for Study

Alzheimer's disease: A disease that impairs the cognitive, physical, and emotional functioning of the patient. The disease usually affects older people, but it can appear in a person as young as 45 years old.

Autonomy: A state of independence and self-sufficiency needed to function as an adult in society. Adolescents often struggle to achieve this with their parents.

Closet gay: A homosexual who chooses to conceal his or her sexual orientation from society or certain people in society. Because of negative attitudes toward homosexuality, this choice is common among gays. They practice concealment to avoid hurtful feedback and other negative consequences that may occur if people know of the person's gay sexual orientation.

Differentiation: A process whereby an adolescent/young adult establishes a mature identity and the capacity for intimacy needed to assume adult roles and responsibilities.

Disengagement: Behavior toward children in which parents do not relate to the child in a nurturing manner; the child feels little support and sense of belonging.

Domestic elder abuse: Maltreatment by someone who has a special relationship with the elder.

Enmeshed: Descriptive of a state in which an individual lacks a sense of separateness from others with whom he or she has an emotionally intense relationship.

Individuation: See *differentiation* on the previous page.

Institutional elder abuse: Maltreatment of an elder that occurs in residential facilities such as nursing homes and board and care homes.

Public guardianship: A program often provided through a department of social services that serves as a public caretaker for the elderly. If an elder is being abused or has no one to care for him or her, the county will serve as the caretaker and make decisions for the elder should this person become incompetent.

Self-advocacy: An intervention strategy that aims at increasing feelings of power among the elderly. The elderly population is encouraged to speak out about injustice being done to the elderly and to assert its needs.

Self-neglect: Condition occurring when an elder abuses himself or herself or does not provide adequate medical care to himself or herself.

Epilogue

How a crisis worker listens to all these problems without becoming depressed is a common concern for the beginning counselor. Any person going into counseling must perceive the job realistically. Knowing where one's responsibility starts and ends is a first step. If the counselors know that they are truly listening and are doing their best to keep informed about community resources, they can feel good about their work, even if the client doesn't seem to get better. Remember, the client must accept at least 50% of the responsibility for getting through the crisis!

It can be exhausting, however, to be inundated with crisis situations daily; that is one reason that crisis workers often go for their own personal counseling on a regular basis. In addition, the crisis worker must maintain a healthy lifestyle including exercise, proper nutrition, and leisure activities. When crisis workers go through their own crises, they should seek help.

Good luck to all of you who plan to help others through the many kinds of crises life brings. You are serving an important purpose in your community. Although this book cannot cover every type of crisis possible, the situations presented here should help you deal with many concerns of human beings. Also, by using the ABC model, you should be able to help clients through all the many other types of problems not addressed in the book.

References

Aguilera, Donna C. (1990). *Crisis intervention: Theory and methodology* (6th ed.). St. Louis, MO: C.V. Mosby.

American Psychiatric Association. (1994). *Diagnostic and statistical manual of mental disorders* (4th ed.). Washington, DC: Author.

Arredondo, P., Toporek, R., Brown, S. P., Jones, J., Locke, D. C., Sanchez, J., & Stadler, H. (1996). Operationalization of the multicultural counseling competencies. *Journal of Multicultural Counseling and Development, 24,* 42–78.

Association for Continuing Education (1997). 1-800-777-6839, CA: Author.

Baker, Clay. (1991). In AIDS diagnosis: Psychological devastation! *The California Therapist, 3*(5), 66–67.

Bambas, Judy. (1994). *Interventions with battered women.* Presentation at California State University, Fullerton.

Barnett, O. W., & La Violette, A. D. (1993). *It could happen to anyone: Why battered women stay.* Newbury Park, CA: Sage.

Boehnlein, James K. (1987). Culture and society in posttraumatic stress disorder. Implications for psychotherapy. *American Journal of Psychotherapy, 41*(4), 519–528.

Bowlby, J. (1980). *Attachment and loss, Vol. 3: Loss, sadness, and depression.* New York: Basic Books.

Boyd, V. D., & Klingbell, K. S. (1979). *Behavioral characteristics of domestic violence.* Unpublished paper.

Brenner, C. (1974). *An elementary textbook of psychoanalysis.* Garden City, NY: Anchor Books.

Brown, M. (1990). *AIDS awareness survey.* Fullerton: California State University.

Bugental, J. F. T. (1978). *Psychotherapy and process: The fundamentals of an existential-humanistic approach.* New York: Random House.

Bulnes, A. (1989). *AIDS crisis intervention.* Presentation given at California State University, Fullerton.

Caffaro, J. V. (1992). A room full of fathers. *The California Therapist, 4*(2), 37–44.

California Teachers Association. (1989). *AIDS/HIV education: Teacher's handbook.* Author.

Caplan, G. (1961). *An approach to community mental health.* New York: Grune & Stratton.

Caplan, G. (1964). *Principles of preventive psychiatry.* New York: Basic Books.

Colao, F., & Hosansky, T. (1983). *Your child should know*. Handout from M. Wash of the California Department of Social Services at California State University, Fullerton.

Cole, C. (1993). *Psychiatric emergencies*. Presentation at California State University, Fullerton.

Corey, G. (1991). *Theory and practice of counseling and psychotherapy*. Pacific Grove, CA: Brooks/Cole.

Corey, G. (1996). *Theory and technique of counseling and psychotherapy*. Pacific Grove, CA: Brooks/Cole.

Corey, G., Corey, M. S., & Callanan, P. (1993). *Issues and ethics in the helping professions* (3rd ed.). Pacific Grove, CA: Brooks/Cole.

Corey, G., Corey, M. S., & Callanan, P. (1998). *Issues and ethics in the helping professions* (4th ed.). Pacific Grove, CA: Brooks/Cole.

Cormier, L. S., Cormier, W. H., & Weisser, R. J., Jr. (1986). *Interviewing and helping skills for health professionals*. Portola Valley, CA: Jones and Bartlett.

Corsini, R. J., & Wedding, D. (1989). *Current psychotherapies*. Itasca, IL: F. E. Peacock.

Cusick, M. (1992). When your client has been battered. *The California Therapist, 4*(4), 47–49.

Darwin, C. (1965). *The expression of emotions in man and animals*. Chicago: University of Chicago Press. (Originally published in 1872)

Davis, H. (1982). *Enabling behaviors*. Unpublished paper from Recovery Services/Family Recovery Services. Orange, CA: St. Joseph Hospital.

Drass, D. (1993). *Dreams under fire: The gang crisis*. New York: KNABC-TV, Franciscan Communications.

Erikson, E. H. (1963). The A-B-C method of crisis management. *Mental Hygiene, 52,* 87–89.

Fair Oaks Hospital. (1984). *The coke book*. Summit, NJ: Author.

Fenoglio, Patty. (1989). *Battered women and their treatment at the Woman's Transitional Living Center*. Presentation at California State University, Fullerton.

Garfield, S. L. (1980). *Psychotherapy: An eclectic approach*. New York: John Wiley.

Gilliland, B. E., & James, R. K. (1988). *Crisis intervention strategies*. Pacific Grove, CA: Brooks/Cole.

Hackney, H., & Cormier, L. S. (1988). *Counseling strategies and interventions*. Englewood Cliffs, NJ: Prentice Hall.

Haley, Jay. (1976). *Problem solving therapy*. San Francisco: Jossey-Bass.

Health Communications. (n.d.). *Facts about cocaine*. Hollywood, FL: Author.

Heller, Mikel. (1992). *Sexual assault*. Presentation at California State University, Fullerton.

Hong, George K. (1988). A general family practitioner approach for Asian-American mental health services. *Professional Psychology: Research and Practice, 19*(6), 600–605.

Ivey, A. E., Gluckstern, N. B., & Ivey, M. B. (1997). *Basic attending skills* (3rd ed.). North Amherst, MA: Microtraining Associates.

Jacobs, J. (1994). Gender, race, class, and the trend toward early motherhood. *Journal of Contemporary Ethnography, 22*(4), 442–462.

Janosik, E. H. (1986). *Crisis counseling: A contemporary approach*. Monterey, CA: Jones and Bartlett.

Johnson, M. E. (1988). Influences of gender and sex role orientation on help-seeking attitudes. *Journal of Psychology, 122*(3), 237–241.

Jones, W. (1968). The A-B-C method of crisis management. *Mental Hygene, 52,* 87–89.

Kashiwagi, Soji. (1993, April). Addiction and the Asian family. *Treatment Today,* 43–76.

Kenner, K. L. (1996). *Gangs.* Santa Barbara, CA: ABC-Clio.

Kinzie, J. D., Fredricksone, R. H., Ben, R., & Fleck, J. (1984). Posttraumatic stress disorder among survivors of Cambodian concentration camps. *American Journal of Psychiatry, 141,* 645–650.

Kübler-Ross, E. (1969). *On death and dying.* New York: Macmillan.

Kugler, Daniel. (1992). An opposing view on partner abuse. *The California Therapist, 41,* 43–45.

Leick, N., & Davidson-Nielson, M. (1991). *Healing pain—attachment, loss, and grief therapy.* London: Rutledge.

Levine, E. S., & Franco, J. N. (1983). Effects of therapist's gender, ethnicity, and verbal style on client's willingness to seek therapy. *Journal of Social Psychology, 12*(1), 51–57.

Lindemann, E. (1944). Symptomology and management of acute grief. *American Journal of Psychiatry, 101,* 141–148.

Lopez, S. R., Grover, K. P., Holland, D., Johnson, M. J., Kain, C. D., Kanel, K., Mellins, C. A., & Rhyne, C. (1989). Development of culturally sensitive psychotherapists. *Professional Psychology: Research and Practice, 20*(6), 369–376.

Ludt, N. (1993). *Bereaving parent support groups.* Presentation at California State University, Fullerton.

Magallon, D. T. (1987, June). Counseling patients with HIV infections. *Medical Aspects of Human Sexuality,* 129–147.

Marshall, L. L., & Kratz, N. Z. (1988). Preexisting differences in evaluation of counselors. *Psychological Reports, 63*(3), 889–890.

Maslow, H. A. (1970). *Motivation and personality* (rev. ed.). New York: Harper & Row.

McGoldrick, M., Pearce, J. K., & Gordana, J. (1982). *Ethnicity and family therapy.* New York: Guilford Press.

Minuchin, Salvador. (1974). *Families and family therapy.* Cambridge, MA: Harvard University Press.

Moline, Mary. (1986). Lecture notes, California State University, Fullerton.

National Center on Elder Abuse. (1994). *Elder abuse: Questions and answers.* Washington, DC: Author.

National Council on Alcoholism. (1986). *Facts on alcoholism and alcohol-related problems.* New York: Author.

National Council on Alcoholism of Orange County. (1986). *Facts on crack*. Santa Ana, CA: Author.

Nelson-Jones, Richard (1990). *Thinking skills: Managing and preventing personal problems*. Pacific Grove, CA: Brooks/Cole.

Orange County Social Services Agency. (1982). *Battering parent syndrome*. Handout #7. Santa Ana, CA: Author.

Peake, T. H., Borduin, C. M., & Archer, R. P. (1988). *Brief psychotherapies: Changing frames of mind*. Newbury Park, CA: Sage.

Pomales, J., & Williams, V. (1989). Effects of level of acculturation and counseling style on Hispanic students' perceptions of counselor. *Journal of Counseling Psychology, 36*(1), 79–83.

Price, R. E., Omizo, M. M., & Hammitt, V. L. (1986, October). Counseling clients with AIDS. *Journal of Counseling and Development, 65*, 96–97.

Roberts, Albert R. (1990). *Crisis intervention handbook: Assessment, treatment, and research*. Belmont, CA: Wadsworth.

Rouse, Beatrice A. (Ed). (1995). *Substance abuse and mental health statistics sourcebook*. Washington, DC: U.S. Department of Health and Human Services, Public Health Services.

San Francisco Child Abuse Council. (1979). *Identifying children at risk*. San Francisco: Author.

Segel-Evans, K. (1991, July–August). The dangers of traditional family therapy when intervening in domestic violence. *The California Therapist*, 45–48.

Sequoia Y.M.C.A., Youth Development Department. (1987). *AIDS education project for sheltered and incarcerated youth*. Redwood City, CA: Author.

Simpson, C., Pruitt, R., Blackwell, D., & Sweringen, G. S. (1997, April). Preventing teen pregnancy: Early adolescence. *ADVANCE for Nurse Practitioners*, 24–29.

Singer, Erwin. (1970). *Key concepts in psychotherapy*. New York: Basic Books.

Slader, S. (1992). *HIV/IV drug users*. Presentation at California State University, Fullerton.

Slaikeu, Karl, A. (1990). *Crisis intervention: A handbook for practice and research* (2nd ed.). Boston, MA: Allyn & Bacon.

Southern California Coalition of Battered Women. (1989). *Am I in a battering relationship?* Santa Monica, CA: Author.

Steiner, Lucy. (1990). *Suicide assessment and intervention*. Presentation at California State University, Fullerton.

Steiner, Lucy. (1994). *Date rape*. Presentation at California State University, Fullerton.

Sullivan, H. S. (1954). *The psychiatric interview*. New York: W. W. Norton.

Szasz, Thomas. (1986). The case against suicide prevention. *American Psychologist, 41*(7), 806–812.

Tower, C. C. (1996). *Child abuse and neglect* (3rd ed.). Boston, MA: Allyn & Bacon.

Turning Point. (1994). Channel 7 news program, Los Angeles, CA.

Tustin Community Hospital. (1987). *Progression and recovery of alcoholism*. Handout. Tustin, CA: Author.

United States Public Health Service. (1985). *Cocaine users: A profile*. Chicago: Dupont and Associates.

Vega, William A., & Rumbaut, Ruben G. (1991). Ethnic minorities and mental health. *Annual Review of Sociology, 17*, 351–383.

Watkins, C. E., & Terrell, F. (1988). Mistrust level and its effects on counseling expectations on black client-white counselor relationships: An analogue study. *Journal of Counseling Psychology, 36*(2), 194–197.

Wesley, Jonnie. (1989). *Rape*. Presentation at California State University, Fullerton.

What are the treatments? (1990, September 20). *Orange County Register,* p. M3.

Woods, Kim. (1992). *Domestic violence fact sheet*. Presentation at California State University, Fullerton.

Worden, W. (1982). *Grief counseling and grief therapy*. London: Tavistock.

Wright, Jerome, W. (1993). African-American male sexual behavior and the risk for HIV infection. *Human Organization, 52*(4), 421.

Wyman, Stephen. (1982). *Suicide evaluation and treatment*. Presented at a seminar sponsored by the Orange County Chapter, California Association of Marriage and Family Therapists.

Zimbardo, P. G. (1992). *Psychology and life* (3rd ed.). New York: HarperCollins.

Author Index

Subject Index

TO THE OWNER OF THIS BOOK:

I hope that you have found *A Guide to Crisis Intervention* useful. So that this book can be improved in a future edition, would you take the time to complete this sheet and return it? Thank you.

School and address: _____

Department: _____

Instructor's name: _____

1. What I like most about this book is: _____

_____

_____

2. What I like least about this book is: _____

_____

_____

3. My general reaction to this book is: _____

_____

4. The name of the course in which I used this book is: _____

_____

5. Were all of the chapters of the book assigned for you to read? _____

   If not, which ones weren't? _____

6. In the space below, or on a separate sheet of paper, please write specific suggestions for improving this book and anything else you'd care to share about your experience in using the book.

_____

_____

_____

_____

_____

Optional:

Your name: _____ Date: _____

May Brooks/Cole quote you, either in promotion for *A Guide to Crisis Intervention*
or in future publishing ventures?

Yes: _____ No: _____

Sincerely,

Kristi Kanel

IN-BOOK SURVEY

At Brooks/Cole, we are excited about creating new types of learning materials that are interactive, three-dimensional, and fun to use. To guide us in our publishing/development process, we hope that you'll take just a few moments to fill out the survey below. Your answers can help us make decisions that will allow us to produce a wide variety of videos, CD-ROMs, and Internet-based learning systems to complement standard textbooks. If you're interested in working with us as a student Beta-tester, be sure to fill in your name, telephone number, and address. We look forward to hearing from you!

In addition to books, which of the following learning tools do you currently use in your counseling/human services/social work courses?

_____ **Video** _____ in class _____ school library _____ own VCR

_____ **CD-ROM** _____ in class _____ in lab _____ own computer

_____ **Macintosh disks** _____ in class _____ in lab _____ own computer

_____ **Windows disks** _____ in class _____ in lab _____ own computer

_____ **Internet** _____ in class _____ in lab _____ own computer

How often do you access the Internet? _____

My own home computer is:

_____ Macintosh _____ DOS _____ Windows _____ Windows 95

The computer I use in class for counseling/human services/social work courses is:

_____ Macintosh _____ DOS _____ Windows _____ Windows 95

If you are NOT currently using multimedia materials in your counseling/human services/social work courses, but can see ways that video, CD-ROM, Internet, or other technologies could enhance your learning, please comment below:

_____

_____

_____

Other comments (optional): _____

_____

Name _____ Telephone _____

Address _____

School _____

Professor/Course _____

You can fax this form to us at (408) 375-6414; e:mail to: info@brookscole.com; or detach, fold, secure, and mail.

BUSINESS REPLY MAIL
FIRST CLASS   PERMIT NO. 358   PACIFIC GROVE, CA

POSTAGE WILL BE PAID BY ADDRESSEE

ATT: MARKETING

**Brooks/Cole Publishing Company
511 Forest Lodge Road
Pacific Grove, California 93950-5098**

NO POSTAGE
NECESSARY
IF MAILED
IN THE
UNITED STATES